For Jean and C

With warmest wishes,
as always,

Peter Rose

SPOILS OF WAR

A Trans-Atlantic Tale
(an autobiography)

by Peter Rowley

Also by Peter Rowley

Books: New Gods in America
              Ken Rosewall: Twenty Years at the Top
              The Chronicles of the Rowleys

Plays: God Save England
              Tob
              Social Climbers

Film: Mother and Daughter (in development)

Jacket illustrations

Front cover: Watercolour portrait of Peter Rowley at about age nine. Painted by Owen Ramsay.

Back cover: The Step-father – U S Army Air Force Major Jack Humphrey against sunlit snowy background of English marshes, holding cigar. He loved bombing Germans. Photo credit: Freda Humphrey.

SPOILS OF WAR

A Trans-Atlantic Tale

Peter Rowley

FYDELL PRESS

© Peter Rowley 2005

Peter Rowley has asserted the moral right to be identified as the author of this work

Published by Fydell Press 2005

ISBN 0-9550915-0-0

Fydell Press
10 High St.
Morcott, Oakham LE15 9DN
England

Printed and bound in Great Britain by Piggott Black Bear, Cambridge

FOR TEREZ AND CAROLINE ROWLEY
AND DAVID COZENS

Acknowledgements

I thank the following persons for helping me with this book: Bob Burn-Murdoch, Ned Chase, David Cozens, Mary Cozens, Mike Hallam, Trevor Hann, Sandra I'Anson, Neal Peirce, Terez Rowley, Mark Stern, and Peace Sullivan.

CONTENTS

Introduction

All the persons, events and places are real, except for the names of Janet, Sylvia, Harry Belmarsh, Joe Bottomley, Dave and Sofia Brown, Edward Fount, Ben Govern, Barbara and Donna Jenkins, Morgan Johnson, Betsy Livingstone, Sam MacArthur and Steve Maddox, which have been changed. The identifying characteristics of one individual have been altered.

Chapter 1

England

Owsley Rowley, my father, was a wealthy landowner, suffering all his life from ill health. At Eton his house master said he was courageous to hunt while afflicted with asthma and bronchitis. He was six feet tall and handsome with a rather square face, though in profile it had an angular beauty. Freda Eyre, my mother, was a pretty woman with brunette hair with a submissive personality but capable occasionally of an acute observation. She too was taller than average. She was flat-chested but had good legs.

For her it was a first marriage, for him a second. He was 21 years older than her, being born in 1886, she in 1907, and they were only able to marry because of some legal trickery. He went to a hotel in Brighton and was photographed in bed with a maid or prostitute by a photographer hired for the purpose on the mutual agreement of his lawyer and the solicitor for his first wife, Lady Marjorie Rowley. That was in about 1932.

Of course it was all about money, as Marjorie and Owsley Rowley had been separated for nine years. In 1923 my father had tried to divorce her, and was defeated in a sensational divorce case - featured in the London newspapers - by her barrister the famous Marshall Hall, better known for saving defendants from the gallows in murder trials, and her father, the Earl of Dundonald. The court said the marriage must continue. My paternal grandfather and his butler testified for my father, but they could not prove Marjorie had committed adultery with a certain major of the British Army.

Only years later would my father agree to a very modest annuity for his first wife. In the interim he and his younger brother, Dick, developed quite a reputation in the county of Huntingdonshire and farther afield for chasing every skirt in sight. Eventually he met and installed in his house, Morcott Hall, in Rutland his "secretary", my attractive mother, who was a Roman Catholic. Freda had changed her name from Winifred, though her mother persisted in addressing her by the latter. <u>Her</u> father, the cynical, domineering Stanislaus, who secretly maintained a mistress in Paris, immediately disinherited his daughter for marrying a divorcee. The rules of the Roman Catholic Church must be observed, he decreed, and, while Stanislaus and my father were both members of the Carlton in London, the Conservative club, they never spoke. Stanislaus may have started and certainly maintained a charity owning a number of almshouses restricted to Catholic elderly along with a private mortuary-church for his own family in Bath. For the first 10 years of her life my mother spent most of each year at Stanislaus' Irish estate in County Kilkenny, living in Uppercourt. Though of the same religion as the vast majority of his neighbors, her father loathed the Irish to such an extent that when his wife, my mother's mother, attended a dance a British soldier sat on the roof of the back of her carriage. In 1916 he was forced to sell his property, and purchased another large house in Hertfordshire. There daily my maternal grandmother and her unmarried sister devoted much of the day to pacing the drive together, saying the rosary.

Apparently it was a happy marriage of my parents at the beginning. My paternal grandfather died. Nine months to the day afterwards I was born. My mother always said I was forcibly delivered by the doctor who was in a hurry to go on holiday. Freda and Owsley moved from Morcott Hall in Rutland when I was a year old to their other manor house, Priory Hill, which had two curved corners opposite each other on the front side. It was surrounded by far more land and had a park, which Morcott Hall lacked. Also Priory Park in St. Neots, Huntingdonshire, was an hour closer to London, said to be more advantageous for my mother's friends and siblings to visit. She had three sisters and a brother, and although one of them, Dorothy, had escaped into a convent for life as soon as she was 21 in order to free herself from Stanislaus' control, the other sisters, Violet and Jane, and her brother, Willy, and their husbands and wife were undoubtedly supportive to her on weekends at the big house, while she coped with her aging, domineering husband, who happened to be the Lord of the Manor of the town. This is a title I rarely use, being a republican at heart and a U.S. citizen by choice. The reason my only Christian names are Peter William is that my mother was determined that I have less names than my half-brothers.

On moving in to Priory Park my parents installed electricity and central heating, as my late grandfather did not believe in these modern inventions. In fact Fydell, as he was known locally, deplored the motor car, even though he was the local magistrate. The police took advantage of his views and operated a very successful speed trap on the Great North Road. For this my grandfather achieved minor national notoriety, which was at least better than the publicity surrounding him in the early 1880's when he narrowly escaped going to jail thanks to a hung jury for allegedly bribing with gold coins in a parliamentary election the voters of Boston, Lincolnshire, an old small city on the North Sea.

Guests at his house had to arrive by horse and carriage, and, if they came by car, they left their vehicle at the railroad station and climbed into a horse-drawn one. He always ate the same meal every day for a month at breakfast and lunch, though his artistic wife, Alice Nina Corbett, daughter of a Shropshire baronet, had some say over the dinner food. For breakfast in August it might be sausages, bacon and eggs followed in September by porridge, kidneys and fried tomatoes. My mother always said they lived together "in married misery for 50 years."

While Fydell served as the chairman of the County Council, Alice carved by hand the pews for the St. Neots Church. She would ride into the town from her stately home on the hill in a pony and trap. Among Fydell's other peculiarities was his emphasis on saving pennies. If he had to go to London to see his solicitors, he rose very early in order to catch the workers' train, which offered a cheaper fare. Frequently he dressed like a farm laborer, and, once during a thunderstorm, as he walked towards the wrought iron gates leading to his house, he was spotted by a shepherd struggling to herd his sheep into a field. The man asked him for help, which Fydell gave willingly. The shepherd was then very surprised to see his helper walk though the front gates, which featured at the top in metal two facing "R"s. At his funeral, attended by a 1,000 people, most of them from the local area, he had prescribed in his will that he "be buried with the least possible expense." His remains now lie under a flat stone in a nondescript cemetery a quarter mile from the church. His mother was the last Rowley to be buried in the big vault outside of St. Mary's church. Its proximity to the entrance is a reminder to one and all that the wealthiest are the closest to God - at least on this earth.

Within a few years after my grandfather's death my father sold six of the eight Great Auk eggs. These had been collected in the 19th century by Dawson Rowley, my great grandfather, a noted ornithologist. They went for 500 pounds each, and helped my father pay inheritance tax. For the same reason he also sold Fydell mansion, described as "The Grandest House in Town". It was located in Boston, a beautiful old community often surrounded by fog near the North Sea. Soon after Joseph P. Kennedy, the American Ambassador to Great Britain, gave the money for its restoration.

By today's standards my father and mother lived an extraordinarily luxurious life, but it was not unusual for the British upper classes of the nineteen thirties. There were 11 servants - a butler, a footman, the cook, a pantry maid, the head housekeeper, her assistant, a chauffeur/groom, my nanny or later governess, and three gardeners. A maid was paid about 50 pounds a year, and my mother once fired one of them because she was pregnant. Frequently lower class people had all their teeth pulled in their late 'teens and early twenties because dental care was too expensive for them.

Eleven course dinners were typical, and my mother told me she once attended a dinner party in another country house where after the first course no food arrived. Eventually the hostess went into the kitchen to discover the reason for the delay, and found one of her guests' chauffeurs making love to the cook on the kitchen table. After breakfast my mother's first task was to tell the cook what the day's menu would be and how many guests were coming. My father went to his library, filled with stuffed birds and new and rare books, and supervised his two estates and his stock market investments. The stuffed birds and the rare books were the legacy of Dawson. A scholar at the Smithsonian in Washington, D.C., credits him with assembling all the known information about the extinct Auk, which was probably used for the definitive book on the subject. Dawson was also the author of the three volume *Ornithological Miscellany,* which is today in the collections of the Smithsonian and the British Library.

I have no memory at all of my nanny, even though she was with me until I was four. I have since been told that she was an excellent young woman. One or two photos of her show her holding me in the presence of my mother in the sunlight some distance from the front door of Priory Park in Huntingdonshire, and she appears to be pretty and caring. Beside them are the park railings and in the distance elms. Wherever you are and whoever you are I thank you.

At four my mother decided to begin my education, and thus Patricia Holmes was hired because my mother liked her, and because she was a

Roman Catholic. A small, homely woman, amply bosomed with a substantial nose, she was for the most part kindly, but her heart remained in France where for 10 years she had been the English governess to the d'Ailliere family, who lived in Paris and also at a chateau in the middle of the France. Monsieur d'Ailliere had only one lung, having been gassed by the Germans in the First World War. Years later Madame d'Ailliere told me, "Je déteste les Boche."

When Patricia left their employ and came to me, the mutual separation was occasioned by the fact that the four d'Ailliere children were largely grown up, and fear of the approaching Second World War. Years later she told me that when she was 18 there had been a man who wanted to marry her, but she refused him because he was divorced. Many, many years later she asked me to call her "Patricia" rather than "Holmie." She adored my mother.

My mother's favorite activity next to tennis (she had installed a clay court, which she proudly noted was not grass, the usual surface in those days) was supervising her gardeners' work on "my herbaceous borders." She had three of them. I wheeled my tricycle among them. Every two weeks or so Holmie would walk me down the road between an avenue of elms, the park on our left, our farm land on the right, to my grandmother's house, where we would have tea with her and her maid Millie. At that point relations between my granny and me were amicable.

We took, when I was four in the winter of 1938/39, a cruise ship to Capetown. Normally my father and mother rented a villa in the south of France for the winter to alleviate his chronic asthma and bronchitis, but fears of the oncoming war led to this change. On the deck there was a swimming pool and I was frightened by a game where a grownup dressed up as Neptune supervised a contest in the open air deck swimming pool. Two passengers fought with pillows while sitting on the diving board until one fell in the water. In Capetown below Table Mountain we stayed at a hotel near the beach for several months. I was careful not be stung by jellyfish which we called "blue bottles."

At about the age of five in September, 1939, when the Second World War started I had light blonde hair, a round friendly face and light blue eyes like those of a robin's egg. My ears protruded slightly, and at night I was forced to wear for some months a sort of hair net at night. Photos of me full face and in profile reveal an innocent trusting child, smiling at the camera.

At home in Huntingdonshire I was addressed at a very young age as

"Master Peter" by our butler, Habbits, who was very fat. He was married to Ruth, the cook. I would hear my mother say, "Ruth is hopeless. I teach her French recipes, but they always come out as stodgy English food." I could hear Habbits' voice outside my bedroom door - "Good morning, Master Peter." Habbits was the champion beer drinker in the pubs in the town of St. Neots. When in previous years we had gone to Nice or Cannes, Habbits delighted the French in their cafes by his ability to quaff more wine than any of the natives.

Once he stopped my father hitting my mother. She had taken one pound from his wallet without telling him. A few years earlier, when my parents lived in the other big house in Rutland, Habbits had returned from an evening's drinking in the local pub. Because of his weight he had been advised by the young groom to wear a kind of bandage on his knee soaked in an oil used for treating horses. This poultice had not worked, causing Habbits even more pain. He was helped into bed by Ben, the young groom, and Ruth. He took a pistol which was hidden beneath his pillow and fired a shot in his anger at Ben. The bullet lodged in the ceiling. When my father heard of this incident, Habbits was reprimanded.

In my bedroom there was a tiny holy altar and statues of baby Jesus and the Virgin. My second floor room led upstairs by a few steps to an enormous play room with a black floor. Here I kept about 3,000 lead toy soldiers. Occasionally I would have a tantrum and smash the formations of armies I had made. Tears would follow, and with Holmie's help plus match sticks and glue I would repair the heads and torsos of the broken ones. Outside in the kitchen garden behind the big house I made mud pies and stuck tiny twigs in them to represent fortifications and French or British tanks on the Maginot Line by which I expected our soldiers to stop the attacking German armies. To me the war was a thrilling experience.

I remember seeing my oldest half-brother John Charles Cochrane Fydell Rowley in his brown khaki uniform of a second lieutenant in The Dragoons in my parents' bedroom just after he had returned from Dunkirk. Thin and tanned, he smiled at me in a friendly way. At the time I was not told that he had suffered a breakdown during the retreat to the beaches. I do not remember if I saw John until a year later.

I was not a lonely child, but I had very little contact with other children. Occasionally my first cousin, Rosabelle, who everybody said would be a beauty when she grew up and who was two years younger than me, was brought over by her nanny for an afternoon of play, but when I was six, my mother gave a birthday party for me with a conjurer as entertainer and I felt strange and alienated from my young guests, none of whom I knew, except Rosabelle with her mass of curls.

Her father, Uncle Dick, was described as the handsomest man in the British Army during the First World War. My father due to his chronic ill health could not serve his country, but Dick went to the front in France, and many years later wrote me a letter describing how he had had to crawl across a field of dead bodies at night. He said he was ordered to deliver some ammunition to the front, and as a young officer fulfilled his mission, but his commanding officer was drunk, claimed Dick had not done so, and accused Dick of cowardice. This resulted in him being sent home to England.

Meanwhile my father donned the uniform of an officer in the Yeomanry, and accompanied by a drummer boy walked around the village of Morcott in the tiny county of Rutland, persuading healthy young men to enlist and go to their possible deaths in France.

While Uncle Dick was in France, his wife, the beautiful daughter of a baronet from Liverpool, left him to become the Second Duchess of Westminster. The Duke was the richest man in England, and there was a scandalous story that he had bought Dick off. Another complication was that Violet Nelson had insisted Dick become a Roman Catholic, which he did much to the annoyance of my grandfather, who as a strict adherent of the Church of England deplored the Roman Church. For years afterwards Dick attended Mass in the morning and Evensong at the end of the day.

Uncle Dick was a very good athlete, and won the British Army boxing championship. Particularly after the First World War he developed a reputation of being fearless while riding to hounds. For extra exercise at the end of a day's hunting he would hold onto his horse's tale and run over fields and dale. Then he married wife no. 2, whose existence was concealed as much as possible subsequently. She was said to be a loose American woman. Eventually around the time my parents married Dick married wife no. 3, Aunt Sylvia, Rosabelle's mother, who was much younger than him and equally fond of horse and hounds.

I usually saw my mother for about 20 minutes at tea time when I was brought into the grand drawing room with its French door and floor-to-ceiling windows surrounded by brocade curtains. One end of the room was curved, looking onto the garden and park. There were a number of beautiful pieces of antique furniture. My mother sat in front of a silver tea set engraved with the Rowley coat of arms, serving cups to the family and whatever guests were present. I remember learning at a very early age that upper-class people drank china tea, rather than the stronger darker Indian tea, which was the choice of the middle and lower classes. I seem to vaguely remember that at about the age of two I disgraced myself by urinating on the "Axminster" carpet.

My mother tried to interest her two stepsons in sports. John was in love with her. His own mother, Lady Marjorie, was never present, rarely saw or wrote him, and lived much of the time as a voluntary patient in nursing homes. As John was 16 years older than me, I saw little of him. My other half-brother, who was 12 years older than me, was only a pudgy adult in my life. George was an undergraduate at Magdalene College in Cambridge, where in the dining hall he drank a potent combination of beer and whisky. He would tell his companions that he was studying to be a solicitor and would arrange their divorces for them. Our father deplored his inability to hunt, shoot or do any other sport. My father even had specially made a weird shot gun for George, whose left eye was stronger than his right. The barrel was curved so that he could hold the weapon since he was right-handed but squint down the sights through his left eye. But he still could not shoot game accurately. He wore thick glasses. He spoke in a lower middle class accent like the servants, with whom he spent most of his free time. He was clever - a good student.

Aunt Sylvia and Uncle Dick were asked by John if he could leave Priory Hill and move into their house. However, they decided such a step would enrage my father, and regretfully had to tell John that it was not possible.

The only time I saw my father was for a few minutes before my bed time. Before dinner during cocktails Holmie would bring me into what was called the morning room, which had a curved wall surrounding the French windows to the garden - a smaller, more intimate room than the grand drawing room. My father would be sitting heavily in a low arm chair, and some words would be exchanged between him, Holmie and my mother to the effect that I was learning satisfactorily. He looked down upon me in an approving way, and that was it. The interview was over. After I had said good night I was removed from their presence.

In the early part of the war we were forced to accept a number of evacuee families from the east end of London. We installed them in an unused wing of the house. I remember the adults in my family making fun of these cockney families because they kept their coal in the bath tub. I was not allowed to play with them for fear of catching one of their suspected diseases, or having their lower class accents affect my upper class tones.

Granny Rowley moved out of her house into ours. Until the war started, she had lived in her own house with a full complement of staff, but because the war meant most of her servants were drafted into the military or to work in munitions factories, she was forced to move back in with us. She had left Priory Park for Riversfield, her dower house a mile away, only five years earlier when my grandfather had died. She was always dressed in black as a sign of mourning, even though her husband had been dead for half a decade. At breakfast she appointed herself the toast-maker for the family, a job that our butler Habbits normally would have done. "It's my contribution to the war effort," she insisted. Due to her age she usually forgot to take the bread out of the old-fashioned toaster, and then smoke would spiral up from the four blackened pieces, exasperating the rest of the family. Because national government and family policy was to consume everything on our plates and thus save food, we had to eat scraped toast.

Many nights the family descended to the basement along with the servants. There were blankets and mattresses. The possibility of German bombs at night was a constant fear, though the nearest was an incendiary a mile way. For this reason the skylights were blacked out, curtains drawn and the windows of the big house were taped along their edges with black tape to ensure no light escaped to guide German pilots. My grandmother had been asked on numerous occasions not to allow her pets into the family quarters, but she had ignored these pleas. Because there was darkness over the main staircase, Holmie tripped over one of my grandmother's cats and fell down the stairs. She cut and bruised her leg, and my father ordered the cat to be shot.

One of her cats had produced a litter of kittens on some hay in a barn among the other farm buildings to the rear of the mansion. I poured petrol on the little creatures. But I did not put a match to the liquid. My grandmother bitterly protested, demanding that I be punished, but I was defended by my parents and governess.

The previous winter, after the war had started, we stayed for three months in a hotel in Bournemouth, as it was hoped this would be a slightly milder climate than dank, cold, dreary Huntingdonshire, where the wind blew steadily from the south west over the flat landscape. Because the war was going so badly for the British and it was feared the Germans might cross the channel at any moment, my parents decided to remain at Priory Hill.

One chilly morning in November, 1940, I saw my father silhouetted in the front door of our house. If the weather had been better, he might have played golf with my mother, a sport more suited to his physical condition than tennis. He was wrapped up in a scarf, wearing a hat. He was about to go for a walk. Soon he had a cold, which turned into bronchitis. After that wintry morning I never saw him again. There is some reason to think that drink may have been a contributory cause of his death at the relatively young age of 56. Many years later I interviewed a man who had been his groom when he lived with my mother at Morcott Hall. He said that my father resorted to a flask of whiskey before hunting on horseback to calm his nerves in this frequently dangerous sport. That was in about 1933, and it is a sad guess that under the far greater pressures of the war, a possibly adulterous wife and two very disturbed sons he may have drunk fairly heavily. Among all levels of society alcohol was an even greater escape then than now. The house was hushed. He had retreated to bed, suffering a series of heart attacks. Then on January 10, 1941, when the snow was falling softly, he died. Granny Rowley arranged for a local photographer to take pictures of what she described as his "handsome face."

I was sent away for two weeks to my aunt and uncle's house 10 miles away in Alconbury. This was where my cousin Rosabelle lived. My mother decided to keep Holmie with her for moral support. My father's death meant very little to me, but gradually over the following months I was affected to some extent by a feeling of gray loss. Friends of my mother would say, "Oh, you poor little boy. You lost your daddy." It dawned on me that perhaps I had lost something.

Granny Rowley went out to the kitchen garden, dug a hole, making sure no one in the family was observing her, and buried her jewels, including her emeralds and diamonds. She intended to dig them up after the war, assuming the Germans had not murdered her previously.

From my little boy's viewpoint wrapped in a cocoon of ignorance through my mother's design there was a great deal going on in Priory Park which I was blissfully unaware of. I had not the faintest knowledge that my oldest half-brother, John, who was 16 years my senior, was in a mental hospital in Northamptonshire, recovering from shell shock. He was not released for the funeral. And finally I was unaware that my late father suspected that my mother was having an affair with a neighbor. He was said to be a dashing Army colonel, whose rich landowning wife was a friend of my mother.

That my brother John had suffered a breakdown on the retreat to Dunquerque I knew nothing of. I only learned years later that he had violent disputes with our father about which regiment to join at the beginning of the war. John had just graduated with a degree in agriculture from Trinity college, Cambridge. He had earned a Third, the lowest academic distinction, but the psychological pressure of an impending war probably distracted him from his courses. John hoped to join the local Huntingdonshire regiment, but Owsley, who was a snob, insisted he accept a commission in one of the smart regiments, the Dragoons. Through influence our father obtained a commission for him. One night, wearing the ceremonial uniform, he ran down the staircase of our house wielding a sword hoping to kill our father. He was slightly built in relation to Owsley, and the older man disarmed him. John stayed occasionally with us at the Brankston Towers hotel in Bournemouth on leave from the Dragoons. John said that he was being watched by German spies. However, the whole country was paranoiac. He then went to France as a transport officer for his regiment.

The first few months in northeastern France were peaceful. This period was known as the phony war. John met a British nurse, Eunice Roose, in a small village near Amiens. She was a nursing Sister in the Queen Alexandra Imperial Military Nursing Service. Borrowing horses from the French, they frequently picnicked and read poetry. They fell in love, promising to marry each other when the war was over. Then the Germans, using their panzer divisions, overran Holland and Belgium, circumvented the British and French massed behind the Maginot line, forced the French to retreat in disarray towards Paris and the British to flee toward the beaches at Dunquerque.

During the retreat John suffered a nervous breakdown, and lapsed into silence, crying. The nurse found him by accident. Eunice was driving an Army lorry because the driver was shell shocked. She stopped the vehicle to pick up a group of British soldiers sitting by the roadside. She was also looking for someone stronger than herself to hold the wheel of the heavy military vehicle. John was among them being comforted 'by a Sergeant-Major, who could do nothing with him' - in Eunice's words. It was then that Eunice saw her lover, but John did not recognize her. After they had been driving for a while, Eunice halted the transport and asked John to help her free some dogs trapped in an abandoned farm house, but he failed to react in any way. Then they were separated a second and final time.

After his escape with 300,000 or so other British soldiers across the Channel, he was given a medical discharge. My mother said that he saw no fighting and had a very easy time of it in France. How she knew this I have no idea, unless John in his very repressed way had mumbled to her while stammering that he was fine and had not been injured. Such a statement from her coincided with her usual policy of pretending that everything was going well.

My father's death was a cataclysmic event in the dynamics of the family. There was a vacuum. The heir, John, was in hospital. George, his sibling, was too young to step into the breach. Then there were my mother and my father's mother. I do not know the exact truth of the incident, but one version was that my grandmother wanted me to play with the evacuees' children and also those of the farm manager. My mother, afraid of disease and the influence of unsuitable speech patterns, forbade me. It may have been the other way around. But the two women fought over this issue. Having been married to the Lord of the Manor, my mother was also a middle level officer of the county Red Cross, and the head of the Huntingdonshire branch was Hester Barrie-Goldie, a horsey-faced, stocky, cheerful spinster of middle age who offered to rent mummy Hester's family house, an old rectory in the village of Brampton about seven miles away. My grandmother regarded the Priory Hill mansion as hers. She had lived there for 50 years with her late husband, and only had to move out because my mother and father ousted her. The new owner of the house was obviously unable to express an opinion as to whether either or both ladies should stay. It might be said that my grandmother won the battle of wills, but then it could also be argued that my mother both for her own good and mine was fleeing an unhealthy atmosphere.

Under my grandfather's will John inherited almost everything, although there were trustees, Coutts Bank, who saw to it that he spent only the income and was not allowed to touch capital. Then there was my father's will. His estate was much smaller, though still substantial. He left 1,500 pounds income annually to my mother. I was allowed a similar income and my two half-brothers John and George received the same amounts as me, even though John scarcely needed any more money. My father's will stipulated three trustees. There was Uncle Joss, my father's best friend and the husband of my aunt Violet, an older sister of my mother. There was Uncle Dick, my father's brother who bitterly resented being largely cut out of my grandfather's will. My mother said he would come into our house, brandishing a bible, complaining at the unfairness of his father's will. And there was a Captain Harry Linton, a friend of my father who lived nearby. Linton drank so heavily that one night he fell out of a second floor window of his home and broke his leg.

My grandmother had her house back in her total control. She could hold seances, communicating with the dead, as she was a keen spiritualist. Her cats could breed without fear of being shot by her son or their kittens soaked in gasoline by her grandson. The servants were invited to join these sessions. Holmie did take me back to Priory Hill a month or so after our move for an afternoon's visit with my brother George, who was home for a night from Cambridge. I discovered he had an electric train set in a drawer of his bedroom. "Can I borrow it, please, George?" "No," was his curt reply. I was deeply hurt. On that afternoon visit I did not see my grandmother, but I can't say I missed her. She never forgave me for my kitten crime. I never saw her again.

However, my mother had a victory over granny Rowley on another front. A very tall young lawyer, a Mr. Higginson, whose hobby in his spare time was poetry, came down from London. He was from Bird & Bird, dubbed "Birds" by George, the very same firm who in 1880 had got my grandfather into deep water for allegedly bribing the citizen voters of Boston, Lincs, and then hiring very expensive barristers who persuaded the jury that they could never come to a decision as to his guilt or innocence. The prosecution alleged that Sir Ernest or Sir William Bird had supplied 2,000 pounds worth of gold coins for this purpose. Local lore was that my grandfather fled to France. However, the truth was that he did not have to, but after this experience, during which he was so ill he could not even appear at his own trial, he gave up his parliamentary ambitions, and settled for being the leading political power in the county. In the early 1920's he was offered by Lloyd George a peerage in exchange for his switching from the Conservative party to the Liberals plus a contribution of 10,000 pounds to the party. Perhaps having been burned by money once, he refused.

Mr. Higginson said his firm had been bombed, many papers destroyed, such a big estate would take longer to file for probate. The will also allowed my mother to choose furniture with a total value of no more than 1,000 pounds. . Even by the economics of the 1930's, this was very little money <u>but</u> my father and his lawyers had not foreseen that antique furniture prices would be at rock bottom levels at the time of his death. England was in perilous danger of being invaded by the Germans. Hitler dominated continental Europe. Who wanted to buy antiques and silver when rapacious German soldiers might wreck or steal them? The result was that my mother, who had good taste, chose the finest pieces, and there was nothing my grandmother could do about it, other than inwardly fume. She chose for example two particularly beautiful Venetian cabinets inlaid with ivory, and a set of Chippendale dining room chairs. She plundered the silver, such as the lovely tea pot and tray decorated with the Rowley coat of arms, which now belongs to my half-sister in Philadelphia, taking only the best, as she had every right to do. When some months later my father's brother, Uncle Dick and his wife, Aunt Sylvia, came to dinner at our Brampton rectory, Dick denigrated my mother's selection. After they left, I remember my mother being indignant in her discreet, upper-class way which was all the more devastating for the concealed anger. Dick, who was his mother's favorite, was obviously parroting my grandmother's sour grapes party line.

About a month or so after we moved into the rectory, John visited us one afternoon. He had been released from the sanitorium - cured. He was now the Lord of the Manor, owner of two mansions and nearly 3,000 acres. When he returned to the big house on the hill overlooking the park, where herons sometimes perched in the high trees, he found himself alone with beant granny wearing her usual black, now in mourning for both husband and son, and the remaining servants. Gone were his father, young step-mother, Holmie and me. Our grandmother urged him to join her spiritualist meetings. Only his brother visited on some weekends, and George was jealous that John got almost everything, while George had only two small trusts barely enough to pay for his alcohol and the prostitutes he was starting to visit.

After lunch John walked out into our much smaller garden and smiled down on me, and I showed him a secret hideaway I had discovered inside a very bushy tree along the drive. It was useful for war games, I explained to him. My memory is that he liked me. Around that time Bird and Bird persuaded him to write a new will, leaving everything to George, and, if he died without children, everything to me. The previous will favored solely his mother.

Shortly after his visit to us he was turned down by a local beauty he hoped to marry. The rejection was from a girl whose parents had for years been urging her to marry John. She elected to elope with a young officer in the Royal Navy. A lesser challenge to his psyche was explaining to the town and his neighbors why he was not still in the army. Every eligible young man was; why not him? One day he took a .22 rifle from the gun cabinet, went up to his bedroom (until very recently his father's and my mother's), lay down and shot himself in the mouth. He was found unconscious by Habbits, who immediately telephoned Doctor Harrison, the local physician who had cared for our father. Harrison had been briefly famous a few years earlier as he was the doctor for the St. Neots quadruplets, a record number of babies in one birth for that time. Harrison called an ambulance and dispatched his patient back to the Northamptonshire mental hospital. Suicide or attempted suicide was a crime then, and he faked the paper work to make it look as if it was an accident. I of course was told nothing of this.

For me life was pleasant at the old rectory. In the morning and early afternoon I had lessons with Holmie. The rest of the time I was free to conduct imaginary war games against the enemy. I constructed a field "telephone" by running string from metal cans attached to trees in the garden. I cut off willowy branches, hid behind bushes, and hurled them at the gardener who would be digging holes to plant vegetable seeds. They never hit him, but for an instant he was a German Panzer division. I discovered I could run along the top of the walls around the garden. There was an opening in a wall that separated the garden from the vegetable one, and a path below. Here I placed three parallel wooden planks. While fleeing from the Germans, I put both feet on an outer plank, lost my balance and tumbled to the stony path below. Unconscious, I was taken to the hospital, suffering from a concussion. My mother, who was away at the time, rushed back.

Then some months later we visited my mother's youngest sister, Aunt Jane, at her country house in Shropshire. A few miles away another sister, Aunt Dorothy, who was about three years older than my mother, was headmistress of a Sacred Heart convent in the region. Jane's son was my cousin, David, one month younger than me, a very dark curly-haired boy, who was even thinner than me. There were rumors that he had rheumatic fever as a child, affecting his heart. We visited our aunt, Mother Dorothy, and David and I played in the convent gardens while the sisters chatted. Then Aunt Dorothy came outside, looking for us. Because of a garden wall, we did not see her and were shouting, "To hell with the nuns." She heard us, and laughed.

Returning to cousin David's home, he and I played outside by a big oak tree. His parents lived in a sizable cottage and still owned the nearby park, full of bracken with a lake. We had bicycles, and one of them we turned upside down. David still had a father, Uncle Reggie, who was away in the Army. We began to twirl the foot pedals in order to make the rear wheel go faster and faster. It became a competition between us to see which one could achieve the greatest velocity. Somehow I caught my right index finger in the chain which sliced off part of the top digit in the sprocket wheel. Blood spurted, and then my tears and screams. Fortunately a skillful local doctor managed to sew most of the torn flesh together, leaving me with a slightly shortened finger. To this day I know I could never be a spy because I have a readily identifiable deformity, and when I serve in tennis I have to "band-aid" the tip. Of course I was put to bed to recuperate, my finger heavily bandaged. When the adults were not looking, I cut some locks of my blond hair and made a nest into which I put the shells of a broken robin's egg David and I had found, and placed it on the pillow beside my head.

Then my cocker spaniel was run over by an American army truck in the high street outside of our home. His leg was broken. The gardener shot him.

I listened to my mother and Aunt Violet, the oldest sister, who came to live with us for some months as her husband, Uncle Joss, was in the British army in Yorkshire. They happily discussed how they were learning to cook. Neither had ever done so before, always being dependent on servants. They did not even know how to boil an egg. They talked of Cordon Bleu cooking. They bought hundreds of fresh eggs, stored them in jars filled with water and a substance that preserved them for a year or two. As the widow of the late Owsley Rowley, my mother bicycled the seven miles to Priory Hill, returning with essential foods which the big estate diverted from the shops, as there was strict rationing. Everywhere we went by bicycle due to the virtual absence of petrol, and I became adept at flying along with my hands off the handle bars, and guiding the machine by shifting my weight. Frequently we bicycled to Huntingdon, passing by the stone wall of Hinchingbrook House, a castle, still the home of a Lord Sandwich. My ancestor had been the lawyer for the 4th Earl who was blamed for losing the American colonies. As First Lord of the Admiralty his political opponents said he had failed to bring a British fleet up from Jamaica in time to rescue Cornwallis at Yorktown.

Occasionally Holmie would take me to visit one of Holmie's sisters who lived in Bedford. I would climb on her bed to test the springs and jump up and down for the sheer joy of it.

One afternoon at tea time there appeared on the sofa of our drawing room an overweight American in a neat brown uniform. His name was Jack Humphrey. Bald, he was middle-aged, a major in the U.S. Army Air Force. In profile with his officer's cap on he had a strong handsome face. He was stationed as an intelligence officer at the nearby Alconbury air base. He was exceedingly friendly to me with his broad smile, bringing gifts of candy every time. I don't think I was suspicious, but I wondered why he was doing this. Showing us pictures of them, he said he had a wife and three sons in America.

How had he met my mother? A quarter mile away on another road of our scenic village lived a Mrs. Evans, who was rotund and convivial. She liked to give parties, and as her contribution to the war effort she was happy to invite our new allies, the American officers. When my mother walked into her cottage, there was a man standing on his bald head, his legs leaning against a wall for support. A short time later she saw the same person sitting in a chair sticking a pin into his thigh for the entertainment of onlookers. It was of course Jack.

A color photo of Jack around that period shows an energetic, aggressive man in his officer's uniform with its form-fitting jacket and trousers plus the gold insignia, holding a cigar, grinning widely. It may have been the angle of the photo, but it shows him less fat than I remember him. In the background are wild rushes and patches of snow of an English marsh. The photo must have been taken by my mother.

Many years later Mrs. Evans told me that two American airmen were driving in a jeep past the local crematorium, and, thinking it was a restaurant, as it was a hot day, thought they would stop for some refreshment. Entering, they saw a lot of people formally dressed, the men in top hats and morning suits. Innocently, the Yankees said, "What's cooking?" They were thrown out.

Coinciding with this friendly American invasion, plans were afoot to send me away to boarding school. Holmie would leave our employ and start training as a nurse. I greeted this idea with enthusiasm. I was only eight and three quarters, and naively assumed a world of happy fun and games with other boys lay ahead of me. My half-brothers were unavailable to advise me.

George I never saw, and John had lapsed into total silence. Psychiatrists and neuro-surgeons were consulted. Because of the attempted suicide John was blind in one eye. It was suggested that removing the .22 bullet might improve his mental health, but the doctors were afraid to operate, fearing that the surgery might kill him.

John had gone to Eton because all the Rowley males before him had been there, but George with his extreme shyness, inability at sports, and fat physique was sent to Stowe, a much newer boarding school with a reputation for being kinder to boys than Eton and the other prominent "public" schools.

In April of 1943 my mother and I took the train north to York. At the big railroad station, which seemed vast and noisy to me, she escorted me to another train, which would travel about 50 miles west on a local line to the prep school, Gilling Castle. I was told to climb into a carriage where there were about five other boys.

After she had gone, and, as the train started, they said to me, "What is your name?" "Peter Rowley." That was the first mistake of my new career. Boys never used their first names, as it supplied easy material for taunts such as "Peter, weter, peter, peter darling, darling" etc., delivered in deadly sing-song sopranos. My second mistake, though this occurred some days later, was to reveal my birthday. I was one of five new boys, and the social structure among the boys, ranging in age from eight to 12, dictated that an older boy was allowed "to give cheek" to a younger one. One of our five newcomers, a boy named Fattorini, said, "My birthday is July 20." I of course said that date was also mine. "Which of you was born first during the day?" said another boy. I said, "Mummy said I was born in the afternoon." Fattorini announced triumphantly, "I was born in the morning." "Fattorini can give cheek to you." I did, however, learn to keep carefully concealed letters from my mother, reading them only when I was sure no other boy was looking over my shoulder. If he had seen the word "Darling" at the beginning of the letter, he would have started chanting in a derisory way, "Darling...darling," running around the big recreation room.

Gilling was indeed a castle. There were about 150 students and five Benedictine monks and two or three lay teachers. We were located on a hill side and looked across the valley to Ampleforth College. The British use the word "college" to describe what would be known as a high school in the U.S. Boys from Gilling were expected to go across the valley to Ampleforth when they were 12. However, I had been "put down" for Eton, and, when the monks heard of this, they said I would be risking my soul by going there. The flames of hell would be perilously close, hinted Father Hilary, a young sharp-faced Benedictine monk.

Many years later my wife and I visited Gilling. Immediately I felt a sense of cold depression settle on me as we approached the castle. Inside a monk showed us the dining hall. "There's something different about this refectory," I said. "Yes," he replied, "When you were here in the early forties there was no paneling. Now there is, because we bought it back from the Hearst estate. In the 1930's it was sold, and sat in a warehouse near San Simeon for decades."

My other principal memories of the refectory were that we would enter in a line, snapping our fingers together in a gesture I can still perform today. It involved letting the forefinger hang loose. It was then whipped against the index finger, held in place by the thumb. We only did this when we saw food that we liked particularly. The lay masters would often give us their jam off their plates.

Our favorite snack was a jar of Ovaltine, which occasionally was sent as a gift to a boy. Because it had sugar, he would pour small portions of it into the open cupped palms of other students, who would walk around happily licking it in the recreation room. When I went to America a year or so later, my first purchase was a jar of Ovaltine, but, because there was an unlimited supply, I soon lost interest. I discovered I had an inadequate singing voice, when in a competition we were gradually eliminated. We stood in a circle, and the losers were forced to go into an outer circle, like those of Dante's Hell, except that the inner circle for the youngsters with the purest sopranos was heaven. I was hurt.

That first spring term was a happy one for me. Life at school was novel and exciting. We were for the most part treated well by the masters and older boys, just because we were new. Before the summer holiday began, I caught measles, mumps and chicken pox, and was confined along with other sufferers to the infirmary. As we lay in our row of beds, to combat the boredom during our convalescence, I told fantastical stories to the other boys, usually dramas about the war. "Tell us another, Rowley," they would say, and I would comply, inventing on the spot - so to speak - these verbal entertainments where we were the heroes and always triumphed at the end.

That summer of 1943 I went to Scotland with my mother, and we stayed in a hotel in Aboyne some 30 miles west of Aberdeen for about six weeks. Aboyne was two railway stops before Balmoral. The hills were covered with mauve heather speckled with red and green. Every day I went out in a rowboat with her on the nearby lake, and we trawled for pike, occasionally catching one. Usually it was raining or drizzling, but I didn't care. One day I actually caught a six inch salmon in the nearby River Dee with a fly rod - my greatest fishing thrill. On the rare days when the sun shone I played on the moors near the hotel, and insulted my mother by calling her "a twerp." I had learned this and other pejoratives at Gilling. My mother was not amused. "I am going to write Father Paul [he was the very tall headmaster of Ampleforth] and he will discipline you." I suppose this threat produced a degree of fear within me. "I am all alone as your mother, and I have no other choice. You force me to. He will punish you."

Around that time I finally learned from my mother what had happened to John. I now knew that he lived in a mental hospital. Referring to his attempted suicide, she added, "He bungled it."

The autumn began. I took the train west from York, and depression settled over me. As I looked out the train window at the gray landscape, dusk falling, I fantasized that I would fall asleep for three months, only waking up on the way home. Father Paul never materialized. She may have written him, but he had better things to do than cross the valley and chastise a small boy in the junior school for calling his mother "a twerp."

My mother did, however, take the train north to Yorkshire, and visited me at the school. She had moved to a flat in London. Brampton was no more. From her viewpoint putting even more miles between us and Priory Hill must have been both an escape and a relief. Years later I learned that she had visited John in the hospital a few times, but on each occasion he said less until - after about nine months - he said nothing at all. Uncle Dick and our grandmother had the same experience with him.

In 1943 George, who had just "come down" from Cambridge with his law degree and was starting to work as an articled clerk in a London solicitor's office, for which he was not paid, applied to the Ministry of Defense for a full pension for John. Our grandmother submitted an affidavit, saying, "If he had only taken up spiritualism, as I told him to, he would still be in the Army." This legal statement combined possibly with the history of John's mother's frequent sojourns in nursing homes gave the government sufficient ammunition to deny the application. Men existed to fight the Germans; if you didn't, you were a coward. I of course knew nothing of this. John had just disappeared.

So my mother arrived for a night's visit. She stayed with a nearby landowner, an elderly gentleman, who was, I think, a widower. Even a small boy such as me could tell that he was interested in her. I have often thought since then that my life would have been very different, if she had accepted his proposal, but her heart was with the American. She and I visited the school chapel, and prayed there for a few minutes. In this chapel, closing my eyes tightly after gazing at the sacred host on the altar, I used to pray that the war would end, that sweet Jesus would bring the combatants to their senses. Coming out of the long room with its wicker chairs, the altar at one end, I said to her, "Mummy, did you pray for daddy's soul?" "No," she replied. Surprised, I said, "Who did you pray for?" "Someone else."

Sometimes we were allowed to play in the bracken on the hillsides. This provided ample opportunity for war games, as we dashed and hid among the hillocks, tumbling to the ground, laughing and screaming. One dark night the entire school walked down the hillside, crossed some fields and stood by the railroad tracks. We were there to watch the King's train pass by on the way north to Scotland. Loyally we cheered. In the winter we walked down into the valley to play rugby, which I was bad at. By the end of the afternoon we would be covered in mud. We were allowed one bath a week, but what we called "a spray," i.e. a shower, twice a week. For daily ablutions there were also rows of wash basins, which had a grim extra utility.

Punishment was either by caning, which happened only when a boy ran away and was then caught; being struck by a whalebone covered with leather on the open palm - the usual form of discipline; or at night the bottom of a tennis shoe, which was swung against the small offender's naked behind. The victim was ordered to climb out of bed, kneel beside it and drop his pajama bottom while bending the upper part of his torso across the bed. Tennis shoe therapy was usually prescribed for offenses such as talking in the dark after lights were out. The master on my floor was a Father Christopher Topping who would suddenly appear in a dormitory room, his dark form silhouetted in the dim light. There were about 20 of us to each room in single beds. At the beginning of one term we noticed that he was wearing new tennis shoes. This was bad news, because they would be harder and less supple. The moment he appeared in the first of the linked dormitory rooms - a figure in his cassock outlined by the electric light behind him - a whispered message would flash through the bedrooms, "FCT is coming. FCT is coming."

I was never struck by FCT's shoe, but I was once hit with the whalebone. My crime was talking during math class, and the Benedictine, a Father Bede, a big tall man, ordered me to visit the headmaster just before lunch. A group of other boys, who had also committed various sins, waited in a line outside the office of the elderly head of the school. Each one of us entered separately, and would then emerge a minute or so later, crying, and holding his injured hand with the other one. He would run as fast as he could to the wash basins, turn on the cold water tap, and hold his burning palm to the stream of water. When I appeared before the monk, he asked me what my offense was. He was a little old man. I told him. I then held out my open palm. He raised his arm, and I was struck by the whalebone, which was about a foot long and resembled in shape a ruler. I was lucky. I could have been hit two, three or four times.

The school held boxing matches one day. I was not liked by my fellows, but I was respected. I was the best student in the class, and at night before going to sleep just before our holidays began I would lie in bed, calculating where I stood in relation to my classmates in each of the 11 subjects we studied. I was usually the best in about six of them. However, I decided on the occasion of the boxing matches to see if I could improve my popularity. There was a boy in the class who was taller and bigger than me, who was neither liked nor respected. So I challenged him. We had big gloves. In the ring he was just too strong for me, and, though I was comforted by a lay master who was fond of me, and by a couple of my classmates, I lost the match.

When our vacation came, we climbed into a school bus. It headed down the hill to the local railway station, and we sang songs. "No more pencils, no more books, no more teacher's dirty looks." Twice a week we were compelled to walk in pairs up a path on the hillside. This was for exercise when there were no sports that day. So we sang, "Walking two by two, Up the dirty old avenue." These songs with their blatant rebelliousness gave us great pleasure, because we knew the authorities could do nothing about it. They could hardly expel us from the school, since we were going home anyway.

That Christmas of 1943 I returned home to our new London flat, which was in Burton Court in Chelsea. Nearby was the Guard's chapel, and some months later hundreds of them would die when it received a direct hit from a German V-1. Outside in the small park opposite our apartment building I could see the cables which held balloons flying several thousand feet above in the gray sky to deter enemy bombers. My report card for the autumn term arrived, containing mostly "A"s in my courses and a comment from the headmaster, "Sometimes Peter is absent-minded." I asked my mother, "What does 'absent-minded' mean?" She told me. I was puzzled at this characterization, and did not know what I could do about it.

That same holiday she received a telegram, and her face became wreathed in smiles. My mother and I rode up the lift to our flat.

She said, "How would you feel if I married Colonel Humphrey?"

"I don't know, mummy. Isn't he already married?"

"Yes, but when you are sixteen I will explain to you why it is all right with the Catholic Church." As I was nine, this seemed a very far away promise. At the time I did not know that among my mother's accomplishments was the turning of Roman Catholic teaching on marriage and divorce upside down. Somehow she had found a Jesuit at the Farm Street church in London who, she said, had sanctioned their union, despite the fact that Jack had been previously married. And then there was her sister, the nun, who by then had been promoted to the exalted position of Reverend Mother. She had approved the marriage. Both the priest and the nun further assured my mother she would not go to hell.

A little voice inside me told me that Jack Humphrey spelled trouble for me in the years ahead, though I could see the happiness in her eyes and the smile on her lips when she spoke of him. He had been transferred back to Washington, D.C., but this had not stopped the romance.

What I did not know was that when he returned to America (whether it was by plane or boat in the middle of the war I have no idea) he and my mother had decided that he was going to stay married to Katherine, his wife. His job was in the Pentagon, and he said years afterwards that he was offered a promotion to brigadier general. Simultaneously he and Katherine resumed their relationship which had been interrupted, so she thought, solely by his patriotic service to his country. He was after all way beyond the age for conscription, and had volunteered after Pearl Harbor. Because of his relatively brief flying experience in the First World War, he was offered a commission as a staff officer. According to Jack, he told her of his love for my mother, concluding that he had broken it off out of loyalty to Katherine. Jack said that her reply was that she only wished she had known about this a year earlier, because there had been a man who wanted to marry her. Now she had lost her chance. He decided that such an attitude merited his changing his mind yet again and asking Katherine for a divorce. The Army Air Force agreed to transfer him back to England, but it would cost him the promotion. Angrily Katherine agreed to establish residency in Reno, Nevada, and obtain the divorce there, accompanied by the oldest of their teenage sons. He promised to give her all his assets in America, except of course for most of his military salary. He knew of course that I brought a trust fund with me, and there was my mother's fund, which would be automatically reduced to one third of its size if she remarried.

Meanwhile my mother and I spent the second summer in Scotland. I do not remember there being any mention of him on the moors or in the Scottish hotel, and I returned to another depressing term at Gilling. On the weekends a smaller tow-headed boy and I played chess indoors. When the weather was bad, there was nothing else to do. One day in November, 1944, I was given a telegram. "Darling Peter. I have married Colonel Humphrey. Love. Mummy."

His job as an intelligence officer was to interview the pilots and crews of the American bombers in the Eighth Force who had returned safely to their English airfields after bombing various parts of Germany. Occasionally he went on these missions himself, though he did not have to, but he was very fond of war and was prepared to take the risk. He knew months in advance that the Germans were preparing to attack London and the southern half of England with strange unmanned planes, which carried lethal explosives. These were technically known as V-1s but popularly as "buzz bombs." They flew at about 300 miles per hour and the engine in the rear, which was a kind of primitive jet, made a buzzing noise. It was possible to shoot them down, though they would then explode on hitting the ground. Another technique used by British fighter pilots was to fly very close to the V-1, slide the fighter's wing under the tip of the buzz bomb's wing and then try to turn it into a swooping dive towards the ground before it reached London. The V-1s were inexpensive to manufacture, and there were so many of them that some penetrated the shield of British fighter planes, anti-aircraft fire and balloons. Before the V-1 attacks began, Jack was not allowed to tell my mother of this alarming future development, and it would be treasonable to tell her too of the rockets, which were expected to follow in a few months the V-1s. These were called V-2s, were small in number, and very expensive to make. The crippled German economy could only produce limited numbers. They performed a sub-stratospheric arc at great speed, were impossible to detect and caused even more damage. Nevertheless, he used all his considerable powers of persuasion to urge her to move out of London to a hotel, the Red Lion, about 40 miles west in High Wycombe. She strongly objected, but eventually she gave in. In the 1945 general election Winston Churchill addressed the crowd in the High Street below him, speaking outside from the roof of the front door portico with its pillars.

There I spent Christmas, 1944, and a little girl of about 10 and I became friends. She was living with her family in the hotel too. Once we exposed our sexual organs to each other. We also made fun of my mother and new step-father. On the hotel staircase, walking up to our bedrooms after dinner, Jack would speak to my mother in his Midwestern American accent, "Honey…" We would mimic within their earshot, "Honey, honey…" He turned angrily towards us, saying "That's not funny." But he restrained himself from further reprimand. After all we were still living in England, my country, where I had trustees and relations. If he hoped to take his new bride - encumbered, as she was, with a son - to America, he had better be pleasant. On a cloudless day at the spring holiday I looked up into the clear blue sky and saw in the distance a small black object. That was the only "buzz bomb" I ever saw.

In April, 1945, I was told by the monks and by letter from my mother that I would not be coming back to Gilling. We were to take a ship to the United States. I was warned by other boys and even by their visiting parents, "America is a dangerous place with Red Indians." Others said Americans were "very rude." I was filled with both foreboding and excitement. I had also made a friend at the school, and he expressed a willingness to come and stay at my home as my guest, but obviously this was not to be.

Chapter 2

America

My mother and I were among the thousands of passengers on the 20,000 ton *S.S. Argentina*, converted from a passenger ship, traveling in the last convoy of the European part of the Second World War from Southampton, England to New York. President Roosevelt had died a few days before we embarked, and everybody knew the war against Germany was almost over.

My English maternal grandmother, dressed in black, without my grandfather knowing about it, had said good-bye to us at Victoria Station in London before we took the train to the Southampton docks. She had whispered to me, "Peter, promise me you'll never become an American citizen." "Yes, granny."

Except for the few other women and children in our cabin for two (we were eight) the boat was filled with soldiers. They were Americans who had been prisoners of the Germans, and they were the first to be returned to their native country. Because my new step-father was a colonel, he had finagled us onto the vessel, knowing that the moment the war was over, the fighting men would be given priority over dependents.

Standing at our porthole, I could see the destroyers on the horizon, patrolling on the white-capped waves. We sailed at the speed of the slowest ship. In the distance the fast destroyers went around us in circles. The week before an identical convoy had been attacked by Nazi submarines. Occasionally we could hear depth charges being dropped for practice, making loud muffled noises, and I could see the spumes of water. During the voyage I had an ear infection, which must have been cured by a ship doctor, though I have no memory of him. Except for our bedroom on a higher deck the lower ones, which were designed for four adults, slept 20 soldiers in hammocks, five tall, that swung out from the walls.

On the May day we approached New York it was sunny, and the main deck was covered with soldiers in shirtsleeves and brown trousers, playing poker with match sticks as chips. One of them said to me, "When you're in New York, kid, and you see a black car, grab the nearest manhole cover, and jump down. They're gangsters, and they'll shoot you."

My mother and I checked into a bedroom on a high floor of the Hotel McAlpin near 34th street, and I looked out the window at the gray clouds and the city below and burst into tears. That night we walked up Park Avenue, and ran into the only person we knew in New York - John Harlan, a lawyer, who had been in the Army Air Force in England with my step-father. A tall, charming man, he later became a justice of the U.S. Supreme Court. He immediately invited us to stay in his apartment for two days. The next day my mother had to take the subway to the Brooklyn Navy Yard on an immigration entry problem. The same day the war in Europe ended - VE day. There were subdued celebrations in New York, as the conflict with Japan continued.

Then we took the night train to Detroit, and changed to another one the next day to Saginaw, Michigan. This had been my step-father's childhood home, and one of his two sisters, Gladys Sample, a kindly white-haired woman who was married to a psychiatrist (possibly the only one in Saginaw), welcomed us, though it soon became clear she sided with my stepfather's first wife, Katherine Strong Humphrey. There was an argument between "Aunt Glad" and my mother.

So we moved to a respectable hotel in downtown Saginaw. I was enrolled for three weeks in a Catholic parochial school, where I was astonished at a holiday fete in a public park to see my girl classmates wearing lipstick. Nevertheless, the Samples took us to their country club where their friends greeted us warmly, exclaiming over our British accents.

My mother and I were taken to see Jack's mother, who lived in a white bungalow when she was not wintering at her house in Sarasota, Florida. A very plump sweet old lady, she always spelt President Franklin Delano Roosevelt's name with a small "r." What she thought in her cool polite midwestern way of her youngest son marrying a middle-aged English war bride I have no idea. All his life Jack spoke of her reverentially.

When the summer vacation began, the Samples encouraged my mother and me to stay at a resort on Lake Michigan near Traverse City called Indian Trail Lodge. I endured the incredible heat in the old railway carriages carrying us through the scrub pines of the upper part of the lower peninsula of the state. In the woods near the resort I saw for the first time a chipmunk - a delightful little brown and white speckled creature sticking its head up from a hole in the sandy forest floor. There we heard of Churchill's defeat by the Labor Party in the British election, which shocked my mother.

In August we moved to Joplin, Missouri, the home of Jack's youngest sister, Win, married to an older man, a stocky congenial character, Pat, who was a wheeler-dealer in the lead and zinc mining industry of the Ozarks. They were friendly, and never mentioned my step-father's other family. They lived in a large rambling wooden house with a porch, surrounded by fields, and I happily caught baby rabbits in the long cut hay, running excitedly after the tiny creatures. I did not hurt them.

Then the atomic bombs over Hiroshima and Nagasaki went off, the war against Japan ended, and we knew my step-father would meet us soon in Washington, D.C., which was to be his new military assignment, working in the Pentagon. We had to drive there, but because my mother was unfamiliar with American roads the Sample's son, Dick, a sturdy young buck, deeply interested in girls and beer, reluctantly offered to be our unpaid chauffeur, stopping along the way in Cleveland, Ohio.

We stayed with Jack's brother George, who was later to become Eisenhower's Secretary of the Treasury. George was six years older, and used to regularly beat up his younger brother when George was in his late teens. He was the President of the M.A. Hanna Co., an enormous mining conglomerate, and during the Vietnam War was characterized by Norman Mailer in *Why Are We in Vietnam* as the quintessential corporate tycoon. He and his wife lived in the wealthy suburb of Shaker Heights, and, though they were polite during our overnight stay, there was a distinct cool in the air. American soldiers, who fought overseas, were not supposed to leave their wives and children back home and take up with foreign hussies. That evening which was VJ Day young Dick groaned that he could not go out and celebrate with his buddies.

After Jack arrived, one of the first orders of business was to get me out of the way. The happy newlyweds found a boarding school outside of Washington called Georgetown Prep. Run by Jesuits, it was housed on a hill in large dark red brick buildings. I was on my own. Most of the other students were the sons of wealthy Irish-Americans, who were not fond of the English. I was repeatedly pushed on a bed by a fat boy as the others watched. I was also given "a pink belly" which consisted of the victim being held down and his torturers slapping his stomach. The only saving grace was that one weekend a group of us went to a drugstore in nearby Bethesda, Maryland. I had not yet lost my desire for sugar after British rationing. I ate five butterscotch sundaes in a row. Of course I was sick and for 30 years could not eat another.

One of the Jesuit teachers asked me to tell the class about my experiences in wartime Britain. Standing on a platform in a small dark auditorium, I was embarrassed because no bombs had fallen directly on us and had no idea what to say. I felt I was a disappointment. Every other weekend I was alone at the institution, as most of the other boys went home to their families. I wandered the dispiriting campus, climbing and descending the small hills and valleys, as the sun set. It was the fall, and russet leaves lay everywhere, their dark red color matching the buildings. Occasionally a passing Jesuit greeted me. I developed an obsession that I was losing sight in my right eye. One fall weekend Georgetown Prep's football team played their arch rivals, St. Alban's, the episcopal private day school in D.C. - a contest that baffled me and left me feeling even more alone. On the other weekends I was allowed to visit my mother and step-father 10 or so miles away in Washington. They would visit the National Gallery, admiring the paintings, me trailing behind. To this day I'm reluctant to visit museums.

When the Christmas holiday began, I found myself in the latest of the six different places my parents had found to live in over the space of less than a year in Washington, as there was a housing shortage because of the recently ended war. In the evening I would listen upstairs in my bedroom to American radio such as the adventures of "Superman," which were a new escape for me. After I had gone to bed one night, I heard my mother and Jack talking in the living room, and crept to the head of the stairs. My step-father was giving my mother wise counsel on what was wrong with me. I could hear "Peter this... Peter that." It was usually his voice.

My step-father never hit me. He didn't have to. A constant theme of his conversation was how tough he was and what a good athlete he had been. Wrestling. Acrobatics. Football. Military combat in both world wars. In the First his only "action" had been when his Army biplane in France during a practice flight struck an enormous roller on a grass field when attempting to land. His large body and forceful manner were a reminder that one swipe of his hand, and I would have been history, so to speak. He only had to raise his voice a little bit, or project a harder tone, and I was cowed into silence, This meant that he could continue his almost endless monologue. As my mother and I were the only two human beings in the world who accepted his stories about himself without question, we were an audience essential to his ego. His first wife and his three sons obviously did not share this unbounded admiration of Jack Humphrey, and his older brother was even more dubious of his younger sibling's superiority, not to mention those corporate competitors at the General Reinsurance Co. in the late 'thirties who had undermined his position near the top. Thank God the Second World War had come along just in time to rescue him from Wall Street and Katherine.

It was not easy for them to find a boarding school in America who would accept a boy a year below the minimum age. Fortunately for them my grades at Georgetown Prep had been good. I was about fifth in a class of 30. What better solution than to jump me a grade so that I could be admitted. This was in early January, 1946. So I went from the sixth to the seventh grade and was enrolled at the Asheville School in North Carolina. It was five hundred miles from Washington. My parents could truthfully write my trustees in England that I was going to a prominent boarding school while continuing to pocket much of the income from my trust for their residence. After all a room had to be kept for me. More than once during those years Jack said to me he thought my father's will was unfair to my mother. My mother assured me that, even though the new school was not Roman Catholic, the Dean of Students, a Mr. Coffey, was of our faith. He would protect me.

Asheville School for Boys. We pronounced the "a" in Asheville with a flat sound, but the southerners spoke it with a drawl, enunciating the "a" like the sound of the first two vowels in "iambic." Some put a slight emphasis on "for Boys." The school song began, "Where the pines and laurels…" and extolled the glories of its education and the surrounding hills and mountains. In the distance was Mount Pisgah, a vast shape rising gradually to a peak. Around the school there was green forest as far as the eye could see. The small city of Asheville was about five miles away and invisible. There were as many privies as houses in the countryside. Occasionally dogs could be heard barking. Moonshine, an illegal very potent whiskey, was distilled in the region.

Asheville was a "northern" prep school in the south. It existed because two headmasters from Cleveland at the beginning of the 20th century wanted to found an educational institution with the same high academic standards as the famous New England ones like Exeter and Groton but located in a healthy climate. There would be no cold winters. Because Asheville was in the mountains of western North Carolina the summers were cooler than were usual in the south. In fact the town and its immediate environs were well-known throughout the U.S. for harboring sanatoriums. In the winter there was little snow, and in the summer there were pleasant breezes. The school itself faced south. There were three large wooden buildings of imitation Tudor style of uninspired design for dormitories and classrooms, an imitation Gothic stone chapel, and a rickety wooden dining hall. Each of us had our own small narrow bedroom with bed, desk, lamp, chair and a closet. After Gilling I found such accommodation luxurious. My window looked out on the grass, bushes and trees of the campus and Pisgah. The headmaster was David Fall. To an outsider he appeared to be handsome and charming.

Almost all of the boys came from wealthy WASP families. Their families lived in fashionable suburbs such as Lake Forest, Illinois, and Upper Montclair, New Jersey. Their accents were very different from the southern drawls of the local whites and blacks. With few exceptions the masters and their wives were from the north too. All the waiters in the dining hall were Negroes (as they were called in those days), and deferential.

On arrival I discovered I was the smallest boy in the school. There were about 150 students. After a day of classes I realized my five peers (there were six of us in the youngest form) were bigger and smarter than me, not to mention all the others. There was a tall boy with a wide mouth who liked to make fun of everyone else. There was a very rich 12-year-old from a family that owned a famous facial tissue - a sensitive, quite pretty youth. The class was taught by a tall, dark-haired young man, who looked like what would today might be called the ideal yuppie. Recovering from an illness he was there temporarily, planning to return to his family's Chicago bank. And then there was Ted who like me was alienated from the others. Ted was a very fat youngster with rather thin sensual lips. He walked with a slight swaying motion, and his American parents, who lived in Maine, were young and impecunious. Ted and I became friends, giving each other sympathy in the face of the others, tentatively questioning their characters. During one class the wide-mouthed boy turned round (he was in the front row) and said, "Look, Rowley's sucking his thumb." There were giggles.

Ted quoted the exhortation,
> "Early to bed
> Early to rise
> Makes a man
> Healthy, wealthy
> And wise."

But he then rephrased it as,
> "Early to rise
> Early to bed
> Makes a man
> Healthy, wealthy
> And dead."

American culture surprised me. I had never heard a song like "Shoe Fly Pie" in England. I thought I liked it, but I wasn't sure. My school mates were very enthusiastic about such popular hits. One of their other favorite hobbies was reading comic books. These I appreciated too, eagerly awaiting the monthly arrival of "Captain Marvel," "The Green Hornet," "Spiderman" and my favorite, "Superman." When I imagined I was one of these heroes, I escaped from the school.

Boyd Fall was in the eighth grade. I was in the seventh. Nevertheless he lived on the same dormitory floor, and he was the younger of the headmaster's two sons - a fat, red-faced bully who knew he could get away with a lot more than the rest of us. I was very careful whenever he was nearby, though once he succeeded in throwing me against the wall of my bedroom.

All of us were forced to attend a 20 minute daily service every week day morning. On Sundays Mr. Coffey, stocky, white-haired with a stern but kindly face, took the few Roman Catholics into the 8 a.m. mass at a church about two miles from the school. We walked there and back, and we then had to attend the Protestant service in the chapel, On one such walk Mr. Coffey said to me, "Boyd's dangerous. He may try to force you to do immoral things." He did not explain exactly what these were, but I was grateful for the advice.

The chapel was described in the school brochure as a haven of peace and beauty. The services were "non-denominational," though in fact they were similar to Episcopal and Presbyterian ones. Mr. Fall, wearing a dark gown, sat in a pew on a raised platform beside the altar. Showing us his profile, his face displayed holy gravity. The chaplain was a pleasant-looking middle-aged man who wore tweeds and affected a caring manner. He earnestly delivered a boring 10-minute homily Monday to Friday. Fortunately he did not give the sermon on Sundays where the quality of the addresses by the visiting clergy was slightly higher. Although the purpose of our attendance on weekdays and Sundays was to edify our minds and soothe our souls, I do not remember their having any effect on me other than using up time. But little more could be said of my weekly trips to the Church of Saint Whatever it was other than satisfying my mother's wish that I remain a Roman Catholic. Then the summer holiday began, and Mr. Coffey retired. A few of the other masters made snide remarks about him, welcoming his departure.

I took the train alone to Atlanta and changed to another train, getting off in Montgomery, Alabama. The small city was deep in the south with a history of fervent support for the Confederacy. My destination was Maxwell Air Force base, the home of the Air War College. The Air Force had not yet achieved its independence, and was technically a part of the Army. My step-father had been transferred there from the Pentagon, and as a full colonel was given a substantial house on the edge of the base golf course. Less than a mile away was the muddy brown Alabama river, which in an odd way was beautiful. Very occasionally I saw catfish which had been caught by fishermen - large unhappy creatures who were wide and mostly flat. They had protruding eyes and the characteristic wet antenna. Their happier brethren patrolled in large numbers the bottom of this broad river slowly cutting its way through the fields and forest on the way to the Caribbean.

As a veteran of the strategic bomber command in Europe Jack's job was to teach the majors and lieutenant colonels who were sent there as students by the Air Force from posts all over America and the world. Jack loved the base. His enthusiasm extended to his commanding officer, Major General Orville Anderson, nicknamed "O.A." In about 1936 the then Major Anderson and another officer set an altitude record by ascending to 56,000 feet in a balloon over Kansas. The general had commanded a large number of fliers and bombers of the Eighth Air Force in the raids on Germany. Occasionally he visited our house as the guest of Jack and my mother. He would enter, bound up the stairs to the second floor to visit the bathroom, cursing happily while yelling over his shoulder to my parents and me. He was of Scandinavian origin, and it was his strong conviction, which he expounded to the officers, that the only way to deal with the Russians, our ex-allies, who were becoming increasingly uncooperative, was to drop an atom bomb on Moscow. After the general left my step-father in his discussions with my mother and me endorsed the idea whole-heartedly - or almost.

We had a black maid who could have been the model for Aunt Jemima of the Pancakes. She came every day from the colored (as it was referred to) section of Montgomery. Jack had a good opinion of her housekeeping skills, but said she had the brain of a 10-year-old like almost everyone else in her race. She could not be trusted with the vote or anything else important. She always smiled. Eight years later one of these ladies like her refused to move to the rear of a Montgomery bus from her front seat, and thus was born Dr. Martin Luther King and the civil rights movement.

My step-father was very solicitous of my mother. Although she constantly had to listen to his views, worries and accomplishments, he never struck her, criticized her in the gentlest way possible, asked that she do tasks for him or the household in a polite manner, praised her frequently and equally often gave her gifts - usually clothes or costume jewelry - as much as he could possibly afford. For her part she reciprocated his admiration.

I returned to Asheville for the fall term. To my surprise the bully was no longer there. Once a week my mother wrote me a letter, beginning "Darling Peter…" There were then two pages of sweet nothings. Then she would end with "Lots of love. Mother." I spent a large amount of my time daydreaming. I would become Prime Minister of England or a great detective like Sherlock Holmes. Everywhere I looked for clues. I found it frustrating that I never found any. Another escape was the weekly issue of *Time* magazine, which I read cover to cover, imagining myself the famous person on the front cover.

The school sponsored in conjunction with *Time* a contest, which was mandatory for the student body. We sat in the auditorium answering the multiple choice questions. When I took the test I won it for the first and second forms, and was rewarded with the gift of a book. One year I chose *The Complete Works of O'Henry*. I could tell that most of my classmates were unhappy with my triumph..

In the afternoon like every other boy in school I was ordered to play American football. We trooped down to the basement of one of the buildings where there was a room with lockers. Amid much clatter we donned what struck me as rather heavy unwieldy equipment - shoulder and hip pads, trousers with knee pads and helmets. My heart sank. I had never played this strange game before. I suspected that there was bodily contact. Ted Fount wore his uniform with an air of willowy resignation, and the other players laughed at his appearance.

On the field I was told to play guard. I was not fast enough to be a running back, nor tall enough to be an end. I learned that the players in the line were supposed to be muscular and brave. In play after play the back on the opposing squad holding the ball ran directly at and over me. Rather than resist after a weak attempt to put my arms around his churning legs I was pushed to the ground. It was strongly hinted that I was a coward. Eventually one of the players offered to teach me how to tackle. After practice he ran at me time after time, and I, though I did not like it, succeeded in stopping this larger boy by seizing his legs. At the end of the season the school engaged a photographer to take a picture of the junior football team. There in the front row beside the center crouched me, holding the same pose as an NFL regular, faking a smile. When I returned home for Christmas, I gave this photo to my mother and Jack. They looked on it as further proof that my transfer to Asheville was a success.

Among the new boys that term was Bob Luchars from Upper Montclair, New Jersey. With bushy eyebrows and an honest face, his personality was sometimes gruff. Of course his distaste for the school included football. Ted, Bob and I became friends. We formed a little group. One day I asked him which of us he liked best. He replied Ted, and Ted preferred Bob over me.

I joined the dramatic society. My friends also did. We were advised by a Mr. Baker, a jowly, portly man who also taught senior English. There were two older boys who were active in the club. Both of them were outsiders within the school, and one of them, Jerry, was thin with a long jaw and dark eyes. Because of them we discovered there was an elegantly furnished one-story building called The Music House. The bay window faced south. A wealthy alumnus had given it to the school in the hope of encouraging appreciation of classical music. No one from the rest of the school ever visited it.

My first role in a light comedy was the French maid. I had no lines. When the curtain went up, I walked on stage swinging a feather duster against the pictures and chairs. I was asked to wear high heels. I found it very difficult to learn how to walk in them, teetering precariously. I wore a dress, stockings, white apron, and a little white cap. Then I was made up with a blonde wig, lipstick and rouge. Andy Riggs, a star of the football team, said, "Rowley, if you were a girl, I'd ask you for a date."

One night I woke up to find myself on the dormitory floor below me in the presence of a tall older boy with short dark hair, who was a prefect. I was standing in the corridor in my pyjamas. The senior said to me solicitously, "Rowley, you were sleep-walking. Did you have some bad experiences in England during the Second World War?" I could not think of any to tell him, but he persisted with his questioning in a kindly way. I struggled to think of some, but I could not. Eventually he gave up.

That same term I experienced feelings of puppy love for the very wealthy young man. However, other than glancing at him in a friendly way, I never dared to go any further, and there were never any thoughts of physical intimacy. I think he too shared similar feelings, and also was afraid to admit to them. After a while he was cold to me, and I reciprocated with an equally standoffish manner. One day he ran away from the school. His parents had one of their several homes some 30 miles away and this was where he fled. He was persuaded to return, and suffered no penalties for his brief escape. Asheville allowed him and the wide-mouthed boy to share a bedroom - the only such arrangement in the school.

I also developed a habit of imagining that I was carrying a blanket under my right arm. Whether I was in my room or outside, I would clutch my elbow to my chest time after time, and became quite worried by my unusual behavior, though fortunately no one else noticed. Eventually my neurosis faded away.

Occasionally at night I dreamed I was shot into outer space. I traveled deeper into the dark of the universe, hoping to return to the earth. There were some distant stars. I went farther and farther into empty space never reaching a destination, nor ever returning to earth. The sense of loneliness and terror was frightening. I woke up relieved to discover that I was in my bed room.

After two years of Asheville I rarely smiled. In the dining hall we were forced to sit at round tables under the supervision of a master. Usually the other boys tried not to sit next to me. Frequently I was ridiculed. When a boy made a devastating rejoinder to me, another would say, "Flush." If we were in the privacy of one of our bedrooms or in a common room where there was no faculty member, the "flush" would be accompanied by the other boy mimicking the sound of water emptying from a toilet. With the exception of my three friends I became suspicious of my fellow students.

Asheville did well in sports, winning most of its football and basket ball games. Our opponents were local high schools, their players from low and middle income backgrounds. For the more important games we were transported by bus, if it was an "away" game. Our role was to cheer for the Asheville team, which wore big "A"s on their jerseys. The school colors were blue and white. One song was "Seven come eleven, come a blue, come a white, come on team, fight, fight, fight." My friends and I could not care less whether our school won or not. Mr. Fall rarely mentioned the academic accomplishments of the best students but he was enthusiastic in his praise for the outstanding athletes. Asheville students regarded themselves as superior to the North Carolina youths - taller, smarter and better coordinated. Our opponents looked upon us as hated northern preppies.

However, most of the time Mr. Fall was not at Asheville. He and his glamorous wife were traveling through the mid west and the north east, raising money from alumni and friends. The old dining hall was torn down, and a new one built. The school decided they could not afford a full complement of black waiters, and so students were offered on a voluntary basis some of their jobs.

During the spring vacation from the eighth grade my mother and step-father suggested that I go to summer camp. The thought of being alone at another new organization dismayed me, and I resisted. Were they worried that I might complain to my trustees in England? What would happen if the trustees decided to bring me back to the U.K.? What would occur if the trustees asked for an accounting of how my income was spent? Where would they find the money to replace what I was contributing to their upkeep and mine? Did sympathy for me enter their hearts? They dropped the plan.

After the Christmas holiday at the beginning of the winter term despite my dismal performance in American football I went out for the newly organized soccer team. On the squad I discovered I had a talent for "dribbling" the ball past an opposing player. This involved a bit of trickery of pretending to push the ball with one foot in one direction and then kicking it a little harder with the other foot in the opposite direction. I was assigned to play end on the squad. Frequently the player opposite me was the redoubtable Andy Riggs, who I outplayed time after time with this little trick. Visions of being on a regular sports team swam through my head. I would be given the school sweater with the big "A" on it. But shortly before our first game against a team from another school I developed a "crick" in the groin of my right leg, and was unable to run. The school doctor prescribed rest.

I noticed my classmates refer to the four of us as "The Boys." Said in a mocking tone, this description was voiced loud enough so that we could overhear it. Other times they said it directly to us. "What does 'The Boys' mean, Ted?" I said. "It's a nasty remark," he replied. "But what does it mean?" I repeated, but he wouldn't tell me. After I learned the truth from someone else (I do not remember who) my feelings were a mixture of indignation, confusion and hurt. The others in our little group reacted variously. Sometimes they were annoyed; at other times they accepted these insults with amused resignation.

The school cancelled the annual *Time* current affairs contest. I felt that it was a conspiracy on the part of the school authorities to deny me my only distinction.

When vacations came, I did not really care whether I stayed at Asheville or returned home. And I felt neither pangs of regret or feelings of joy when it was time to leave home and go back to school

By the fall of 1947 my mother had persuaded Jack to resign from the Air Force. With her reserved manner my mother had found the American wives of the other officers a challenge, a situation she had never entirely overcome. Driving north while reading and talking about the Hiss-Chambers case, we arrived in Chicago, where he had taken a job as the first head of the Chicago office of the CIA. His office was a Greco-Roman white marble building on Lake Shore Drive about a quarter mile north of the Drake Hotel. Opposite was Lake Michigan. The government rented him at a reduced rent a town house on Ritchie Court. The back of our residence looked across an empty lot onto the Drive. At the end of the block was the old Potter Palmer mansion. A few blocks to the west was Clark Street notorious for its bars and crime. Nearby was the Pump Room, a fashionable restaurant, and Jack became a member of a private club which had an indoor tennis court and swimming pool.

I took the Southern Railway sleeper from Chicago to Asheville. Every month the school published on a bulletin board the grades of every boy. To my surprise and everyone else I placed third out of 150.

This entitled me to study at night anywhere in the school I liked. I was excused from study hall. I also achieved a modest measure of acceptance from my fellow students.

I developed a passion for baseball. Whenever I got the chance, I played it, practicing with the junior squad, though I was not yet good enough to be put on the team. In my spare time I read the major league baseball scores every day, published in the *Asheville Citizen-Times*, which was available in the school barbershop. I was a fan of the Detroit Tigers and admired their pitching staff which consisted of four starters "Prince" Hal Newhouser, "Dizzy" Trout, Paul Hutchinson, and Virgil "Fireball" Trucks. When at the end of the season, they invariably lost to the New York Yankees, I was disappointed. I subscribed to the weekly *The Sporting News*, and could recite within 10 points the batting average of the 400 major league baseball players. But my greatest individual hero was Bob Feller, the famous fastball pitcher for the Cleveland Indians. I read his autobiography and resolved to be as much like him as possible.

Puberty was raising its head among my classmates. In our spare time the most frequent topics of conversation were masturbation and sex with girls. The only teen-age girls we saw were the daughters of two masters who sometimes sat with their parents in the dining hall, but - other than laughing at us - contact was non-existent. The school allowed a few dances a year. One of them was at graduation, which was obviously limited to the senior class, as the rest of the student body had gone to their homes. Another one was sponsored by the Dramatic Society. Some girls from a private Roman Catholic day school in the town were invited. As I and most of my classmates knew none of the local girls and were too shy in any case to approach them, these rare dances were a non-event.

Throughout the day and evening my classmates and I interpreted every other remark for sexual meaning, producing guffaws and leers, and of course there was much boasting about sexual exploits with girls on vacations, though I - never having even kissed a girl - could not speak on the subject. Even classic books we were assigned to read for our courses were retitled - "The Sail of Two Titties" and "The Virgin of Menace". It was common knowledge that a group of students would meet in one of the boys' bedrooms. They sat in a circle on the floor, masturbated, competing with each other to see who could ejaculate first. These were called "Circle Jerkles."

I became obsessed with being popular, and spent a large amount of time, worrying how to achieve this state. But the more I thought about it, and the more I tried to ingratiate myself with my classmates, the more frustrated I felt at my failure. My grades ceased to be very good. The best teacher in the school was Wilbert Peck, who taught the fourth formers algebra. Mr. Peck was unusual in another respect. He was the only faculty member not to live on the campus. One afternoon after classes were over, I was summoned to appear before him. Middle-aged, he had a broad brow, hair combed on either side of a parting in the middle, and a grim visage. I stood before him. "Rowley," he said, sitting at his desk staring up at me. "You're an egotist." I was baffled by this remark.

My ego suffered another setback. I was a reporter on the school newspaper, the *Ashnoca*, which was published on glossy paper once a month. The faculty adviser was Mr. Baker, the English teacher who also directed the dramatic society plays. The student staff prepared an issue which carried the headline HEADMASTER VISITS ASHEVILLE, describing Mr. Fall's return from one of his many trips. The article had gone to the printer when Mr. Baker learned of it. Just in time he managed to cancel it.

For one issue I was assigned to write three articles. Normal procedure was to assign only one to an individual. A new rule had been introduced whereby any person who submitted an article after the 7 p.m. deadline would be dismissed from the paper. On my third and last article I was 10 minutes late. Thinking I had a very good excuse, I thought nothing of it, but two days later Sam MacArthur, who belonged to our little group, told me I had been fired. It was particularly galling because the editor, Mike Buhl, an upperclassman, was distantly related to me through marriage. But I was afraid to protest.

The summer holiday began, and we went to Indian Trail Lodge for six weeks. My step-father did not like the resort, but it was inexpensive and within driving distance of Chicago. Perhaps so many of his fellow mid westerners reminded him of his childhood in Saginaw. I loved the life there. While my parents occupied one of the cottages, I slept in a room in the lodge itself. I was free to run between the beach front cottages, delivering newspapers. I liked the white sandy beaches. I appreciated the friendly guests. The Lodge was owned and operated by the three Green sisters, none of whom were married.

I learned my mother was pregnant. Jack had been opposed to having a child, but she won out. The baby was due in mid-September, 1948.

About a week before the birth my old governess, Holmie, arrived from England. Initially I was pleased. My mother and step-father had persuaded her to leave Britain, where she had been working as a governess, and move to America. She agreed to be paid only one third of the going rate for baby nurses. My half-sister was born by Caesarean, and was named Dorothy in honor of my aunt, the nun.

Baby Dorothy's appearance in my life made no difference at all. I had naively assumed that Holmie and I would resume the loving relationship that had existed before I went away to boarding school in 1943. I soon discovered that this was not the case, that she was there solely for the benefit of my new half-sister. Relations between her and me cooled.

On vacation in Chicago I read an English translation of the short stories of Guy de Maupassant until my mother removed the book from my hands, saying it was unsuitable for a 14-year-old boy. She and Jack decided that I needed advice on sex, and so he asked me into a room at the house that he used as an office, and said that sex was like going to the bathroom, and that some people found it pleasurable. I did not know what to make of this information and had difficulty associating one activity with the other. My mother never gave me back the de Maupassant book.

Around this time his career in the CIA came to an abrupt end. He had resigned, he said, after a dispute with Admiral Hillenkoetter, the director in Washington. My step-father's main task had been to interview the heads of big Chicago-based corporations and persuade them to give him the reports from their foreign employees. Jack said he promised anonymity to the CEOs. According to Jack, Hillenkoetter demanded to know their identities.

Jack's mother, Mrs. Humphrey, had just died. Her estate after taxes was worth $180,000, and her will divided it equally among her four children. He decided he would support his family by investing on the stock market. He expected that there would be a bull market, particularly after Dewey beat Truman in the upcoming presidential election of 1948.

From then on through the rest of my teen-age years I listened - not always willingly - to Jack's views on stock and bonds. The Dow Jones average and a p/e ratio, which is the price of the stock divided by its annual earnings, appeared at every family meal. Long hours Jack spent in his office with a slide rule and calculator, the predecessors of the personal computer, calculating the fortunes of companies like IBM. Bored as I was, years later I found his expertise useful.

My mother and I had been away from England for four years. So we flew in a Constellation, a four-engine propeller plane, to Gander, Newfoundland. There was a snow storm. Visibility was so bad that the pilot could not see the airfield. Three times the plane circled it. I could see my mother becoming increasingly nervous. On the fourth attempt the pilot found the clouds had risen just enough to enable us to land.

After arriving in England we started a tour of friends and relations' houses, distributing as gifts cans of food. Although the war had been over for several years, there was still rationing. We visited my mother's brother, Uncle Willy, who owned a farm in Gloucestershire. My mother and her sisters severely criticized his wife, also called Dorothy, behind her back for not wearing fashionable clothes. They deplored the fact that she had converted one room of their house into a village shop. "Poor Willy. She's very unfair to him. The least she could do is wear some makeup, and she's always running into the shop when the bell rings."

We then went to Bath and stayed with my maternal grandparents. They lived in a town house on the Royal Crescent. My grandfather was very old, and obviously would not live much longer. My grandmother had persuaded her husband to drop his ban on the errant daughter, my mother. Even he must have realized that he was soon going up to heaven and that he had better see the sinner before it was too late. It was the first time I had ever met my grandfather. My mother had not seen him for 18 years. Conversation at dinner was entirely devoted to superficialities. He was very beant, and, when we went to the theatre, he sat in the front row and used an ear trumpet.

Then my mother and I stayed a few weeks with Aunt Jane and Uncle Reggie beside their small pretty estate in the tiny village of Acton Burnell eight miles from the historic town of Shrewsbury. They employed two keepers to raise pheasants and partridge which would be shot, starting in the autumn, at a paid shoot they ran. Cousin David and I were allowed to accompany stocky tweedy Bert, one of the keepers, in the evening, carrying a shotgun. We took turns shooting at rabbits and pigeons. For us it was the thrill of the day, and any game we killed were eaten.

Lying in our separate beds at night we chatted. David made a veiled reference to an unpleasant habit some of the boys in his boarding school practiced individually on themselves. I was afraid David would discover how unsure I was of myself as a result of my years in an

American boarding school. I tried to pretend I was normal. One night we decided to escape from our parents. I would steal my mother's and my Pan American plane tickets and cash them in. We would take pound notes from Uncle Reggie's wallet and Aunt Jane and my mother's handbags. Then we would go to Shrewsbury and take the train to London, making sure people at the ticket office and in the railway carriage noticed us. We would go separately into the men's toilet. When the train stopped at the second railroad station from Shrewsbury on the way to the capital, we would sneak off, and walk back to Acton Burnell park. We would have already hidden the shotgun and some shells in the woods. We would lie in the bracken and trees, shooting animals for food, sleeping in the open, avoiding the keepers and searching parents. If the adults were out, we would creep back into the house for extra supplies. I was determined to do it. When the appointed day came David said nothing. His nerve had failed him.

Then we went to Huntingdonshire and were the guests of my late father's brother and his wife. They took us to dinner in the private dining room of a country hotel in Buckden, and among their guests was a small wiry retired Army major with a moustache. He said of me, sticking out his tongue, licking his lips, "He is such a beautiful boy. I want to kiss him." The other adults laughed happily, and the major pursued me around the round dining table. He laughed uproariously, but I was quite frightened. I was glad to return to Chicago.

I had missed five weeks of the baseball season. The coach of the junior baseball team was a Mr. Bates, the French instructor. Although I had difficulty throwing a baseball overhand, as in England we either threw underarm or sidearm, I developed a sidearm fastball. One afternoon in practice I threw as hard as I could and struck out several of our batters. Mr. Bates noticed this. The next day we took a school bus to play our arch rivals, Christ School. I had a sore arm. Mr. Bates asked me to be the pitcher. This was my chance, and I was afraid to say "No," fearing I would never be asked again. Of course, I threw the ball slowly due to my stiffness, and by the third inning I was relieved, having been hit by the opposing team with ease.

That summer between my sophomore and junior years we went to Indian Trail and I met Nancy Brinker. She was an attractive 15-year-old with a stutter and a good figure - an accomplished swimmer. She said I was "cute", which surprised me. I was not even quite sure what this meant, though I guessed it was a compliment. In my little bedroom in the lodge one afternoon after hours of persuasion she lured me into kissing her. We then had trysts behind trees and cottages, holding each other while standing on the sandy ground. Then she went home to Grosse Pointe, a wealthy suburb of Detroit.

The summer continued. I became friends with Jim Reindel, a tall boy also from Detroit. He and I played tennis for hour after hour on the one concrete court.

At the end of the summer I went to Detroit for a few days to see Nancy. I asked Jim to come over and meet Nancy and me at her house. It soon became obvious that she preferred him over me. I was heartbroken. We returned to Chicago, and I wrote her letters, but she never answered me.

Returning to Asheville, I was more depressed than usual because of Nancy. I neglected my studies. Ted had not come back to the school. Presumably his Maine parents had run out of money for his tuition. My few friends and I heard that Jerry, who was a senior, was not well. Jerry was convinced that Mr. Hutchins, the assistant headmaster, had stood outside in front of the ground floor window of Jerry's room at night and watched him for three hours. Hutchins tried to persuade Jerry that this was not true. One evening Bob suggested that the four of us go and see Jerry to try to be of help. I was frightened, but I followed the others, and we found him in the senior common room. I did not know what to say, and stayed in the rear of our little group, but Bob engaged him in a strained conversation. Jerry's eyes looked hollow-eyed and dark. A few days later the men in the white coats from one of Asheville's mental hospitals arrived and took him away.

Such an event in a small community such as Asheville could not go unnoticed. Mr. Fall and the other faculty summoned the entire student body to the auditorium. Standing on the stage in front of us, Mr. Fall said that Jerry's illness was not the fault of Asheville School. It was because Jerry had been in summer stock theater.

For its fall production the dramatic society had decided to stage a play by J. B. Priestley. The melodrama concerned a middle-class British family (the father was an industrialist) whose daughter becomes pregnant outside of wedlock. I played the role of the girl's mother. After rehearsing for weeks and building the sets we performed our dress rehearsal.

The next day after lunch Mr. Fall summoned Mr. Baker, the cast and stage crew to a meeting in a corner of the new dining hall. He announced that he had canceled the play. He explained that Mrs.

Bement, the widow of the late saintly headmaster, had read the text and told him of her concern. Mr. Fall said it had an immoral theme, and there might be ministers from the town in the audience who would be shocked. We stood there in silence, meekly accepting this edict. But then Bob objected forcefully. Mr. Fall angrily told him that he was not going to change his mind and that he had better shut up.

When the Christmas vacation arrived and I returned to Chicago, it became clear that my step-father's plan to support my mother, Holmie and Dorothy (other than my contribution) through financial investments was not succeeding. After Truman was elected, the stock market went down. He had stayed up all night to hear the shocking news of Dewey's defeat. They decided to move to Princeton, New Jersey. My mother felt this would be more to her liking than the usual American suburb. Jack could find a job in the insurance industry and commute to New York.

That spring I continued to do very little work on my studies, though slightly more than in the fall. Nevertheless I was failing chemistry. This was taught by Mr. McCleary, a self-proclaimed expert on boys' sex habits and promoter of Yale University to the student body. Our small group detested him, and I am sure the feeling was mutual. The majority of the class laughed at his jokes, but we sat stony-faced. Near the end of the school year we had to write a scientific paper. By then my family had moved to Princeton and rented a house on the outskirts of the town. They had made friends with a Professor Luigi Crocco, an Italian, and his French wife, Simone - an expert in nuclear physics and rocket propulsion. With Professor Crocco's help, supplied with photographs by him, I wrote a 10-page treatise on the Cloud Chamber. It is a device used for detecting atomic particles. Mr. McCleary was astonished. He had to give me an A+ on the paper.

During that spring I suddenly began to grow rapidly, adding six inches to my height in a few months. I was now five foot eleven. Then the final exams began. Chemistry was an important course, and it was essential to pass it in order to be considered for admission to a good university. When I looked at the exam questions, I realized that on only some of them did I have any knowledge of the answers. A passing mark was 60 out of a 100. I concentrated on the subjects with which I had some familiarity, virtually ignoring the ones where I was weak. When Mr. McCleary graded our exam papers, he discovered I had scored 59. I was given a grade of 60 for the course.

On arrival at the school for my senior year I felt this was my one chance to seek a life which might be better than Asheville. I determined to study hard. I gave up all hope of becoming popular. I even took Mr. Peck's Advanced Algebra and Trigonometry course, which was said to be excellent preparation for entrance to an Ivy League college.

One of my four courses was English, and the teacher was Mr. Baker. For the first few classes he stood before us, rambling on in completely disconnected sentences, jumping from one subject to another in a totally illogical way. My classmates and I sat there in silence. None of us laughed. Then the men in the white coats arrived and took him away to one of Asheville's sanatoriums. In retrospect one can see that whatever may have been the other reasons for the poor man's breakdown there was the fact he had narrowly escaped from losing his job when he had discovered the outrageous headline about Mr. Fall. One of the star performers of his dramatic society had been locked up in a mental hospital. A play he had approved of as faculty adviser had been banned just before opening.

The school reacted swiftly, although the authorities did not seem to think it necessary to summon the student body for an explanation of what had happened to Mr. Baker. Perhaps as a faculty member his sudden departure only saved them money whereas a student was a source of money, or more likely madness of a student was a little more surprising than that of an adult. Within a few days a new English teacher appeared. He was a Mr. Edgar, who had just retired as the head of the English department at the Hotchkiss School in New England. He was white-haired, slim of build, and obviously fond of teaching boys. He had a particular liking for John Galsworthy, and - as we read *The Man of Property* - encouraged me to write a paper about each chapter..

Mr. Peck's mathematics was a major challenge. I had no hope of achieving a high mark. Many hours were spent struggling with problems for homework every night, but we were assured the admissions departments of the great universities would be impressed. Mr. Peck had a well-known reputation.

I also took American history, and "Uncle Will", the baseball coach, urged me congenially to read as many books as possible in my spare time of a 50-book series about the United States. They were short books of only about 150 pages each. For every book report I submitted to him I would receive extra points towards my grade. Plump and affable "UW" was the only master at the school to ever show more than a perfunctory interest in me during the five and a half years I was a student there. However, his approach was a sort of hands-off avuncular one.

He invited me and three or four other seniors to come to his house for "Wit'n Waffles" every Sunday night. In his living room one of us would read a brief paper on some subject, usually political. Then we would talk about it, "UW" encouraging our free discourse. The Korean war was a frequent topic as all of us were approaching the age to be drafted. Echoing Jack's views, I favored dropping nuclear bombs on China.

I took the SATs, and achieved a high score in mathematics and a very high score in English. Like my classmates the question of where to go to college was on my mind. Taking trips to see other colleges was never even considered by my parents. There was always Princeton down the road, so to speak. What could be easier for my mother and Jack than to send me there.

Then the director of admissions for Princeton University, William Edwards, arrived on the Asheville campus. Mr. McCleary had proselytized so enthusiastically for Yale that one third of my class hoped to go there. All the seniors including me were told to sit in a classroom and listen to a talk from Mr. Edwards. We were instructed to go to Mr. Fall's residence after the talk if we were interested in applying to Princeton. When I walked into the headmaster's living room, except for Mr. Edwards I discovered I was the only one there. He must have traveled a considerable distance in order to visit Asheville, and here was the only fruit of his labors - a tallish boy, thin with a blond pompadour, looking years younger than the sixteen I was, wearing an ill-fitting jacket and trousers. I was nervous, and in my usual way shy. I was very careful to say as little as possible. I sat on the edge of the sofa, my knees pressed together. I do not remember any of the questions he asked, except for one. "What do you like to do?" he said. "I like to read, sir," I replied. I sensed that he approved of my response.

The decision for me to go to college immediately after graduating from Asheville was influenced by the Korean war. If one entered college, one received a deferment from the local draft board. Of course the 19 Asheville seniors intended to go to university in September after the June graduation. For once my parents accurately analyzed my character or absence of it. They knew I lacked the maturity to attend college. However, if I put off going there for a year, I would then be 18, and the draft would take me into the war.

I decided to try to get the top grade in American history. Perhaps I would win the history prize at graduation? But my competitor, an obnoxious but popular six-footer, did not take Mr. Peck's math course. I had never received any honors at Asheville, except for the canceled *Time* prize which was not even a school award. After nearly six years perhaps I would earn <u>one</u> academic or athletic distinction.

At spring vacation I persuaded my mother to spend a small amount of my money on seven tennis lessons. She chose as my instructor, Dick Swinnerton, the freshman tennis coach at Princeton University. What a splendid idea, I thought. Surely he could teach me a backhand. My tennis game, learned entirely from books plus occasionally playing with my mother who had a good forehand, consisted solely of a forehand. When there was no one else available, she would play with me. I had no serve and a hopeless backhand. An Englishman, Swinnerton was stocky and elderly. He was short and gruff. His idea of a tennis lesson, the purpose of which was to teach me the backhand, was for him to stand just behind the net on one side with a large basket of balls. He would then hit one at a time hard into the opposite corners on my side of the net. It was all I could do to reach the ball and just try to hit it back. I never developed a backhand stroke.

Then I returned to Asheville and tried out for the tennis team. But it was immediately obvious to the tennis coach, the same Mr. Bates who had frustrated my pitching career, that I could not possibly win a match. And so I was relegated to the practice players, and there went my last hope for an "A."

At night in Mitchell Hall as we were going to bed on the ground floor, where the seniors lived, I would see in the dim half light in the distance a classmate who was homosexual dashing across the corridor into another boy's bedroom just after lights were out. One of them was on the football team, as were in fact most of the gay boy's nocturnal friends. The athlete would wear a grin of complicity the next day as if to say he was not a homosexual but living in an institution where there were no girls. Therefore he had a right to enjoy sexual pleasure.

In early April a small envelope turned up in my school mail box. I opened it. I was admitted to Princeton's freshman class. I was not overjoyed, as the registrar Mr. Copenhaver had predicted my acceptance. Nevertheless I felt a twinge of excitement.

Then the time for graduation came. I was amazed to discover that my mother was planning to come to the ceremony. She and my step-father had not set foot on the campus since they deposited me there in January,

1946. Jack was too busy to attend, but my mother hitched a ride with Bob Luchars' parents for the trip from New Jersey to North Carolina. The car would also contain Bob's sister, Sally, who was to be my date for the graduation dance. I am not sure if I had ever met her before, but she proved to be a nice girl. There were the usual rumors that the school had put saltpetre into the food in order to prevent any of the boys achieving erections and bringing about pregnancies among the young ladies. The mashed potatoes was said to be the likeliest target. I have no idea whether there was any truth in these stories, though I would not have put it past the Asheville authorities. For Sally and me the dance was a relatively painless affair.

The next day was graduation. I told anyone who would listen, "I've been here so long I know every blade of grass in the place." The sun shone. On the lawns looking towards Pisgah I introduced my mother proudly to Mr. Peck, but he did not seem enthusiastic about meeting either her or me. We seniors sat in the front rows, wearing our Asheville blazers. The prizes were given out. The history prize went to my competitor who proudly marched up to the lectern to receive the award, head high. Then we sat back to listen to the commencement address. The speaker was a Lieutenant General Ira Eaker, who my step-father had despised, having known of him in the Eighth Air Force, calling him a "political general" unlike Major General Orville Anderson, his hero, who had wanted to wipe Moscow off the face of the earth. His speech to us was so unmemorable that to this day I have no idea of what he said. Then the diplomas were handed to the seniors by Mr. Fall. Each of us went up to our handsome headmaster. I of course received one. Asheville had given me a withdrawn personality and an education. I left the school for the last time - never to see again the beautiful institution I hated.

That summer I elected to go back on my own for six weeks to Indian Trail - the one place I had been happy in America since arriving on a troop ship six years earlier. I played tennis for hour after hour. The Lodge held a tennis tournament. Only a few guests entered it, but I reached the finals. My opponent was a middle-aged man with gray hair and well-balanced features who had drunk a lot of cocktails the night before. I won. The Traverse City newspaper ran a small story about a Princeton freshman winning the Indian Trail Lodge tournament. Among the guests was a very pretty dark-haired girl with long tresses - Cathy Greig. She and I kissed at beach parties at night where occasionally we could see northern lights. She gave me a photograph of herself in a bathing suit, which I put in a little leather case.

I started as a freshman at Princeton, naively thinking that Princeton custom required that every fall weekend at home (the ones in between were devoted to football games at other colleges) I should have a date come and stay. In those days at Princeton there were no girl students. As my mother and step-father lived only a quarter mile from the campus, it was easy to arrange for her to stay at our house.

My three room-mates in 1903 dormitory were a Jew, an Episcopalian and a Presbyterian. I was the Catholic. We did not know each other beforehand, and we could think of no other reason the university had placed us together. In character each of us was completely different from the others. There was a tall, relatively quiet Groton boy - the Episcopalian. There was a Jew from Queens, who studied a lot. The third was Harry Belmarsh, a muscular dark-haired boy with a deep tan, who, while flexing his triceps, liked to roar, "mwah…hah.hah". He was the Presbyterian. Gordon Gray, the Groton graduate, and I shared a small room with an upper and lower deck bunk. I took the ground level one, and placed Cathy's picture on the small bedside table beside my head. The other two were in the bedroom next door. There was a living room with a couch and arm chairs.

One of my first weekend girl friends was Sylvia, a sophisticated pretty girl. Harry led a group of boys who jumped on top of her while she and I sat on our couch. With laughter they disentangled themselves. Sylvia took it as a compliment, but I was humiliated. A few nights later Gordon had gone to sleep in the bunk above me, his cold manner symptomatic of his general distaste for me. I lay in my bunk beneath him, trying to go to sleep. Our bedroom door opened, and I saw Harry's muscular hand and arm knock Cathy's picture to the floor. I was too frightened to protest.

My second date, Janet, was a nice serious girl with glasses, who was not pretty. I had met her at Indian Trail. While she and I were sitting on another sofa in one of the Princeton clubs for upperclassmen, a fellow freshman, a small tough preppie, passed by and made a face at her to let her know he thought she looked like a pig. Janet remained expressionless. I died inside for her. My third date was Sarita van Vleck from Vassar - a level-headed, attractive young woman who was unfazed by Princeton. She later went on to write a book about birds which was among those recommended by *The New York Times Book Review* for several weeks.

Courses for me were relatively easy that freshman year due to my prep school training. I had to do little work in order to pass. In fact I did not understand the second half of the introductory math course - calculus - at all, but thanks to Mr. Peck's training I still received a "C." The four of us went our separate ways after Christmas, and I stayed on in the suite, inviting to join me a fellow "townie" who I had become friendly with. Joe Bottomley was a large convivial charlatan with a constant amused smile. Pleasantly overweight, he regarded himself as a friendly counselor to one and all. After we had been room-mates for a few weeks, he complained to me, "Rowley, you never show any emotion." I did not really know what he meant. But he started to spend more and more time downstairs with Harry Belmarsh, who had moved into a suite directly underneath ours.

That spring Harry and Joe, who until then I had thought was a friend, led a group of students upstairs to our living room. On the same couch where they had jumped on Sylvia they held me down forcibly and shaved my head. During the haircut I was frightened, but not terrified, as shaving heads by brute force was a cruel Princeton tradition. The beginning of that freshman year was, I believe, the first one where the university had halted the annual charge by hundreds of freshmen against a massed group of sophomores gathered under an arch of Holder Hall. Accompanying this mayhem had been a "sport" whereby sophomores shaved the heads of as many freshmen as they could capture. So I knew I was being abused in a manner familiar to the undergraduate mind, though my tormentors were fellow freshmen, and it was the spring. I was of course deeply embarrassed. My sense of being unpopular and an outsider was clearly being continued. The next morning I went to our local barber in Princeton, who trimmed the tufts as best as he could. I decided I would let it grow into a crewcut. Crewcuts were a male fashion in the early 'fifties, and they also conformed to a popular undergraduate appearance.

The undergraduate body for the most part was very conformist. Gray or brown sweaters were okay. Most of us wore dirty white buck shoes. Tan trousers, but not blue jeans. The only freshman I remember wearing the latter was Ralph Nader. Princeton in those days was similar to a glorified prep school. We were addressed by the faculty and deans as "men," but in fact we were treated as boys. No undergraduate was allowed to own or drive a car within the vicinity of the campus and the town. The official excuse was that there were insufficient parking facilities, but an institution as rich as Princeton, which thought nothing of erecting Gothic buildings using the most expensive stone in imitation of Oxford and Cambridge, owning hundreds of acres of nearby farm land, could easily have afforded parking lots. The university also banned women of any age from undergraduate rooms after 7 p.m., even if it was one's mother. Expulsion was automatic. A campus police force of six men known as "proctors" enforced these two principal rules. We were forced to attend a religious service of our choice during the first two years there. Attendance was taken at the academic courses, and freshmen and sophomores were permitted only 12 "cuts" a semester. We were even denied the right to marry, though one member of the class of '54 was given an exemption as the girl, a respectable young lady from the town, was expecting.

The diametric opposite of Nader was Donald Rumsfeld, class of 1954, who was far more representative of undergraduate mores and thinking than Nader, who was elected into one of the least fashionable clubs. Rumsfeld on the other hand was a BMOC, "big man on campus," though I remember him being relatively short of stature and always surrounded by admiring classmates. He had dark hair and what one might describe as the classic Princeton look of the nineteen-fifties: clean-cut, short-haired, handsome, cool. I think he was president of his class, chosen in a class poll as "most likely to succeed." Whether ordering the killing thousands of people in Afghanistan and playing a major role in getting us into a war in Iraq is a sign of a successful life re Rumsfeld or whether saving thousands of lives as Nader has done in his campaigns against the auto industry and the environmental abuses of corporate America are two very good questions. Some 14 years later I was introduced to Norman Mailer at a party in Greenwich village. My date, Carolyn Gaiser, a writer, said to Norman, "Peter went to Princeton." Mailer looked up at me. He said in a friendly way, "I was at Harvard. I always think seven out of eight losers go to Harvard while seven out of eight winners go to Princeton." I said, "I always think Princeton is rather junior chamber of commerce."

Near the campus on Mercer road (also the street where Einstein occupied a modest old house) was the duplex apartment in an old house of the literary journalist, Anne Fremantle, a middle-aged red-haired English woman, who on warm summer evenings in April and May attracted a group of Catholic intellectuals to sit around and discuss theology over wine and cookies - led by a Dominican priest from Egypt with a charming smile and benign manner on his round face. Even though I was only a freshman, because my mother was a friend of Anne's, I was allowed to join them, although my mother rarely, if ever, attended. Perhaps my mother did not want to be reminded of her equivocal relationship with the church. Poor woman, she was still trying to arrange an annulment of my step-father's marriage to Katherine. The cooperation of the first "wife" in these matters is essential, but, as I remember, Katherine, having mothered three sons by Jack, was not keen to testify that there had never been a valid marriage. Faithfully my mother would go to mass every Sunday, but not receive holy communion, which by the theology of those days would have been a mortal sin.

We sat on the floor or on chairs and discussed in an erudite fashion why Catholicism was the best religion. At one of these gatherings I met a brilliant graduate student with a very acute delicate mind, Jim Kritzeck, from a poor family in Minnesota. What a relief he was in comparison to my undergraduate classmates like Harry Belmarsh.

I had been thrown off my prep school newspaper, *The Ashnoca*, three years earlier because I was 10 minutes late with the third of three articles I had written. The junior who fired me was a cousin by marriage - Mike Buhl. I was not even informed of my expulsion in person but only heard via a friend. For no other reason than to prove I had been unjustly fired I applied to be a freshman reporter on *The Daily Princetonian*. Lacking confidence and often depressed by Princeton, I was an average candidate but somehow I was elected on the second attempt. I could now call myself an assistant editor.

The academic year had ended. The *Prince* ceased publication. I happened to go to New York City for the day and learned that Audrey Hepburn was about to sail for Europe. So pleased was I that I had been elected to anything that I decided to see if I could attend her farewell press conference before her passenger liner left the harbor. She had just had her first Broadway success and was going to Rome to film *Roman Holiday* with Gregory Peck. I found myself going up the ship's elevator with a group of hardened professionals from such papers as *The Daily News*. One of them said, "I hear she's going to be married by the ship's captain in mid-voyage." There I was on the top deck, worried that someone might discover that my newspaper was not even going to appear for the next three months. The sun shone. A ring of reporters gathered around her, me on the outside. Suddenly she came forward

)k my hand - this young, delicate, beautiful creature. I was
...med, but managed to ask some question such as "Are you
looking forward to the voyage?" She smiled prettily and softly.

That fall, Arthur Krock, the famous Washington correspondent of *The New York Times*, addressed our annual dinner, saying, "On the masthead I notice there are far more chiefs than Indians on the 'Prince.'"

I became friends with Neal Peirce, a red-headed sophomore who was probably the most talented writer and certainly the hardest working on the campus newspaper. Neal was also an outstanding student. When the upperclassmen of the "Prince" refused to elect a freshman named R.W. Apple, nicknamed "Johnny," because they thought him too provincial, Neal objected strongly, and finally the snobbish seniors gave in. Apple is now the very distinguished Washington correspondent of *The New York Times*. Neal became president of his undergraduate eating club, Terrace, and in the middle of January, 1953, when all the sophomores applied to join the upper-class run clubs one of the applicants was a black student, one of only two or three in the entire student body. The alumni board of Terrace attempted to prevent his election. Neal fought them, and eventually prevailed. The black's last name was White.

I was even more depressed that first term of my sophomore year at Princeton than usual. Whereas freshman year at the college I had just been moderately depressed, as I had been in my prep school years at Asheville, when September, 1952, began I sank into a deeper malaise. Joe Bottomley, my room-mate the spring of freshman year, and I were no longer together, and I found myself alone on the ground floor in a single room, which was usually dark, looking onto the quadrangle of 1901 Hall.

One of my courses in the English department was public speaking, popular with football players for being a "gut" course requiring relatively little work, which was the same reason I had for taking it. After about three weeks I had to give a speech. My topic were the lampreys, a bloodsucker who had attached themselves to the fish of Lake Michigan. From start to end my voice quavered nervously. The football players stared up at me on the stage, thinking, I thought, what a pathetic psychotic I must be. When my "performance" was over, the instructor, a solid serious man in his thirties with hair smoothly slicked back, parted down the middle, said a few noncommittal words in the deathly silence.

However, the previous spring Jim had given me a copy of a letter from the administration of the Graduate College to him. Dated a year earlier, it had forbidden Jim as a graduate student to share a suite with undergraduates on the main campus or anywhere else. The graduate students were supposed to live in a beautiful quadrangle with a Gothic tower on a hill nearby or else in rented accommodation in the town. In fact, due to the influence of the famous Catholic philosopher, Jacques Maritain, who was a member of the philosophy department, this discrimination against Jim had subsequently been overturned, and Jim had shared a suite his last year at Princeton with underclassmen. Now, having received his doctorate in oriental studies, he had been made a prestigious junior fellow at Harvard. He was free from reprisal by the Princeton administration.

But I as a "Prince" reporter had a story - DISCRIMINATION AGAINST UNDERGRADUATES. We ran a photo of Jim's letter with his name blacked out on the front page. Why were graduate students not allowed to share a room with undergraduates? Did the university think we were too stupid or too immature? We played it to the full in a series of three articles, the Dean of the Graduate College, Sir Hugh Taylor, the target, the history of how Woodrow Wilson was forced out as President of Princeton in a dispute over the Graduate College, etc.! It had been the turning point in Wilson's career which led to him becoming the governor of New Jersey and then President of the United States. An item of gossip in my expose was that although graduate students in England would accept wearing gowns at meals, American ones with more independent minds objected. The result was that Sir Hugh's decree was observed by many of them who were naked underneath their gowns.

Near the end of the dreaded public speaking course I delivered a five minute address to the teacher and my burly classmates about the course itself, producing a lot of laughs. But two weeks later as the final grade the assistant professor gave me a C.

That January of my sophomore year like a butterfly emerging from a chrysalis I suddenly felt confident and popular. *The Daily Princetonian* was perhaps the major cause. My friend Neal, who went on to become a highly respected columnist on U.S. state and local government politics and the environment, made me his assistant on two special issues of the newspaper. One was a new course evaluation issue which proved popular with the students and unpopular with the faculty. We distributed questionnaires to hundreds of our fellow students, who were asked to return them to the editors of the newspaper. Neal's innovation of a special edition of the newspaper evaluating courses by their merits and demerits, including brief frank biographies of the professors, was an immediate hit with the undergraduate body. Many of the faculty condemned it as "superficial," but the entire supply of "Prince"s that day were picked up in the University department store by professors. Neal's idea was subsequently copied by other Ivy League colleges, and today many colleges have unofficial web sites offering honest views about courses and their teachers. The junior professor, who had taught my speaking course, did not have tenure. He came to see me at the "Prince" office. I had given his course a less than complimentary evaluation. Coldly I listened to his complaint, but I was unmoved.

The other special edition was for a February mid-year celebration of the alumni on the campus, called "Princetonians in the Nation's Service." It consisted of interviews with the Secretary of State in Washington, D.C., John Foster Dulles, his brother, Allen, the director of the CIA, the defeated Democratic presidential candidate Adlai Stevenson (not done by Neal and me) and lesser luminaries. When we entered John Foster's office, the size of a small cathedral, in the State Department building, there was the great man standing over a blue overalled telephone technician amidst a mass of cables. Dulles was saying, "The President can hear me, but I can't hear the President." Dulles had a reputation (perhaps inaccurate) of lording it over Eisenhower. He was very polite and helpful in the interview questioned mainly by Neal.

We then went to the CIA, where I was the interviewer. Allen was charming and congenial - "unlike his brother," I said in the article. I implied that John Foster was cold. "You should <u>not</u> have written that," said the mother of my new Washington girl friend, Margot Strong.

However, the Strongs were friends of a congressman from Maine who was a friend of Vice President Nixon, and by the spring I found myself alone with Nixon for 20 minutes. He had agreed to answer a list of my questions approved in advance by his staff. Two of them I had crossed out, as I was afraid he would be annoyed, but he won me over by insisting on answering them. One was whether Communism should be taught in colleges, to which he answered that it should be in order to learn about the enemy. He was intelligent and cooperative, and my interview - after being published in the "Prince" - was picked up by the Associated Press, and I was asked to write a column for *The Trentonian*. Skipping my art history class, I drove to Trenton to do so.

That same January another of Princeton's big weekends with girls on campus rolled around. I was now six feet two inches tall. Under the influence of bourbons and ginger ale, which I had been introduced to by Margot, I proceeded to kiss six different girls in various clubs. Suddenly I was popular with the opposite sex too, and, although I had been told I was handsome some months earlier, I had had trouble believing this.

Around Easter a group of us, including Joe Bottomley, with whom I now had a more careful relationship, went to a deb dance outside of Philadelphia. The five of us, known as "townies," had homes in Princeton. After the dance we returned to Bottomley's house on Library Place in Princeton. The new "me" was determined not to be pushed around by Bottomley and his friends, who I now regarded as rather below-average undergraduates. Next year I would be elected chairman of the "Prince." I had been told I was a leading candidate. After Princeton, there would be Harvard Law School, finally a United States Senator. Margot would by my wife.

Shortly after returning to the Bottomley home (his parents were away), it was agreed among the other four that one of them should fight me. However, I was afraid to fight Bottomley and his friend, John D'Arms, who both weighed more than 200 pounds. Steve Maddox also weighed more than me. I was only 150 pounds. Arguments were interspersed with my collapsing on a couch, pretending to be drunk. Eventually at 5 a.m., when it was still dark, it was decided that Morgan Johnson, who weighed the same as me, though he was much shorter, should be my opponent. I neither liked nor disliked Johnson, who was a somewhat laconic type. He prided himself on doing what the majority wanted. The alcohol gave me courage and deadened my fear. We all went out to the gravel circle of the drive, and Morgan and I started to hit each other. I remember swinging wildly at his white face in the dark. Eventually I genuinely collapsed - defeated - in a bush. I must have passed out as much from the drink as the blows. Some while later I was driven to my mother and step-father's house on Cleveland Lane and walked in the front door at breakfast time with blood on the front of my tuxedo. Shocked, they did not criticize me. A day or so later I ran into Bottomley, who told me that Johnson had two black eyes. My opponent was too embarrassed to leave his home. As for me there were two tiny scratches on my face, which I proudly showed Margot the following weekend when I visited her in Washington.

Returning to the Princeton campus, I continued my new-found conviction that with a smile, charm and verbal trickery I could out best anyone in an argument. A corollary of my new philosophy was that cynicism was the wisest policy - though expressed openly only when propitious - to follow when judging my fellow human beings' characters.

In May the final exams began. I had cut many of my classes and scarcely read a book in any of my courses. I knew I faced a big challenge. Time was very short. At Asheville at the end of my junior year I had rescued myself from a failing grade in chemistry by concentrating only on those questions on the exam I knew something about. Frantically I studied some key points, borrowing notes. Neal, who was a superb student, helped me. In the final exam of my politics course I typed pages and pages of answers, demonstrating the speedy hunt-and-peck typing I had learned on the "Prince." Before the grades were even published (in those days they were posted on public bulletin boards in Alexander Hall) I went to see the course lecturer, Professor Alpheus T. Mason, winner of a Pulitzer price for his biography of Brandeis, who was a friend of Neal and to a lesser extent of mine, and told him my graduate student instructor with whom we met in a small "precept" of nine students was prejudiced against me for my Republican views, this individual being a leftist, or so I thought. Professor Mason told me my exam paper was brilliantly written and imaginative and had little to do with the subject matter of the course. When read out loud, it had provoked, he said, gales of laughter from the instructors who were his assistants. I was confident as I took the Queen Mary passenger liner from New York for England that my career at Princeton would continue.

Traveling tourist class, which was an improvement over the troop ship of eight years earlier, I met the two Seipp sisters from Virginia - likable Ellen with red hair and her cuter but less lovable younger sister Trina. I discovered how easy it was to climb over a rope or a railing and sneak into cabin or even first class. Trina and I kissed. On the last night I met another girl, Ann Noble, a dark-haired pretty creature, who went to Wheaton. I kissed her too. Softer than the sometimes acerbic Trina I preferred her, but she was traveling on to parts of Europe other than England when the ship docked at Southampton.

I then stayed with my aunt Violet on Sydney street in Chelsea. Violet was a tall thin woman with dark curly hair and an owlish penetrating gaze above her pursed lips usually painted a dark red. She was about five years older than my mother with the nun in between them in age. Her husband, Uncle Joss Wickham, one of my trustees, had died over a year earlier, leaving Violet with relatively little money. In the 'thirties Violet had been a secretary to one of the Royal family. Like my mother she had been disinherited by grandfather Stanislaus not only for taking a job (my mother who had briefly been a mannequin in a shop had had her allowance reduced by exactly the sum she earned) but for the more serious sin (in his eyes) of marrying outside the Church, as Joss had been previously married, but unlike my father never had any children from the first union. Aunt Violet was an expert on protocol, titles and who was who among the landed families of Great Britain. The United Kingdom class system despite the war and the inroads of socialism was still largely intact. Violet was very impressed by ancestry, position and wealth, but with the death of her husband, who had had only a minor job as a judge and little pension, these characteristics of my mother's older sister proved very useful. She had two daughters, ages 13 and 10, and a two-year-old boy. With his death she could no longer afford their nanny. She was in effect given the use of the house by the Turtons, a very wealthy Yorkshire family. All she had to do in return was keep an eye on one of their four daughters as each of the young ladies arrived in London "to do the season," in other words be presented at Court and go over a number of months to numerous debutante dances. Mary and Ralph, who rarely came to London, occupied a room on the top floor, and a daughter another bedroom. Lord and Lady Howard de Walden were very helpful with money, and they too had four daughters, and one of them, Susie, occupied another bedroom. A side effect of the Howard de Walden generosity was that ill feeling developed between Violet and the youngest sister, Jane, who had offered with her husband to help the widow. When the Bruce Smythes learned that the peer and his wife were giving aid, they decided because Lady Howard deWalden was Austrian and the English had recently fought the Germans they were not going to help. Violet was being comforted by the "enemy." My aunt had to cook and supervise the cleaning woman known as "a char" or "a body." Then of course there was Reverend Mother Dorothy Eyre, who supplied free education and boarding for Violet's two daughters, Daphne and Claire, at her Sacred Heart convent in Brighton during the school terms.

Into this world, not yet 19, by now thoroughly Americanised with a crew cut and a preppie Princeton accent, stepped me. My aunt said,

"Peter, would you like to go to some debutante dances?" pausing for the significance of her next remark. "Noochie has so kindly offered to arrange it." I could tell from Violet's tone of voice that "Noochie" was a very important person in her eyes. Her upper-class accent rose an octave or so. "Noochie" was Lady Howard de Walden's nickname. I was unimpressed. After all I was a Princeton "man" destined for the chairmanship of the "Prince" and then the United States Senate. I had completely forgotten about my English background and regarded myself as an American.

"Tomorrow morning you'll have to go to their suite at the Dorchester and be inspected," said my aunt firmly. 'How dare they?' I thought. 'I was already perfection.'

John and "Noochie", i.e. the peer and his Austrian wife, took a large part of the seventh floor of the hotel that summer with a view onto Park lane and Hyde Park, in order to launch their sharp-faced moderately pretty daughter, Hazel, onto the social world.

Rising in the elevator to the top of the hotel, I knocked on the door of the suite.

Entering, I saw "Noochie," sitting on a couch in the suite. The sun streamed in. She was quite a pretty woman, middle-aged, expensively dressed as befitting a lady married to a man who owned a shipping line, a racing stables, both sides of Harley Street where many of the most fashionable doctors had offices and God knows what else. A few years later one of the British gossip columns said his lordship was worth 60 million pounds.

Using her Austrian accent, she said succinctly, "Would you like a martini?" Even though I was a Princetonian and supposedly unfazed by anything, her question caught me off-guard. It was 10 a.m.

Standing a few feet away was her husband, the peer, a moderately tall pleasant man of average weight, who gazed at me down his nose with a bemused, superior smile.

"You'll have to do something about your hair," declared her ladyship.

'My beloved crewcut!'

I mumbled something about how it would grow out. My armor of the Princeton man had been severely dented.

However, I passed the inspection and was placed on the list of suitable young men for the dances. Those who failed often had "NSIT" placed by their names - "not safe in taxis."

There was a strict protocol for each dance. Dinner jackets or white tie. Long dresses. Cocktails. Then dinner. Afterwards the dance which could extend to two or three in the morning. Breakfast was often served at about one in the morning. At dinner I was placed on her ladyship's left.

The first course was a collection of small speckled eggs in their shells on my plate. I had not the faintest idea what they were or how to eat them. I glanced at John Howard de Walden to see what utensils he was using but he was too far away at the big round table for me to discover the technique for what I later learned were plover's eggs.

After the eggs I took out a pack of cigarettes.

"We will not smoke until after the coffee," said "Noochie" firmly.

Then we got into her Rolls Royce to go to the dance. I was told to sit in the front beside the chauffeur. I knew the more favored guests were in the rear behind the glass partition with mother and daughter. It was becoming a struggle to maintain my ego.

At these dances the men ranged in age from 18 to 50. Some of them had a ruddy alcoholic look, ex-Army officers looking for an heiress. Conversation was superficially witty. I was told I had to dance with every girl who had been at my dinner table. I was not allowed to leave her alone after we had finished dancing unless another man asked her to dance. If the young lady one was with was plain, one could be stuck with her for a long time until mercifully she escaped to the ladies' room. The girls seemed very shy compared to American girls, and my jokes about sex were not well received.

Neal arrived in London. The Seipp sisters, Neal and I decided to visit Cambridge, but I knew St. Neots was on the way.

It is probable my aunt had invited George over for dinner one night to see me, as she was quite good about showing merciful hospitality to the less fortunate in the world. He was already grossly overweight, excessively shy, never looked one in the eye and stared at his unpolished shoes, smoked Players constantly and occasionally made witty remarks. His suits, including the waistcoats, were stained with food and cigarette ashes. Everyone pretended not to smile or stare. My aunt always advised me to be on good terms with him. As for my other half-brother John he did not exist. Not only did my parents and my mother's English family never speak of him but I doubt if George on his one visit that evening mentioned him. By now I knew John lived in a mental hospital, but my mother and Jack over the years made it an unwritten rule that neither I nor they were to ever visit him. At that time of my life I did not even know that he was a frequently violent patient in a hospital called Ticehurst in Sussex. I certainly did not know he had once nearly killed a nurse.

It was against this background that I played a trick on my friends Neal, Ellen and Trina. On the way to Cambridge I persuaded them to stop by a private park and walk up the hill towards the manor house. I knew that technically this was trespassing, but I was confident that as the half-brother of the mad owner and the tenant, his full brother, I would be released if caught by the gardener or the police. It was a sultry summer day as we climbed through the uncut brownish grass among the trees, holding hands with the girls. The garden was deserted. Then we continued on to Cambridge in the small car I had rented for the summer in England. After we returned to London I told Neal the significance of the house and park where we had walked. He laughed.

With the same cavalier disregard I had shown towards Princeton's academic courses I ignored the needs of my car. In those days automobiles had to have their oil replenished frequently. On the way to a dance in the country "the big end" of my vehicle burned out. I was temporarily stranded with the hostess of the previous dance I had attended.

Then a telegram arrived from my mother and Jack. I had been expelled from Princeton. I flew back to America. Instantly I fell into a deeper depression. The choice was simple - the army or a job. Fortunately the draft boards were well supplied with cannon fodder at that time, so hopefully I would be readmitted to college, preferably Princeton, before the draft got me. The Korean War was over. I was offered by the United States Steel Corp. in Morrisville, Pennsylvania, across the Delaware river from Trenton, at their new Fairless plant a clerk's job or that of brick mason's assistant. One of my many hangups from Asheville was my supposed lack of physical strength, typified by thin wrists. I chose the manual labor one. There were three shifts around the clock, and I would be assigned to a warehouse which supplied brick for the open hearth furnaces, by which the raw steel was made. I would have to become a member of the C.I.O. United Steelworkers union. It was a rapid change from the corrupt glitter and marble of the London deb season.

The night shift, which ran from midnight to 8 a.m., was exceptionally beautiful. Perhaps its allure was aided by the contrast with the day, for in the light of the sun or even under clouds it was just a dirty, ugly steel mill, albeit a new one, but at night there were whooshes of flames against the black background of the sky - usually white, red or gold colored, and only the barest outlines of the smokestacks and buildings. Even the noises were less - just some rail cars shunting and occasional whistles. The man-made electric lights only illuminated a few roads, and the ramp from the warehouse up to the charging floor. Sometimes there was a moon and stars. Often we could sleep for an hour or two on the very late night shift.

When a furnace was down, i.e. not operating because the brick roof and walls had burned out, we brought up by forklift the heavy long bricks for its reconstruction. We also supplied bricks for repair of burnt-out patches in still operating furnaces. At the beginning I was working there in the late summer, and the temperature outside might be 100 fahrenheit, but inside on the floor beside the furnaces it was about 150. We would come outside into the summer heat and feel cool.

Half of the work was unloading the brick from railway cars parked beside the warehouse. This was manual labor, which had to be done by hand until enough of the interior of the box car had been cleared so that a forklift could enter and gently lift out the brick piled up on pallets. I came into close contact with my fellow workers. There was the warehouse boss, Mike Gorka, who wore a tan open-necked shirt and a black stetson - tough. Under him were a couple of expediters, and one of them was a charming late middle-aged man, slightly built, we called "Ellis" who was educated and intelligent. He had been an inspector of steel sheets in Pittsburgh, and through the vagaries of the industry had been forced to take this foreman's job at Fairless, which he regarded rightly as a slight comedown. Nevertheless he could afford to live with his family in a small new Levittown-type house a few miles away. He befriended me, and disliked Gorka, who was something of a bully. Mike's favorite target was a young man who was uncoordinated and unsure of himself (not me), with light brown curly hair whose only ambition was to become a forklift driver, which had a slightly higher pay scale than laborer. But Gorka harassed the "loser" so effectively that, when he was given a test, he invariably mishandled the machine. Then there was "Angie", a muscular Italian-American who could lift a 100 pound can with his arms. I had difficulty hoisting a 50 pound sack of cement powder. After work from his car, as we were going back to our respective homes, Angie would watch me race by in mine. The next day he said to the others at work within my hearing, "He goes too fast, but I notice he stares straight ahead, never taking his eyes off the road."

And then there was "Muff" Cenerino, a big Italian American in his early thirties, who also lived in Princeton. Cenerino had been released from prison after serving several years of a felony conviction for stealing checks from mail he was delivering as a postal employee. He made a point of telling everyone that I lived in the wealthy part of the town. Everyone knew that I could escape from the world of unions and low pay, whereas for them it would be very difficult. However, after a while they accepted me and despite my depression I grew to like most of them. After a few months I was allowed to operate the forklift when someone was sick, and I can still remember the thrill of driving my vehicle up and down the ramp with a load of bricks. Operating the gears to raise or lower the load and slide the two metal teeth of the forklift under a pallet was also fun.

I suppose my manual labor job impressed Jerry Finch, the Dean of the College at Princeton, who interviewed me in November, 1953, to see if I might be given another chance as a Princeton undergraduate. Dean Finch was a diminutive intelligent man who preferred to ask polite questions and listen. I seem to remember him as a dark, slightly depressed personality, who did his job from a sense of duty but without enthusiasm. His predecessor, Dean Francis R.B. Godolphin, had been a friendly loquacious classicist, whose photo, smiling broadly, we ran almost daily on the front page of the 'Prince.' He was an ex-combat colonel of Marines in the Second World War.

My step-father with his long-running love affair with the military persuaded the new head of the Princeton Army R.O.T.C., a Major Purkitt, to write a letter supporting my readmission. But there was a price to pay. The R.O.T.C., now that the Korean War was over, was not popular, and Purkitt needed undergraduates in his program. I had to agree to rejoin it. Purkitt was a somewhat overweight big talker who wore all his medals and thought he was going to make a fortune on the stock market with Jack's help. After I was readmitted under the proviso that I would have to repeat the second semester of my sophomore year, I nearly got into trouble again by sitting on the edge of Purkitt's sergeant's desk. I was made to apologize to the non commissioned officer by Jack and Purkitt before the term even started. They knew they had me.

Before the second semester began, I returned to chasing girls and partying. Trina Seipp wrote me a letter saying, "Jungle drums are beating" that I was a Princeton undergrad again. My Washington girl friend, Margot, had long ago fallen by the wayside in my affections. Even before the Princeton expulsion I had written her a letter from London, enraged that she had not answered my well-written (so I thought) love letters, by saying (wittily, I thought) that "Absence is said to be the acid test for love, but in your case you turned out base". I may have nearly failed that chemistry course at Asheville, but that much I had remembered. I had several Princeton friends who lived in Washington, D.C., and there I went for dances during the Christmas vacation, proud to be the only ex- member of a union there. I had of course resigned from my job at Fairless once I was readmitted. One of the girls at these D.C. dances was a luscious Roman Catholic creature, Ann Phelan, who went to Manhattanville in Purchase, N.Y., with coal-black hair, superb breasts, and inviting full lips. I bet a minor friend, Doug Stenhouse, that he could not kiss her that night, and then treacherously told her while dancing of the wager. Doug was not pleased, and had no hope of winning the bet after my disclosure. However, on another evening Ann consented to go out with me, and I remember being very frightened that she and her parents would notice a tremor in the puffy area beneath my right eye. Doug also had a cute sister, Emily, who I spent many hours necking with.

Returning to the town of Princeton before the term started, I went to a party held at Neal's Terrace Club with Trina as my date. I offered her for sale to friends and acquaintances there, but when she heard of this either from me, who thought it a good joke, or someone else, she slapped me. I seem to remember during this period of my life of talk of a "pig party" at one of the other clubs, where each undergrad invited the ugliest girl he knew with first prize being a pickle inside a condom.

I discovered that my parents had behind my back made a deal with the Princeton administration that I was to live at home rather than on the campus. I was very angry, but they had persuaded the deans I was so immature that the university rule requiring undergraduates to live in a dormitory was waived. I would not be allowed to rejoin *The Daily Princetonian*. Nevertheless, I studied as little as possible and failed my mid-term exams. Self-preservation penetrated my psyche, and, while dashing back and forth between the TV set to watch the Army-McCarthy hearings in my parents' dining room, I worked on my courses in their living room. The interior of the ground floor of our house was painted a bilious dark green decorated with prints of classic paintings, which Jack assured my mother were as good as the original.

In my heart I looked down on his artistic taste, remembering the family portraits in oil in my childhood home in England. I am sure he sensed his step-son's snobbish disapproval.

Although much has been written since the Senator Joseph McCarthy era about persecution of left-leaning academics and artists, I never detected any interest or concern in the town of Princeton or among the faculty or students. We were truly a part of the Eisenhower Presidency complacency.

I passed my sophomore year exams, and continued my feckless flirtation with the speed limits of New Jersey and neighboring states. However, I never drove faster than a speed at which I felt safe regardless of whether this conformed to the highway departments' rules on miles per hour. My caution on the road - even when drinking - was thanks to Jack. A good driver, he constantly warned of the dangers of the road. Though I had passed my New Jersey driver's test at age 17, receiving a license, he had insisted I take more lessons. I received a number of speeding convictions.

One Sunday night in late May or early June Neal, two girls and I returned at about midnight from a day at the beach on the Jersey shore, and I was stopped by the police in Hightstown, N.J., about 8 miles from Princeton, and accused of ignoring a stop sign. I truthfully said I had never seen it, and pointed out to the patrolman that the sign was partly obscured by a tree branch. Princeton students were not popular, and he gave me a ticket anyway. If convicted, I would lose my license, as I had too many offenses already. Less than 48 hours later I returned with a photographer friend at about noon, and in the bright sunlight discovered the sign had been freshly painted, the branch above pruned, and the white warning on the road newly painted. Even the small plastic reflectors on the sign had been replaced. Coming up to us as we took a picture of the sign, the Hightstown police captain denied that anything had been done to it. I found a private detective agency in the Philadelphia phone book, returned to the sign, chipped a tiny bit of the fresh paint off it, and had it analyzed, proving it had been done since Sunday night. I then went to a lawyer in Princeton, who later became a judge. He said he thought I was guilty. He referred me to another lawyer, who said he was not interested in whether I was guilty, but only wanted his $50 fee. I gave it to him. A few days later in the evening a trial was held. The arresting policeman lost his temper on the witness stand. The Hightstown judge noted I was born in England and said something about friendship between our two nations and acquitted me. *The Trenton Times* ran a story along the lines of Princeton junior outwitting the police. Even Jack was proud of my initiative and showed the story to his friends.

Then I was offered a summer job as a reporter on a weekly newspaper, the *Netcong-Stanhope* (N.J.) *News*. I was only 20, and had gone for an interview to Blairstown, N.J., which is in the northwestern corner of the state near the Delaware river and Pennsylvania. A Mr. and Mrs. Ray and Rita Fuller owned the Netcong weekly (circulation about 2,400), the Blairstown one and a small printing business that did wedding announcements and such like. The next day I drove an hour from Princeton to Netcong. The newspaper office on the tiny main street was on the ground floor of a small two-story clapboard building. In the front at a desk sat Olive, a late middle-aged lady with white hair who sold the classified ads - usually over the phone - probably the most profitable part of the paper. She was sweet, soft-spoken and delightful. Inside and around a corner up one step was the editorial office, consisting of two desks. Here I met Peggy, the editor, who immediately told me she was quitting at the end of the week and I would be the new editor. She was exhausted. Had not Ray told me? No, he had not. Peggy's husband, who had a one-man contracting firm, would continue to take the photos. His subjects of course were car accidents and events such as meetings of the Gold Star Mothers of America, the Kiwanis and the Elks. One afternoon a week I would have to go into the nearby larger town of Dover and sell display advertising to store owners. This was the only part of the job which frightened me, and I dreaded that Wednesday afternoon, but I sold a few ads, and was chided and encouraged by the Fuller's advertising manager, Bob Keating, who would drop in at the end of the day. He was a fast-talking utterly charming middle-aged slightly balding man with a modest paunch, neatly dressed in jacket and tie plus fedora hat. "Never carry a rate card," he said congenially. "Always tell each store owner you gave your last one to the previous store. Always say you have sold the entire page except for the last quarter you're saving for him, even though you haven't sold anything yet." Much of the gross of the tiny newspaper chain was due to him.

I poured myself with a passion into the job. Being a newspaper editor at the age of 20 went rapidly to my head. I instituted weekly reviews of the local summer stock theatre. A musical *Wish You Were Here* "made one wish one wasn't there." I severely criticised a performer in a play for over-acting. To my horror the man phoned me, but to my relief said some of his friends had told him the same thing. The theatre's director was Herbert Machiz, who was well-known in New York for directing an original Tennessee Williams drama. He appreciated the free publicity I gave the theatre. I smoked constantly, partied, drove back and forth to Princeton, and once stayed up 48 hours going to a deb party and then editing the paper the next day.

One afternoon I drove past a school bus that was letting off children without stopping and was given a ticket by the Hopatcong, N.J., police chief. I knew my license was again at stake. The local judge, in whose jurisdiction the violation had occurred, occupied an office on the floor above mine. I knew him from running into him on the staircase. He was a slight middle-aged man, always courteous. I went to see him and explained my problem. In a friendly soft-spoken way he said, "Go and see Chief (whatever his name was) and tell him that if it's okay with him it's okay with me to forget about it." I drove back to Hopatcong. The police chief said, "I didn't know you were the press. I'll tear it up." Finally in mid-summer I hired an assistant, Hermione Hobhaus, an English girl, who was a relation of Anne Fremantle staying with her for the summer on a tourist visa. Even though I was only 20, the two hours of daily driving and the responsibility of the job, where I was trying to edit the finest weekly newspaper that I could, meant that I appreciated some assistance. At the same time I had discovered when I went up to Blairstown every Thursday to supervise the production of that week's issue that the Fullers had a pretty tow-headed daughter, Lee. After a week of listening to me talk non-stop in my car from Princeton to Netcong on how to be a newspaper reporter and probably miffed by my amorous preference for the sexy Lee, Hermione quit. I was enraged, and threatened to report her to the U.S. immigration department, as she was not supposed to hold a job. The next day I rescinded my threat. To her credit Anne Fremantle never held this incident against me in subsequent years.

Finally the summer came to an end, and I faced Princeton as a junior - a grim prospect after the summer's excitement. Since I had just been the editor of a weekly newspaper and was only nine months from being 21 years of age, I asked my mother and Jack if I could see the accounts of my trust, which my mother ran. I knew that on my next birthday the English trustees would send the income directly to me. Some training in advance would be a good idea, I said. My step-father, who usually took the lead in telling me what to do, seemed unenthusiastic, but my mother in a rare burst of strength eyed me in a steely way and with the determination of a tiger refused to show me anything.

Afterwards Jack drove me to the Princeton campus, and I said I should have gone to Exeter as a boarding school instead of Asheville. It had more prestige, I argued. He defended my mother in a spirited fashion. Nevertheless, my way was clear - law school, a fashionable marriage to a lovely girl, being elected Senator.

But I missed being an editor. There was a mid-term race for U.S. Senator from New Jersey, and I wrote long interview articles about the Republican and Democratic candidates to be published in both the Netcong and Blairstown papers, but it only gave me a hollow feeling of loss. My roommate was Bill Grigsby, and I had shared a suite with him and another Chicagoan before my expulsion, but it was hard work pretending to be the new mature me before him and my classmates. I tried to be as precise as possible on a mid-term paper on constitutional interpretation for Professor Mason, but was told my effort was mediocre by the instructor. Desperately I drove several hundred miles to a prep school near Harrisburg, Pennsylvania, where Lee had been placed by her parents for her senior year to curb her supposedly wild ways, but the affection between us was forced. I was becoming depressed, but this was a darkness deeper than the previous ones.

Around this time my mother and Jack had started going on a regular basis for their ailments to a new doctor in Princeton - William J. Welch, an internist. A few years later he was described to me by a medical friend and colleague of his in Boston, Mass., as having attracted "the carriage trade" in Princeton. Bill Welch was a tall, very congenial man with a long jaw and an easy manner combined with medical expertise. He had quit a successful career in advertising to go to medical school. He was about 45, and just 20 minutes alone with him was enough to make one feel better. Whether it was advertising bonhomie or warmth I do not know, but he conveyed reassurance and hope. Out of desperation I went to see him. I was so depressed I couldn't go on. I felt suicidal. Come and see me tomorrow, he would say. I had to write a term paper for a history course but I couldn't organize or study for it. I sat on the couch of my parents' living room trapped by those dark green walls and thought about killing myself with a knife, cutting my wrists. I would spend the rest of my life in a mental hospital like John. In the family car parked in our small driveway my mother said, "Pull yourself together." Then she told me how my father had beaten her up for stealing a one pound note from his wallet until our butler, Habbits, had stopped him. Hearing this story did not make me feel any better. Finally after a number of visits to Welch it was decided between him and me that I would have to resign from Princeton before I was expelled for failing my courses. He recommended I go to New York and see a psychiatrist, called Harry Potter. "Don't worry," he laughed. "He won't speak in a Viennese accent and ask you if you masturbate." I went to see Potter in his New York office, but I was as depressed after the session as before. I was afraid to talk openly to him. He was frightening. The only person I trusted was Doctor Welch.

I had to go through the formality of resigning from Princeton. By then the Dean of Students was William Lippincott, a tweedy man with a pipe who accepted my resignation as matter of factly as if he was turning a page in a file. The meeting in his office was so dark and painful to me that I have no memory of who said what. By one of those curious ironies my tormentor of freshman year, Harry Belmarsh, had told Lippincott he was resigning midway through Belmarsh's sophomore year, and then had deliberately insulted the Dean. A couple of weeks later Belmarsh changed his mind, but Lippincott refused to reinstate him.

I had to tell Bill Grigsby, and he never really forgave me in subsequent decades for leaving him alone in the suite for the remaining six months of his senior year. In the middle of all this a phone call came into my parents' house taken by Jack. It was Peggy's husband asking if I could help, as Peggy had been hospitalized for schizophrenia and was undergoing shock treatment. To my abject humiliation I heard Jack say that I couldn't help because I had also suffered a mental collapse. I think the contractor drove down to Princeton to see me to ask if I could be of assistance, and came to our house but I was incapable of helping anyone.

Without my being present a conference was held in Welch's office between my mother, Jack and the physician. He suggested to them that I see his wife, Louise, who was a psychotherapist.

The relationship between my mother and Jack and the Welchs was similar from the Welchs' viewpoint to walking through a mine field. After all my mother fully supported by Jack was paying out of my trust fund Mrs. Welch's bill. It would be very risky for either of the Welchs to persuade me that my parents were not the ideal ones they pretended to be. During my visits to Mrs. Welch there seemed to be a slight cooling off of the enthusiasm felt by my mother and Jack towards the doctor and his wife, but nothing was ever said. Twice my mother and Mrs. Welch had tea together. Mrs. Welch each time said the conversation was pleasant, and that I was discussed very little. My mother was non-committal, but even I in my depressed state knew that the necessity of Louise was somehow a reflection on my real mother's treatment of me. I am sure diplomacy was essential when Mrs. Welch met with my mother, and doubtless Doctor Welch took a similar line when he received my parents as his patients, separately or together. Doctor Welch once made an offhand remark to me about Jack, hinting that he was a strong character he had some reservations about, someone he had to be a little careful with, but it was said in a friendly way.

The first time I was told to go the Welch's house at the other end of Nassau Street from the western area of the town where we lived. Because he was a new doctor in the community - admittedly becoming sought after by wealthy patients - it was not expected that he and his wife live in the most expensive section just yet. The house was a relatively small clapboard one. Louise Welch was a woman of about average height with her dark hair pulled back tightly into a bun with a round face. She was calm, and a slight smile played on her lips - sympathetic, serene. She appeared to be about 50, and, though she was on the plump side, I guessed she had once been pretty. At the beginning I did not know she was active in the Gurdjieff movement, which might be described as a mystical intellectual sect that had included Katherine Mansfield among its disciples, but she never breathed a word about her "religious" philosophy. Her back and posture were perfectly straight. I sat on a couch or chair opposite her. She sat with her back to the light, the half-drawn shade of a window on Nassau street behind her. Her legs were crossed at her ankles, and her hands rested together on her lap. Looking directly at me, she encouraged me to talk and said little. I was so humiliated by my latest failure in life that I was willing to say anything. Why had it happened, I wanted to know. She listened and listened, and I talked and talked. Once I was too depressed to drive to her home, and phoned her to say in a halting voice I couldn't come. It was the only time she ever spoke sharply to me. "Come down here right now," she said firmly. I did.

Meanwhile life continued at my parents' house. Another desperate move on my part was to take instruction in self-defense from Dick Swinnerton, the Princeton freshman tennis coach, but after he had thrown me to the mat a couple of times it was painfully obvious that becoming a he-man was not the answer to my problems. One night Neal, his best friend Bill Beaver who was now a medical student at Cornell/New York Hospital, and another friend of theirs Peter Trent, invited me to meet with them in New York City. Blind dates were supplied. I was still trying to conceal that I had had to resign from Princeton. The girl produced for me was a really pretty young nurse, but I felt within 15 minutes she found me very strange. I had never felt so miserable, and then Beaver took us into the medical students' morgue to show us the cadavers he and his classmates were working on. I stared at some light brown skin, bones and muscle of a dead body. Beaver thought it was very funny.

Then at a Christmas party in a big house outside of Princeton owned by a couple who belonged to the Rockefeller family I was reintroduced to John Harlan, now a justice of the Supreme Court. He asked me what I was doing, and I lied and said I wanted to be a lawyer, knowing in my heart I had no hope of ever going to law school. He nodded his leonine head approvingly.

Fortunately the Korean war was over, and the draft board was seeking less men, and Doctor Welch would have obtained a temporary medical exemption for me, but I still had to do something. Going to see Mrs. Welch two or three times a week was not enough. In six months I would be 21. The only area where I had shown any talent was journalism. I heard that Barney Kilgore, the long-time managing editor of the *Wall Street Journal*, who was credited with turning it into a national newspaper, had just bought a decrepit weekly, *The Princeton Packet*, out of his own money, planning to revive it. I went to see him in his house high on a hill in a Princeton suburb. During the interview he kept twisting his head to one side. He offered me a job selling advertising, but I was terrified at the prospect and turned it down. I wanted to be a reporter, but he had already hired Dan Wakefield, who later became a well-known writer. Dan had just graduated from Columbia.

However, the other and more profitable weekly in the town was a glossy white paper publication, *Town Topics*. I was offered an almost full-time job typing up church announcements and social events, as the owner, Mrs. Samuels, emphasized society. She was an elderly, white-haired woman from the south. She was very plump, and once a week she took the list of births from Princeton Hospital and crossed out the names of the black babies - "pickaninnies." The editor, Mr. Osborne, a quiet, easy-going man of middle years, did exactly what she told him to do, and Mrs. Samuels' affable son sold the advertising. In about April Mr. Osborne went on holiday, and Mrs. Samuels, editing the paper that week, fired me, complaining "your typing is so bad." In a day or so Mr. Osborne returned and rehired me. Mrs. Welch said she was very pleased with me because I had not lost my temper with Mrs. Samuels.

Slowly thanks to Mrs. Welch I was regaining my confidence. One of my best friends at college was Barry Block, a tousled, dark-haired physicist, who had been expelled from the university for operating a car in his senior year. He was immediately admitted as a student to Harvard. Simultaneously Barry had tried to arrange an alibi in a phone conversation with his father, claiming the car was always parked at his home. His parents lived on a farm outside Hightstown, and his father was the bare-chested Jewish director of the central New Jersey farmers' cooperative. By an incredible one-in-a-million electronic quirk the conversation was overheard by one of the proctors, who reported it to Lippincott. The latter phoned the Harvard dean, demanding Barry's transfer be rescinded. Harvard gave in, but Barry, who was a brilliant student, was admitted as a graduate student by M.I.T.

From central Europe his kindly plump mother, who spoke with an accent, insisted on serving the food to Barry, his father and me at the kitchen table without joining us. Barry had heard there was a nearby nudist colony. I was also a stringer, i.e. occasional reporter, for *The Trentonian*. On a hot summer afternoon Barry and I drove in his open convertible up a trail through the woods. A sign greeted us - HAPPY VALLEY SUN CLUB. We had previously agreed we were going to pretend that we were interested in joining. Our car stopped in a clearing, and a man in his thirties wearing only a baseball cap and a whistle on a cord around his neck appeared from among the bushes. While we explained our purpose in being there, two women came from the trees. They too were in their thirties, and one was fat and ugly, and the other thin and ugly. The thin one had a brief towel which was just long enough to cover either her breasts or her pubic hair, but not both. She raised and lowered the towel. The male manager told Barry and me we would have to disrobe if we wished to see the swimming pool and buildings. There was also dancing at night. We said we'd think about it, and he gave us a sheet containing the rules for membership. One could not have any record of sexual deviancy. One had to be 100 per cent American and anti-Communist. As Barry and I drove back down the forest road, the Humpty-Dumpty ice cream truck passed us on the way to the club, its bell ringing cheerfully.

The absurd fear of Communism in America in the mid-fifties was accompanied, though not necessarily connected, with class warfare and racial oppression of Afro-Americans.

Dan Wakefield and I, as we were virtually the only two reporters in the town, became friends, and one night during Princeton reunions he and I went out on a double date. After we had returned the girls to their homes, we went to the parties. The younger classes of alumni usually met on the campus in tents, where free beer was served. I was carrying my camera with flash attachment. It was easy to gate-crash, and I was after all an alumnus. Suddenly there was an uproar, and he and I came upon a group of young alumni forcibly restraining three low-income toughs. They were brothers and one of them was on the ground, being held down by several Princetonians, wearing their Bermuda shorts and orange and black boaters. I took a flash picture, and the alumni crowd turned on me, and one of them tried to seize the camera from me. I lateraled it to Dan, who fled into the darkness of the trees, though not before the flash attachment was torn from the camera body. Dan and I found each other. We obtained another camera. The next day *The Trentonian* was delighted, and ran the story with pictures on the front page.

Around this time, Dan, who disliked Barney Kilgore's Republican politics, became friendly with the very well-known left-wing columnist Murray Kempton while riding the train from Princeton junction to New York. The much older man persuaded *The Nation* to advance Dan $50 to go to Mississippi and cover the Emmett Till case. Emmett was a black boy who had whistled at a white woman and was murdered.

The persistent theme in my conversations with Mrs. Welch was why I had broken down. She did not really know, she said. There were many studies. But she strongly advised me to eat and sleep regularly. One subject she did not want to discuss was sex. The moment I led into this area she stopped me. However, once she laughingly said she thought I would have many affairs by the age of 30. As I had never had sexual intercourse with a woman and had not even touched a vagina, I remembered her off-hand remark. Once she said she would like to conduct a little experiment on me. She asked me to tell her my mood as she raised and lowered the shade behind her. I said I felt more cheerful when the light was greater. On an another occasion she said, "You will do well in the world."

In about May or June I was asked by my step-brother, Bill Humphrey, a very talented electronics expert, to spend the weekend as his guest at his apartment in Boston, Mass. He was the youngest of Jack's three sons and worked as an electrical engineer for Sylvania outside of the city. He was five years older than me, and I did not know him well. His apartment in central Boston appeared to be a single room with white bathroom-like tiles and a bare light bulb, clothes scattered everywhere. He asked me to move up there and share a larger apartment with him. We would rent it together.

Mrs. Welch encouraged me to go. I would have to try and find a job as a newspaper reporter in the Boston area. I could write her and occasionally phone her.

Around this time my cousin David arrived from England to stay for a few nights. I had not really seen him since we had planned to run away at the age of 14. He had a reputation for being very wild and with his parents' approval was on his way to spend a year in western Canada. To me and Barry he seemed uncouth and uneducated. I was afraid of him, but I treated him with a patina of Princeton sophistication. He slept in a bed opposite mine in my small room in the back of the house. In the middle of the night I awoke, facing his bed. He was sitting on the edge, holding his erect penis in one hand. He said, "A woman taught me how to do this." I was so frightened that I pretended to be still asleep, and rolled over facing the wall. I fell back asleep. The next day I wondered if it had been a dream, but the memory had a sense of raw reality.

That summer during an interruption from searching for a newspaper job in the Boston area I went on a camping trip with John Stewart, a friend who was a graduate student in geology at Princeton, in Montana. With him in the west was a young male assistant, a prep school boy. Throughout the 10-day holiday I was jealous of the latter, who I felt John preferred to me. We spent most nights sleeping by the side of the road, where John cooked for us on a Coleman stove. Once we were thrown out of the Banff Springs Hotel for looking like yokels covered with hay. I had futilely pretended we were looking for a room, but we stood out like sore thumbs among the rich Texan guests in their stetsons, and an assistant manager escorted us outside. A day before my wallet had been stolen when we spent the night in the Kananaskis National Forest in Alberta, probably by a lumberjack or construction worker from a nearby site.

Returning to Red Lodge, Montana, where there was a saloon which featured a running spittoon - a stream entering from one swing door, passing along the length of the bar and exiting from the other - we entered another bar the evening of my 21st birthday, but the bartender refused to believe I was of age. I produced my aunt Violet's blue airmail letter congratulating me on this milestone, but he refused to accept this as evidence. Then, half-drunk, we climbed a nearby mountain at 3 a.m.

Chapter 3

Iceland

I rented a U-Haul for the trip from Princeton to Boston. Barry's convertible, which was very useful to him for seducing girls, pulled it, and Barry drove. I sat in the front seat, Holmie in the rear. She was going to Massachusetts for about two weeks to care for one of Bill's brother's new babies. Barry's language was colorful, and my ex-governess, now a middle-aged nanny, groaned with dismay at each four letter word, but he did not desist. "<u>Please</u>, Barry," she would say in her middle-class British voice, but he ignored her. We headed north on the white concrete roads in the summer heat.

The apartment Bill and I rented was 209 Mt. Auburn street, about a quarter mile west of Harvard Square. It was in a two-story brown-painted clapboard house facing Storrow Drive and the Charles river. We had one half of the second and third floors, a kitchen and living room on the 2nd, and bedroom and bathroom under dormers on the third. There was a small parking lot behind the building. Bill took care of the dealings with the landlord, and I gave Bill a check monthly.

Next door was a newly married couple who were freshman students at Harvard Law School. They fought frequently, and we could hear their voices through the walls. "Dick and Jo are at it again," Bill would say, smiling.

Harvard summer school was still in session, attracting young people from all over the world, who sat on the grass among the beautiful buildings of the old campus. Barry and I walked up and down the pavements among them, using the Princeton grading system to rate the girls as we were sure no one there would know what the numbers meant. The number "1" was the equivalent of an "A" while the lowest grade was a "7", meaning an "F." Barry would say, "<u>She's 1+</u>," meaning a girl we had seen was a stunning beauty, and I might say, referring to an exceptionally ugly young woman, "<u>a 7</u>."

I searched all over the eastern part of the state for a job as a reporter. From Brockton in the south to Gloucester in the north. Among the 40 or so publications I drove to was *The Boston Post*, where the associate city editor, Eddie Drohan, a plump gentle man, interviewed me, but I could see on his desk the pile of forms from the dozens of applicants. *The Post* was an important big-city daily, and I knew I had no chance. The publisher of the Salem or Lynn (Mass.) daily was a stocky curmudgeon, who said to me, "I've got an old fart who's a sports reporter on my paper. He's been with me for years. I want to fire him. Do you think you could write sports stories?" I replied, "I'll try." He said. "I'll let you know."

I went for an interview at the *Gloucester Daily Times*. The *Times* was located in a ramshackle old brick building just off the main street not far from the docks and the fishing boats, for which was Gloucester was famous, though the industry was in decline. Boats called "draggers" containing a few fishermen had a mysterious way of sinking when there happened to be another one nearby to rescue them. The owners, who were often members of the crew, would then collect the insurance.

The editor, Paul Kenyon, a tall-middle-aged man had a severely injured thigh and leg - probably from polio - which he had to drag after him when he walked and heave into position when he sat down at his desk in front of a big window. He had written one children's book. Long-jawed with glasses, hair pasted over his scalp and forehead, he had a kindly face. "We had a reporter who was drafted into the Army, and he'll be coming back to work when he's discharged in a few months. His replacement has just quit on me. Would you take his job until he returns?" "Yes," I said eagerly. "The pay's only $50 a week." That was $13 less than I had made in the steel mill. "You'll do the police news and general interest stories."

Coming out every afternoon except Sunday, the Gloucester daily, known locally as the "GD Times," circulation about 6,000, was owned by a cheery WASP with a superior manner - Phil Weld. Wearing a tweed jacket, Weld would sweep past us on his way to his office, giving us condescending greetings. There was a hole in one wall of his sanctum, and we could see him, and he could speak to Paul.

There were four reporters on the staff, and the prize beat was the fishing industry and the summer pleasure sailing. This was assigned to a priggish young man with curly short hair, Bob Brigham, who Weld had once invited to dinner at his home. I was jealous. I thought as a

Princeton alumnus and a member of an old English landed gentry family I belonged to Weld's world, but the tall publisher was blissfully unaware of me. The chief political reporter was short, pudgy Jimmy, an aging Yale graduate, who substituted for Paul when necessary. He had been bitterly disappointed when Weld chose Kenyon over him for editor, as he had been working there for a much longer time. The social reporter was Marilyn, a friendly Italian-American, with a ready smile and a plump figure. I sat the farthest from Paul at a desk with typewriter. There was also an outside correspondent. Her name was Doris Berthold. She described herself as "The Lady with the Feather." She wore one stuck into her brown hair piled on her head. She covered the nearby artistic community of Rockport. Besides the press machinery which occupied one half the structure there was on our floor the darkroom. I had to learn to develop, enlarge and print my photos there.

I was encouraged to attend the City Council meetings. Jimmy occupied a position of prominence next to the Mayor and took copious notes. It was hoped I would add a few friendly paragraphs about the official and unofficial characters in the chamber.

As a young man John J. Burke Jr. was reputed to have murdered the owner of the ship chandlers where Burke had worked, taking over the firm. He had recently been Mayor, and next to the current one, the scion of the only local department store, was invariably a big vote-getter, championing "the little people" - in his words. He was a Harvard Law School graduate, but with his short sturdy body, belligerent face and rasping powerful voice he portrayed himself as a waterfront boss. With his quick mind he interrogated other councillors and made impromptu speeches, demonstrating a greater skill than the much more famous Senator Joseph McCarthy of the same period. Pretending to cut taxes and save money, he terrorized the Mayor and most other people. Whenever he wanted to, he interrupted, growling "Point of Order" or some similar legal phrase. He sat next to Jimmy, who liked him and gave him lots of free publicity.

His only opponent was the white-haired young city manager, Dean Cushing, who Burke tried to bully at every opportunity. With his gentlemanly manner and efficient command of the facts Cushing struggled to bring order and progress to the old sea-faring city. It was the first time Gloucester had a city manager - a hoped-for beacon to the future. I quickly became friends with Cushing. He told me Burke's checks for serving on the council were seized monthly by the United

States government for non-payment of taxes. The *Times* ran a photo of the check. Burke was not pleased, and when I went to interview him in a bar by the docks, surrounded by cronies, he refused to talk, brusquely ignoring me. I was too frightened to remain there longer.

Girls - how to meet them, how to date them, how to kiss them, how (dream of dreams) to have sex with them. That was the major or one of the major preoccupations of Bill and me. Barry was now going steady with a Radcliffe sophomore, Ellen Gillespie, a short, pert, pretty redhead with a good figure. He was above the fray. In my heart a large part of the time when I wasn't thinking of my job, I yearned for a girl friend. It was the first thought in my mind when I woke up, and the last when I fell asleep.

I was aware when Bill and I were together that my mother had broken up his parents' marriage, but we were careful never to mention the subject. He was in touch with his mother who had remarried. Bill always spoke respectfully of my mother, and occasionally made a joke about his father, referring to some incident or other when Bill had been a child and Jack and Katherine were one. Every day he commuted to work as an electrical engineer for the Sylvania corporation a few miles west of Cambridge. He would leave a message on a fellow worker's desk, "Call Mr. Bird at 634 9821." Returning to his desk, the colleague would do so, and hear a voice at the other end of the telephone say, "Audubon Society of Massachusetts." At the end of a day's work, returning to our apartment, Bill would cut off the top of a can of chicken chow mein, and boil it in a pan of water. This was his dinner. I envied his college degree, and his better salary than mine, but I had a trust fund, which made me feel guilty. He was about five years older than me. I was much more at ease with girls than him, and discussed with Barry and Ellen how to help Bill, but we never came up with an answer. We liked him. He was about the same height as me, mostly bald, with a slight smile on his freckled face, and the hair around the back of his head was reddish.

Barry said, "There's a girl you ought to meet. Her name's Calista Dowlin, and she's a friend of Ellen's. She goes to Wellesley." Over the telephone I made a date with her and drove out to her dormitory - Tower Court West - a Gothic building covered with ivy where boys were not allowed beyond the entrance desk. I did not have high hopes. The sophomore who got into my car was a very pretty blonde with a page-boy hairdo. I was stunned. We immediately liked each other. At the end of the evening I parked my car in the circular driveway. "You are a lovely girl - just beautiful," I said. My usual technique when I wanted to kiss a young female was to pay her compliments, though with Calista it was truly genuine. We kissed several times - passionately.

She was the daughter of a surgeon and his wife in Canton, Ohio. Ellen came from the same city. Calista was of about average height and had a good figure, and she always dressed attractively. She liked to play tennis for fun at Wellesley, and never got into trouble with her studies. She yearned for outside excitement, but was very careful not to break any rules such as the 1 a.m. curfew hour for being back inside her residence. We began to see each other two or three times a week. I would take her out to dinner - usually in Cambridge - sometimes just the two of us, at other times with friends. We necked a great deal. There was an amused look in her eye. She listened to my minor exploits as a journalist, and I told her about Cushing and Burke. I was determined to expose the Gloucester demagogue.

After a while she drew a cartoon strip about me. It had six boxes, and I was portrayed driving my car at a fast speed, acting as an ace reporter, driving out to her college to take her out, etc. I was a kind of Ivy League "Scoop." Once she said, "You should smile more often."

One night we French kissed and caressed for at least an hour so that we lost track of time. We knew that Bill was out for the evening, and thus we had the living room couch to ourselves. There we lay in each other's arms, when suddenly my step-brother appeared in the doorway between the kitchen and the lounge. We had not even heard him come in. We scrambled to a sitting position. "It's not what you think," Calista said to Bill. "Nothing happened," I assured Bill after I had dropped her off at Wellesley and returned to our apartment.

I loved her, though I would never have admitted this to myself, and I think she liked me a lot. "I love you in my own little way," she would say. I could have done without the "in my own little way" but I was nervous about expressing my own feelings, which I was largely unaware of. On another date she said again, "You should smile more often."

While my romance with Calista, which I expected to last for ever, was blossoming, I was told by Paul that I would have to live in Gloucester. "The police reporter must be available if there's a fire in the middle of the night." The idea of leaving Bill's and my comfortable apartment in Cambridge, where all my university friends were, filled me with dismay. Fortunately "The Lady with the Feather" suggested that I stay at her house, and Paul agreed that the nights of Monday through Thursday were enough.

Rockport, where Doris lived, was a famous artist's colony considerably smaller and more scenic than Gloucester. There was Motif No. 1, a pier with a lobster man's shack at the end of it. Piled against the gray slates were empty cages for capturing the lobsters under the sea. The little harbor contained many sailboats, and the surrounding hills and valleys were dotted with summer and winter houses nestling among trees and bushes.

Doris was middle-aged and overweight, wearing loose-fitting unfashionable clothes. She had a son, Peter, aged 15, and a ramshackle house high on a hill. The ground around it was patches of grass and bare earth, and there were a few tall trees stripped of their leaves in the winter. The wooden walls on the outside were painted a dark brown. Inside on the ground floor was a living room and open kitchen and bare walls of wood boards. Doris and her son's bedrooms were on the upper two floors. I would sleep on a long wide ledge beneath a ground floor window covered with a mattress and blankets. Nearby were piles of books and chairs. Doris had a ready laugh and an ebullient personality. She was still sad as her husband had walked out less than a year earlier, and gone back to the mid west, sending her an inadequate check for her and their son periodically. The money from her job as a reporter - paid only for what was published - was essential to her. In the last year of their marriage he had refused to speak to her, climbing the staircase silently when he returned home from work in the evening. But she was fond of her son, and he reciprocated the affection, and she liked me. Many nights I would take her out to dinner in a Gloucester or Rockport restaurant after she had prepared a meal for Peter, leaving him to do his homework. Rockport and Gloucester were only an hour's drive from Cambridge and Wellesley.

When I had to stay overnight in the Gloucester area and Doris was attending a meeting in Rockport in order to write and/or photograph it for the next day's edition, I returned to *The Times* office after dinner alone in a diner. I let myself in with a key, climbed the staircase to the editorial floor, and sat at my desk. I read modern classics, either short stories or novels. I had noticed Dan Wakefield and his friends in New York were aspiring writers, and I wanted to do the same.

Christmas came, and Calista and I drove to New York. In the LaGuardia airport parking lot we spent the night in my car kissing until dawn rose, and she took a plane to visit her family in Canton.

Doris was a good friend of Paul, and in March, 1956, she learned from him that the reporter was being discharged from the Army and that Paul would have to fire me to make room for the ex-serviceman. It was the law. Those in the military had to have their jobs restored to them. But Paul, being a nice man, told Doris he hated to have to do this, and had decided to invite me to dinner at his house. Then after dinner and a few beers he would give me the bad news. I was not supposed to know this in advance, but she told me anyway. So I sat through cocktails, dinner and two beers until Paul summoned up his courage to give me the news. I pretended to be surprised.

Calista and I decided to spend the weekend in Cape Cod. Before we left, I received a phone message asking me to visit the *Boston Post* office Sunday night. The city editor, John Mannion, wanted to talk to me. Calista and I registered as a married couple, using a fake name, at a motel in Barnstable, a town on Cape Cod. Despite my best efforts and hers we never achieved sexual intercourse.

The *Post* office was on State street in downtown Boston, a narrow street with skyscrapers on both sides. The city desk was on the third floor, while the presses and composing rooms occupied the other half of the building. A very tall, large, middle-aged man with dark hair and a stern manner, Mannion looked at me. In front of him was the pile of applications. He said, "Eddie Drohan recommended you." He offered me a job as a reporter. I would be on probation for three months. I quickly accepted. Going out to my car, where Calista was waiting, I was elated.

Every afternoon except Sunday and Monday, which were my days off, I would drive to the first of ten police stations in the northern suburbs of Boston. I would ask the officer in charge if there had been any unusual events. He was usually an Irish-American, and I wrote his name in my address book along with any personal detail such as the fact he was installing a new linoleum floor in the kitchen of his house. If there was an accident, I would go to the home of the deceased and ask the grieving relations for a photo. I blocked out any feelings of pity for them, but I promised to return the picture. In the Revere station I was told they had transported a female patient to a mental hospital and raped her in the back seat of the patrol car, but for the most part the cops were hard-working and dedicated.

One evening I was told to go to the Boston morgue. The photographer, young tough Danny Sheehan, said, "I'm going to hide my speed graphic camera behind my back. It'll be focused and cocked.

When the family comes out, go up to them, and I'll walk by them fast, and take a picture."

A mother in one of my suburbs gave birth to her 18th child. I went to the hospital, but had no idea what questions to ask her until one of the assistant editors said, "Find out who's cooking and caring for the seventeen at home while she's recovering." With bedraggled hair the woman looked tired.

Among the other reporters was a good-looking three-times-married reporter who fell in love with a belly dancer at the Club Zara. There was Arthur King who had been fired by every other newspaper. He was often drunk and worked the very late night shift at 2 a.m. One of the tasks of the *Post* telephone operators was to dial numbers for the staff. King would shout to them, "Get me God."

In May Calista said she was going to Yale for the weekend as the guest of a junior she knew slightly - Philip Lottinville. I said, "He'll probably ask you to marry him." She assured me she wouldn't accept. The following Sunday I drove to her dormitory, and she and I went to a coffee shop in Wellesley. We sat at stools by the counter. I said, "Did he propose?" "Yes," she said. I said jokingly, "Did you accept?" "Yes," she replied. The blood drained from my face.

Despite my anguished pleas she wouldn't change her mind. What was so wonderful about him, I inquired? She replied, "He says, 'When your means don't meet your ends, don't reduce your ends, increase your means.'" And what was wrong with me? "Your fingernails are always dirty, and the back of your car is a mess." I had discovered a Canadian record, titled "The Investigator", which was a satire on Senator Joseph McCarthy. I thought it was very funny, but Calista was an admirer of McCarthy, and objected to my playing it, which I did anyway.

A few nights later, having spent the evening with Calista and drunk fairly heavily, I drove north on Route 128, which was the circular highway around Boston. There was a crash, and I awoke, bringing my car heavily damaged on the right side to a halt. I walked back in the dark, and there was another car parked by the side of the road. There were no lights on, and there was no one inside. I was able to reach Doris' house. The next day I arranged for my Chevrolet to be repaired and repainted. I went to see my friend Gardiner McDonald, the late middle-aged local lawyer who specialized in criminal cases. I told him what had happened, and why I would lose my license if the police charged me with leaving the scene of an accident. He said, "You wrote your name and address on a piece of paper, and put it on the windshield of the other car, but the wind blew it away."

Despite the strain Calista and I continued to date. In May her father arrived for a visit, and I was invited to join them for dinner. Because of his profession, I related a medical case I had covered in court. He listened attentively and coldly. Around this time I learned that her mother had had mental problems. Then Calista and I went to Princeton for the weekend. One of the guests at my parent's house was an English girl, Cecilia Turton, oldest daughter of the family that had rescued my aunt. On Saturday night I joined Calista in her bed, and for the first time achieved partial penetration. At that instant the door opened, light flooded in, and Cecilia said, "Calista, are you home?" I hid beneath the sheets, and immediately fled back to my old bedroom.

Then her summer vacation began. I wrote every other day. I hoped that by some faint chance the brief sexual penetration in Princeton had led to her pregnancy and then she would have to marry me instead of Phil. I sent flowers. But to no avail. She and a friend were to take a passenger liner from New York to France so that she could start her junior year abroad. I could come and meet her for coffee in the morning, but Philip would be there. For moral support I brought with me a friend from the *Post* - Sean Ryan, a chubby copy boy. She was staying at the Barbizon Hotel, where the bedrooms were restricted to girls.

We entered the coffee shop. Sitting beside her was Philip. He wore a neatly pressed dark suit and tie. With dark hair smoothly combed over his exquisitely handsome face he gazed equably at me. I told her that I was now permanently a member of the *Post* staff. "I thought you would be," she said wryly. The Italian ocean liner, the *Andrea Doria,* after colliding with another vessel 50 miles from New York, had sunk a week earlier. I said, "I wish you a safe and happy crossing." There was a hollow laugh. Then Sean and I left. I felt defeated, but I still hoped she would call off her engagement.

Suddenly the *Post* went out of business. The reduced circulation, the competition from the other three newspapers, television and a lack of advertising had killed it. But a lawyer stepped in, and three days later revived it. Some of the staff fled to the other papers.

The editors told me to deliver a message to the man who was still technically the owner, John Fox, a wheeler-dealer. He had made a fortune in oil and natural gas in Pennsylvania. He used the paper for his rabidly anti-communist crusades. He was a friend of a Mr. Goldfine, who was accused of making gifts to Sherman Adams, Eisenhower's chief of staff. Fox's office was on the top floor of a nearby skyscraper. I knocked on the door, and a voice yelled to me to enter. There at the end of a long room behind a desk sat the short, burly Fox. Beside him was a bust of Caesar and a chart showing on a daily basis his weight. With a wave of a finger he summoned me to deliver the envelope. He was already making threats to expose Goldfine and Adams.

One night in August I finished work, and went to a diner in Revere, and ordered dinner. It was a large juicy steak, and I was just starting to eat and enjoy it when I received a call from the city desk. "Go out to Logan Airport. Senator Hubert Humphrey is arriving. Interview him." I had to abandon my meal. Humphrey was a candidate for the democratic nomination for President. When the Senator got off the plane, I introduced myself, adding, "I don't know why no one else from the press is here." He said, "Can I bum a cigarette?" I gave him a Pall Mall. A few minutes later I phoned the city desk at 2 a.m.: "Senator Humphrey says Boston is his favorite city after Minneapolis." "Oh, yeah." Years later after becoming the Democratic candidate for President in the 1968 election against Nixon, which Humphrey narrowly lost, the senator died of cancer.

Doris phoned me from Rockport. The Gloucester High School had hired a new children's physical therapy teacher. On arrival he turned out to be an Afro-American. The School withdrew the job offer. The *Post* ran the story on the front page. With some difficulty we located him in a hotel in Boston. The then-liberal *New York Post* became interested. The other Boston newspapers, who were forced despite their jealousy to print the story, started to discover that the black had been convicted of a child molestation charge in his previous job. We found him another job in another state, and hurried him out of Boston. Shortly after the *Post* went out of business again.

I was the youngest reporter on the *Post,* competing with older staffers who were far more experienced than me for the few openings on the surviving newspapers, or perhaps I was afraid to be rejected if I applied. I went back to the *Times* and was hired as the society editor, replacing Marilyn, who had resigned. Attempting to make the accounts of weddings more interesting I re-wrote sections of them including the descriptions of the dresses of the bride and bridesmaids. Soon the mother of one of the newlyweds appeared in front of my desk and angrily told me that I had described inaccurately her daughter's gown. We had to run the story again - corrected.

Meanwhile four thousand miles to the east the Hungarian revolution took place, while the British and French supported by the Israelis were invading Suez. They had been forced to withdraw under American pressure. The Magyar uprising, soon crushed by Russian tanks, was to have a major indirect effect on my life some years later. My step-brother Watts and his wife, Barbara, had a young female friend, who was a doctoral candidate at a university in the Boston area. She was so inflamed by the plight of the Hungarians that she wanted to write about a Hungarian teenager who had briefly taken over the control of a city in Hungary before escaping to the west. However, these events seemed so far away to me that I was bored.

Before returning to my own story I mention that Watts and Barbara who lived in Framingham west of Boston with their growing family frequently asked Bill and me for dinner. On one of these occasions I met Katherine. I had met her fleetingly seven years earlier at Bill's graduation from the University of Maryland. His father and mother sat on opposite sides of the large field for the graduation, but when it was over, Katherine, accompanied by a woman friend, suddenly crossed the grass lawn and came up to Jack, my mother, Bill and me. She had never met my mother, and the tension in the air was electric. Immediately Jack talked with his ex-wife while my mother chatted politely with the woman friend, as I stood by their side. When seven years later I met Katherine for an entire evening at Barbara's dinner, I found her a pleasant quite attractive woman, not as pretty as my mother. To my surprise she asked affectionately in her genteel WASP way a number of questions about Jack, including his interest in speculating in gold.

On the *Post* I had been a member of the reporters' union, the Newspaper Guild. At my invitation an organizer came up from Boston to Gloucester. Our group consisted of Doris, me, and the police reporter. Jimmy had not been asked. The union man said on a such a small daily newspaper there would have to be a unanimous willingness to start a union.

One night my new friend Fred Brent sought my help. He was very depressed, he said. I listened to him for four hours, and promised to help. I phoned Doctor Welch, who recommended a friend of his in Boston. Fred went to see him, and shortly afterwards I received a letter or phone call from the physician. "Fred has an obsession that his ears are a Darwinian throwback." I had never noticed anything unusual about Fred's ears. He began therapy.

I decided to return to college, and applied at four institutions. One of them was Tufts, located in a Boston suburb. Tufts required that one write an essay. I wrote two pages about my step-father. Jack was strong and brave. He was also warm-hearted, kind and the finest person I had ever met. I also sought admission to Boston University, Columbia School of General Studies and Princeton. I met Dean Finch. "We couldn't admit you here for the third time," he said. The other three universities accepted me, and I chose to go to Boston University and major in journalism. My plan was to become the owner of a small rural weekly like the Fullers of Blairstown, N.J. who had lived prosperously enough to send their daughter Lee to an expensive boarding school.

Possibly one of the reasons I applied to Tufts was that a girl friend, who had graduated from there, had taken me to the Boston psychiatric hospital where she worked as a nurse for a tour. "That's a padded cell." I looked in the half light through the small glass window at a naked male body lying inside. The thought of my half-brother John in his sanitarium in England flashed through my mind.

Violet Hart was a middle-aged friend of Doris. She was a widow, her husband having been killed during the Second World War. A pretty woman, she had a 12-year-old daughter. Doris said, "Why don't you ask her for a date?" She added, "Both her breasts have been removed because of cancer." On our living room couch in Cambridge I made love to her. She told Doris. The latter said I could no longer stay the night at her house on evenings when I visited Violet at her home in Rockport. Because of her daughter Violet forbade me to spend the night in her house. One night I was forced to park by the side of the road between Gloucester and Rockport - too tired to return to Cambridge. Using a sleeping bag, I slept by the side of the road, and awoke as the sun rose. I drove over to Doris' house.

Then I was informed by the draft board that I would be inducted into the U.S. Army. There was no escape - but there was not a war on. I decided to go Europe before being forced to serve my country. In London Aunt Violet said, "I predict you'll be back." I went to Paris and met Calista in a café. Taking my hand, she looked at it, and said affectionately, "I see your fingernails are clean." I realized she would marry Philip that summer.

In Berlin I stayed with Neal and another Princeton friend, Tom Carson. The wall had not yet been built. My friends were in U.S. Army intelligence, and could not risk entering East Berlin because of the possibility they might be kidnapped by the East German communists or their Russian allies. However, as I was a civilian, I took the S-bahn into the eastern part of the city, where there was still a lot of damage from the war, and shabbily dressed women could be seen going through the piles of rubble looking for bricks and valuables. A German student friend of Neal also took me there on his motorbike, and I saw the head of Nefertiti in the museum and the site of Hitler's bunker. Near the Brandenburg gate was the ruined church being preserved as a symbol of the war. In West Berlin we visited nightclubs where there were prostitutes and a big indoor cafe catering for lonely hearts. We sat at a table which had telephones and pneumatic tubes. If one saw a girl at another table who one liked, one could phone her. Or one could send her a message.

In the American officers' barracks where I stayed there was a captain who hired a different German whore every night. Before she left the next morning, he photographed her with a Polaroid standing naked, wearing his pistol and ammunition belt. On the wall of his apartment each picture was placed next to the previous one. The last night I was guest of honor at a party where most of those present were young Germans. Even though I did not speak the language, I was trained by Neal and Tom to memorize and say in flawless German to each guest who arrived, "I am honored to meet you and it is a great pleasure for me, and although I would like to speak German and will learn it as fast possible I do not speak or understand any German at all."

I returned to Cambridge, and one morning two letters addressed to me arrived. One was the well-known, "The President of the United States extends his greetings…" etc., and informing me that I was drafted for two years. The other letter was from a U.S. Army Reserve unit ordering me to report for active duty for six months. The second letter held preference over the first - much to my relief. Every afternoon I went to the banks of the Charles and spent an hour doing physical exercises. I tried to get into the Army Public Information Office through a friend of a friend who was a reporter on one of the Boston dailies, but I was a day too late in my application. I was headed for the infantry.

On the fateful day of my induction Bill accompanied me to the Boston army base. Beside the buses lined up to drive the other recruits and me to Fort Dix, N.J., we stood in our first formation, and a colonel said, "Twenty million men before you have done this…" I found this comforting. Bill photographed me, boarding the bus, carrying a bag of underwear, smiling nervously.

Fort Dix is in south central New Jersey - an area of low pines and sand. For three nights we were sent to bed at midnight and woken at 3 a.m. while being indoctrinated. We were issued uniforms, boots and a rifle. Everybody received a compulsory haircut, but my crewcut meant that there was little to shave off. We were asked if anyone had spent time in the R.O.T.C., but I was afraid to take on the responsibility, and so did not step forward.

My new home was H Company, First Training Regiment (I forget the battalion), a recently built concrete barracks. We could have been quartered in the old wooden barracks. Two hundred fifty of us were packed into a room and addressed by a solidly built middle-aged man in uniform: "My name is Master Sergeant (whatever it was)." He added in a loud menacing voice, "Don't ever forget it!" I would sleep on the upper tier of a two-bunk bed in a long room with 50 or so other recruits. Most of us had been to college. The majority of us were white. The others were Afro-Americans, who had a high school education. At meal times we lined up outside the mess hall and were ordered to do a chin up on the bar and threatened that we would not eat if one could not perform the task. I was unable to do it, but like everyone else who failed was still admitted into the food area.

Then we met our commanding officer. He was a young Afro-American who was in superb physical condition far better than any of us. The sergeant who dealt with us on a regular basis was Field Sergeant Cecil Prince from Tennessee who usually said to us in his southern accent, "Ah want evry breathin' ass 'n swingin' dick to stan' tall." He was a dark haired, good-looking man in his thirties with a muscular physique.

After we were taught how to march, he chose me to lead an elite group of six fellow trainees to perform before our commanding officers. However, I was so afraid that I would perform the maneuvers badly that I failed to turn up for the show. A few hours later he demanded an explanation from me, and I lied, "Sarge, I didn't think you meant me." He repeated what I said, mimicking me with a whine, emphasizing the "think."

After a few weeks we were given a Sunday off. My mother arrived with a pretty English girl, Mary Newton, who was the niece of Lady Myra Fox, of Croxton Park, Cambridgeshire. Dressed in a garden party skirt and blouse, she had rosy cheeks and a creamy complexion. Her hair was attractively cut. We sat on a blanket on one of the few patches of grass, me in my uniform, surrounded by the barracks and sand of the base, eating a picnic under the hot sun. I felt I was inferior because I was not an officer, but Mary, speaking in her British upper-class voice, did not seem to notice the absence of any stripes or insignia on my shirt. My hat was called by my fellow soldiers a "cunt" cap, and it too lacked a second lieutenant's gold bar.

It was common knowledge that one should never volunteer for anything. However, when Prince told our company he was looking for a typist, I ran as fast as I could from my rank in the rear of my platoon towards him, beating another hopeful by a step. Prince said, "U fuckin' wa-ell bettuh b' eb-ble t' tarp, Rowley."

I found myself in the company office, and was assigned to type the name and serial number of every one of us on 250 files. With my "hunt and peck" system I could do 45 words a minute before corrections. My other task was to answer the phone: "Hotel Company, Private Rowley, sir." During moments of relaxation Prince would exchange banter with the sergeant in charge of the office. Prince reminisced, "When ah was in Korea, ah could see this little Chinese soldier a 1000 yards away, carrying ammo up th' hill to his buddies. There wuz a white outcroppin, and I fired shots at it with my M-1 until ah got the sights purrfectly lined up. Then when that little chink came up th' next time, ah kill'd 'im."

Because I was in the office I did not have to join my fellows in the field. While they slept in tents, I remained in the barracks. I did finally spend one night in a sleeping bag in a tent, and although I missed one third of the training, there were times when I had to participate. As we sat in the stands, gazing across the flat landscape, one of our instructors attempted to inspire us by quoting Tennyson, "Yours not to reason why, yours but to do and die." In the evening the setting sun made the landscape beautiful.

One day we were ordered to take the infiltration course. In the afternoon we watched four sergeants, each behind a machine gun, fire live ammunition at a height of about five feet above the ground. Besides not standing up, which would have been fatal, we were expected to crawl towards the machine guns while holding our rifles. It was necessary to crawl around low circular mounds. Inside of them were explosives which went off periodically. When it was dark I joined my fellows in a ditch opposite the machine guns. I was frightened. At the command I climbed onto the course by rolling over the edge above me and maneuvered my way towards the chattering guns as the explosives went off. Just past the gunners we fell into a ditch and safety.

Back in the office I was ordered by the office non commissioned officer to carry a message to Sgt. Prince. Dutifully I would run to the other man, come to attention, and say, "Sarge, I have a message from Sergeant Maxwell (or whatever his name was). He says you're too dumb to even drop your drawers and pull your prick." Prince would reply, "Go back and tell that chicken shit dickhead…" I would then perform the same ritual before Maxwell. The latter would say, "Tell that motherfucka…" I would then return to Prince, but by the time I had said "mother…" Prince would grin.

Our language featured the word "fuck." About every fifth word was a variant. While I was there, the parents of a few recruits with strong religious feelings complained to their congressmen about this habit. Dix was much closer to Washington than other bases, and had a reputation for being a political base. As a result the training was less harsh. Our officers asked us unenthusiastically to desist from bad language, but everyone ignored this command. I said to a friend, "The reason we swear so much is that this is the only accurate way to describe our situation."

Our C.O. had two assistant officers, who were R.O.T.C. graduates. One of them was somewhat effeminate, and Prince and the other sergeants treated him with a minimum of respect. On my barracks floor at the other end of the room from my bunk was an Afro-American young man, Kittles. He never washed. One night a group of recruits seized Kittles and forced him into the shower. Another of my fellows developed back trouble, and hobbled around half bent over. Prince ridiculed him loudly, and the back patient was given a medical discharge. In the latter part of our eight weeks' training there was a soldier in another platoon who allegedly failed to perform his duties adequately. He might have lost his rifle or cleaned it inadequately. This resulted in the platoon being penalized, and a group took him out into the nearby woods and beat him up.

We were taught to shoot our M-1 rifles, and I won an award for the third level of marksmanship. When we were not aiming at targets as far as 500 yards away, we sat in trenches beneath the targets and hoisted or lowered them. If the shooter missed, we raised a pair of underpants called "Maggie's Drawers." During rest periods between the target practice, we sang over the telephones a song which went as follows:

"Some mothers have sons in the Army, some mothers have sons overseas, but take down your service flag, mother, your sons in the R.O.T.C...R.O.T.C. It all sounds like bullshit to me, to me...(refrain) Some mothers etc..."

Another exercise was for the shooters to aim at scattered targets. Two individuals would be placed in a fox hole below the ground and have to raise by a lever a target. One of my fellow soldiers on the intercom started to imitate the sound of a pig. Soon others mimicked him, and after a while a whole gamut of animal noises were relayed among the trainees.

After we had completed our basic training, we were allowed a few days vacation, and I returned to Princeton which was only a half hour's drive away. I was invited to dinner by Cynthia Smith, a girl friend I had known when I used to see Mrs. Welch. She had been a patient of Harry Potter, and suffered from a complaint known as hyperventilation. This meant that she inhaled far too much oxygen, resulting in very heavy breathing and often unconsciousness. In fact the night about two years earlier when I had photographed the Princeton alumni fighting with the town toughs, she had partially collapsed on my shoulder. Dan Wakefield had thought it was passion for me, but it was the illness. About our respective therapies Cynthia and I used to compare notes. Arriving from Ft. Dix, I told her, "I'm in the best physical condition of my life," but she and her friends were unimpressed.

I was assigned to learn how to be a clerk typist in a different part of the sprawling base. In the Army it is essential to have a friend in order to protect oneself against the abuses administered by one's superiors and for companionship. John Stearns, who I had known in H co., was married, a father, and prior to being conscripted had worked as a young junior executive in the insurance industry in Hartford, Conn. Wearing glasses, he was a tall serious young man lacking a sense of humor or any spark of originality, and I did not like him. Nor, I think, did he like me, but we became "friends" or allies out of necessity, and we each watched out for the other. We sat next to each other in the office where we were ordered to work. We commiserated with each other over the commanding officer of our barracks. This individual, a captain, decided he did not like the shine on our floor. By now we were living in one of the old wooden barracks. For four nights he forced everyone to rise at 4 a.m. so that the floor could be buffed with more wax.

One weekend the entire base was placed on full alert. If the Russians had attacked and dropped atom bombs on American cities, we were to be ready to repel the invasion and give emergency help to the victims. Almost everyone ignored this order, and thousands left the base, which was technically going AWOL, a court martial offense. Many of us went into Trenton and were spectators at an extremely noisy car race.

There was nothing for Stearns and I to do in the base training office. So we sat side by side at a long table, and I tried to write a short story while he worked at some personal matter of interest to him. Often the officers passed by our desk. One had a helmet on which was inscribed instead of his name - GODDAMMIT. Our immediate superior was an Afro-American sergeant - a friendly, plump man. The number of blacks who were n.c.o.s was larger than their share of the population due to the military giving them an opportunity for a steady job at reasonable pay, which would have been far less likely in the civilian world. This Afro-American was married to a white German woman, who he had met while serving in the military as part of the occupation force after the Second World War. He brought her back to the U.S. Such a marriage would have been almost unthinkable if he had been a civilian. He would say to Stearns and me, "How you boys doin'?" To me he said in his southern accent, "Rowley, why'nt u sign up for six?" urging me to enlist for six years. Such a course of action was unthinkable to me, determined to make my way in the outside world, but at the same time it was a tempting thought. I had to admit I was quite enjoying my military service. I did not have to think. "No thanks, sarge," I said sadly.

Because we were in the base training headquarters I heard that a recruit had died the night before in an accident. Like the others he had been crawling through the infiltration course. One of the millions of rounds from the machine guns in a freak way instead of shooting straight ahead had suddenly dived down into the victim. That evening, even though I knew it was illegal to give out information without the permission of the Army Public Information Office, I went to a telephone box in our barracks and called *The Trentonian*, "Sol, this is Peter Rowley. Do you remember me? I'm a soldier at Fort Dix." I told him what had happened. Sol did not seem that interested. Training accidents were not unusual, but he took the details anyway.

In November I was honorably discharged, having completed my six months active duty. I still faced five and a half years of reserve duty, but this only entailed a few hours one night a week plus two week's summer camp. I had let my crewcut grow out. I returned to Cambridge where I immediately had an argument with Bill. During my military duty I had paid for my half of the apartment, but without asking me Bill had installed Sean Ryan as his roommate. Sean departed on my return, but I was annoyed that my permission had not been asked.

I took Violet to a party in Boston. The other guests were young like me, and some of them were shocked by my date. My friend who had asked me said to them there was no reason why a young man should not go out with an older woman. I said, "Older women are wiser." Violet refused to make love. She would not explain why.

The question of returning to college arose. A friend of mine from Princeton, who was a law student at Harvard, Brice Clagett, and I discussed the matter. "What you're saying," he said, "is that three years of Princeton without a degree may have as much prestige as four years with a degree at somewhere like Boston University."

I ran into someone I had known at Asheville. Mark Reed was two years younger than me. He had very dark hair, and I remember his chest and legs were covered with it. We had not been friends then, but now we became friendly. He was starting graduate school. I think he was lonely, and I was at a loose end, trying to decide what to do with my life. He suggested that we attend a dinner in Cambridge for Asheville alumni. The speaker was Mr. Fall. To my amazement the headmaster, his face registering sympathy, said solicitously, "Peter, how are you? So good to see you." As never in my nearly six years there had he ever shown the slightest interest in me, I was speechless.

I decided to become a great writer. I would live in Paris like Hemingway and Fitzgerald. It would be necessary to learn French, and I started to take lessons from an attractive French woman, who was married. My progress was slow, and she was not interested in me amorously. The only other place I could go was England, where I could speak the language. I discovered that, if I moved to the U.K., I would be drafted into the British Army for two years. I consulted Mr. Turton, who was a British solicitor. Surely, I said, the English would not seize someone who was in the American Army reserves. But the answer was that neither country recognized service in the other's military. The only solution, if I still wanted to live in England, was to renounce the Queen. Thus I would be giving up my English citizenship and would only be an American citizen.

The reason I had American citizenship was that when I was about 14, my mother to please Jack had become an American. As she was my only surviving real parent, I became one automatically. At the time no one had asked my approval. So I went to the consulate in Boston and before a grim-faced English consular officer renounced Queen Elizabeth II. I doubt if Liz knew about it. I found this a painful task, and Mrs. Welch commiserated, but I was now free to arrive in Britain.

Another symptom of my dream of becoming a famous novelist was that I thought writers were supposed to be mostly silent, observing people. My friends, including Barry and Neal, wondered if I was suffering from a mental illness, and Barry asked me, "Would you like some professional help?" meaning a psychiatrist. I said, "No. I'm fine." However, I did develop trouble with my right eye, and started wearing glasses to read. After a few months I needed a stronger prescription, which alarmed me. "What about eye exercises?" I suggested to the eye doctor I consulted in Princeton. "No," he replied firmly, "I'd give the same advice if it was my sister."

I decided to propose to Jackie Wei, a pretty hard Chinese-American girl at Radcliffe whose parents lived a wealthy life style in America. She was a friend of Ellen's and lived in the same Radcliffe house, Slater. The relationship was not the same as it had been with Calista, but in the void in my soul compounded by the limbo of being in America but planning to move to Europe I knew I was in love with her. On the dance floor at some university party in Cambridge, I said to Jackie, "I love you." She replied brightly, "Me, too." I couldn't figure out then or much later whether she meant that she loved me or herself. Of course she dismissed my offer of marriage instantly.

In May, 1958, I booked passage on an American freighter, embarking from New York. It would take 10 days, and my fellow passengers were five elderly American ladies. There was no television or radio. The crew ate separately from us, and each of us had a small cabin with a porthole. The cargo was a mixture of cars and merchandise, and the vessel weighed about 10,000 tons. The sky was gray the entire time, matching the color of the sea, until we entered the English channel. There was nothing to do but read, and I finished *Brideshead Revisited,* which I did not particularly enjoy, finding it lacked passion. The book seemed to blend in with my somewhat depressed frame of mind, and the old ladies, though they did their best to cheer me up with their friendly American conversation, did not succeed. Only in the English channel did the sun appear. On the fore deck was a radio belonging to the crew, and I heard that because of the Algerian war de Gaulle had come to power in France.

After reaching London my aunt Violet said, "How could you want to marry a Chinese girl?! Think what the children would look like."

She added firmly, "When she turned you down, that's why you moved here."

I protested weakly, "I was planning to come anyway."

Violet had found me a boarding house in South Kensington which served breakfast and dinner. The others were young upper-class English men and women, but none of them spoke to me, though they chatted happily among themselves. So lonely was I that on a Sunday afternoon I went to Hyde Park to Speaker's Corner, where at least the crowds supplied some form of companionship. I listened to the gamut of religious and political speakers.

A good-looking middle-aged man with smoothly combed gray hair struck up a conversation with me. After a while he invited me back to his flat, where he gave me a tumbler of whiskey without any water. I noticed his conversation was extraordinarily sexual. After half an hour when I had finished the drink he tried to press another one on me. I became frightened. "Thank you, but I have to go," I said. I started to walk down the stair case from his second floor rooms. He was behind me. Suddenly he crashed both hands on my shoulders hard. Running down the stairs, I escaped out on to the street.

Although it was not my usual practice to go on vacations with my mother, Jack and 10-year-old half-sister Dorothy, when they asked me to join them in Spain I decided to flee temporarily from my dismal existence. We traveled around much of Spain staying in comfortable hotels that had been converted from private mansions or abandoned monasteries or convents. I was bored and read a long novel whose title I do not remember (I think it was *The Brothers Karamazov*), and stared out the side window of the rented car at the passing scenery from Segovia to Toledo. My step-father did all the driving, not trusting my mother and me on the Spanish roads.

Equally uninteresting was my step-father's conversation at meals, including dinner which never started until about 11 p.m. as was the Spanish custom. However Dorothy's presence enlivened the company, and I taught her a song, as we drove up and down narrow Spanish mountainous roads, which went, "Cigarettes and whiskey and wild, wild women..." The sight of my sweet little red-haired sister singing this line amused her and me, and my mother and Jack, who was at the wheel, tolerated it.

Returning to London, I discovered that Violet through her considerable network of lady friends had found a flat rented by one of these women, a Mrs. Duggan, for her son Shaun and two school friends of his, Anthony Record and John Ward. They needed a fourth to share the rent. The address was 26 Buckingham Palace Mansions, a ground floor flat, on Buckingham Palace Road. The building was a large decorated Victorian structure of red brick almost directly opposite Victoria Station. Our rooms were in the rear facing onto the mews, while a flat off the hall in the front was occupied, we suspected, by an office of British government intelligence. There was a fancifully dressed uniformed guard, and mysterious people in everyday clothes plus a few military officers went in and out the entrance door, but the identification of the flat in the hall contained some innocuous name such as Overland United.

I met Shaun, John and Anthony. I was now 24, but they were about 18 years old, and had gone to a public school, i.e. boarding school, which specialized in catering to students whose families had little money. It was historic and heavily endowed, and they had had to wear particularly colorful uniforms representing the school. It was their first taste of freedom from school authorities and parents. They held trainee jobs, and to me they seemed naïve. To them I appeared strange. Every Saturday afternoon they played rugby, and would returned in the evening bloodied and bruised.

There was a cleaning woman, a Mrs.Lloyd, who came for several hours a few days a week, and was paid what struck me as a pittance. She was a small plump lower class cockney with an endearing personality. My share of the rent cost very little. Living in London in those days compared to the American standard of living was very inexpensive, and I was able to save a considerable sum of money which I forwarded regularly to my small account supervised by my step-father at the stock-broking firm where he worked in Princeton. He had started up this subsidiary of Laidlaw & Co. a few years earlier.

My three room-mates and I purchased food, which we usually fried. Sausages and bacon and boiled potatoes were staples. There was a system whereby each person who ate a meal had to pay a few shillings into a joint kitty. Telephone calls were rigidly monitored with a sheet, and the caller was to write down long distance calls and their date. We decorated the flat ourselves, and the others skillfully hung the wall paper in the smallish living room, which was partly below street level.

There was an iron railing. We could peer through it at cars parked nearby and the occasional pedestrian.

Of my three roommates the one I liked the best was John Ward, whose father had died of a heart attack early in the Second World War. An only child, he was raised by his mother, a professional nurse, who lived in a comfortable cottage in the center of the Winchester public school campus. Her job was to care for any of the scholars, who were the best students, who were sick. Several of the rooms were "hospital" wards. John had a deformed ear, a genetic abnormality, which he carefully concealed with his hair. He was short and charming.

Shaun was a little taller, and his mother was responsible for the lease. She was the daughter of a Yorkshire landed family, and had married an Irish doctor, which my Aunt Violet said was regarded as an unwise union, implying that marrying Irish men was inherently risky. The husband had disappeared, and Shaun's grandfather lived alone in the mansion, specializing in some erudite form of astronomy. Shaun was friendly but moody.

And then there was Anthony, whose parents were more prosperous than Shaun's and John's. They were immigrants from South Africa, and Anthony was determined to succeed in the business world.

I started to purchase prints of famous impressionist paintings for about five pounds each including framing. This must have been my contribution to the decoration of our somewhat dark flat, and in the kitchen above the table where we ate I hung a sensational Modigliani nude, lush and normally proportioned unlike some of his elongated, very thin women. My aunt Jane and her husband, Uncle Reggie, visited me one day. "That painting is disgusting," they said. "Are you serious?" I said, proud of my artistic taste. They were keen bettors on horse races, drank heavily and loved to attend fashionable parties. I was mystified by their prudery. They were Roman Catholics. "Yes," said the couple. "Take it down." My roommates and I did not remove my work of art.

At about the same time I was interviewed by the deputy editor of *The Sunday Express*, Robert Edwards, a youngish man full of energy with curly dark hair, who had been the editor of the left-wing magazine, *Tribune*. He seemed to think that because I had an American accent I would be sufficiently aggressive for Fleet Street journalism, and I was hired as a reporter on Saturdays only for the Sunday paper on a two-month trial.

The circulation of the *Sunday Express* was about four million. It and its daily sister, *The Daily Express*, occupied a glass and steel five story structure on Fleet Street. Entering there was marble, a bank of stairs, and Epstein's bust of Lord Beaverbrook, the owner. At one end of the news room was an enormous sign saying "**IMPACT**," and beside it commands telling us to get it into our "leads," "headlines" and "photo captions most of all!!!" The effect was sort of like "Big Brother," and in fact the managing editor, his assistants and the company lawyer sat underneath the sign and stared at reporters such as me like Orwell's TV cameras.

Directly opposite me sat a little man whose sole job all day Saturday was to check John Gordon's column for errors. Gordon had been the previous editor and wrote a column full of gossip and strong opinions. The reporter said, "He's so inaccurate that if I haven't found two five thousand libel suits by the end of the day, they tell me to check again. If Lord Glossop shot his pet deer by accident in Devon, you can be sure the true story is Sir Humphrey Twiddleton blasted off his big toe by accident on his estate in Scotland."

Very little seemed to excite the veteran journalists around me, except when Randolph Churchill telephoned our floor. He was a columnist for another Beaverbrook paper, the *Evening Standard*, and in my opinion a superior writer to his father. As Beaverbrook and Churchill father and son were close friends, the news staff had two reasons to be highly stimulated. Their boss, who had been in Churchill's cabinet during the Second World War, admired Randolph and Winston, and the Churchills were very big news. Although Beaverbrook was nearing the end of his days, he still ensured his papers reflected his right-wing opinions, which emphasized the British Empire in its rapidly fading glory.

One Saturday I was sent to a large hall in London to cover a series of speeches by left-wing leaders deploring Britain's nuclear program, and there on the stage a few feet in front of me (this was typical Fleet Street journalism to imply that I was head-to-head with the subject of the story) was Bertrand Russell, looking very frail. I was in fact about 30 feet from Russell, and it would have been very difficult for me to leave the press section in the front row, mount the stage, pass the other dignitaries and approach Russell. Of course the *S.E.* ran not a word of the story I phoned in.

A large part of the time on Saturdays there was nothing to do, and I decided to investigate the Howard de Waldens, my great uncle Francis Norris and anyone else I could think of. I struck pay dirt in the *S.E.* library when an employee brought me a thick faded brown envelope full of yellowing newspaper clippings about Francis.

I had met Francis a few times at my aunt Violet's house. As usual she was being kind to one of the less fortunate in the world. He was a tall, cadaverous man in his mid-seventies. He was very cynical and laughed wickedly with a cackle at any gossip he spoke or heard. He was my maternal grandmother's brother. Aunt Violet said, "As a young man he narrowly failed the exam for the foreign office. I persuaded him to marry Frances. She takes care of him now and has never been married. Once they were married I told her to make sure they sleep in separate bedrooms." In her mid-fifties Frances was a sort of Victorian virgin with a high-pitched voice like a trumpet. She was always cheerful and had yellow reddish hair.

The *Express* clippings described how Lieutenant Colonel Francis Norris and a Dutch jew named Reszinski starting in the early 1930's were buying Weimark Republic bonds at par. As the notes were worth very little, the papers were puzzled as to how Francis and his partner could be losing millions of pounds, francs and dollars. They were purchasing them from British, French and American banks and financial institutions. I knew that Francis after the First World War had been legal adviser to the Allied War Commission in Berlin, where he must have come in contact with many important Germans. It dawned on me that the only explanation was that Francis and Reszinski were fronting for Hitler. For domestic political reasons the Fuehrer could not be seen by the German public as honoring the discredited Weimar bonds, but at the same time the dictator needed to restore the confidence of the international financial community in the German economy. Francis was described in the British press as the "Colonel Lawrence of High Finance," a reference to Lawrence of Arabia. There was even an interview by, I think, the *Daily Mail* with him high in a New York skyscraper, as they put it.

The clippings then described how Francis and Reszinski swapped women. Francis's wife was Elizabeth, a beautiful Swede. Reszinski's mistress was Sonia, a white Russian, who lived in Paris. Reszinski and Elizabeth were married in a lavish ceremony at the Savoy Hotel in a double wedding with Francis and Sonia. According to the press, the affair cost 60,000 pounds, and guests were flown in from continental Europe, and the champagne flowed freely. On and on went Francis and Reszinski's seemingly money-losing activities, but they were clearly living very luxuriously.

Then in the late 1930's a French court convicted Francis on a charge of a minor financial fraud. He would have been arrested if he set foot on French soil, and a Member of Parliament rose in the House of

Commons, demanding to know why the British government was not protecting Colonel Norris. However, the minister who answered dodged the question.

After the Nazis invaded Holland, Belgium and France Reszinski died in a concentration camp, and Elizabeth fled back to Sweden. Francis, who because of his First World War record was qualified to serve in the British Army during the Second World War, was never asked by the government to go on active duty again. Sonia died of natural causes after WWII, leaving Francis with a valuable collection of Russian icons, swords, and umbrellas, one of which had a poisoned tip. They were on display in his west London flat.

One of my problems at the *S.E.* was that I was not allowed to work in England, as I was now solely a U.S. citizen, and when I returned late Saturday night to our flat, I would bring back an early edition of the paper. My roommates were mystified as to how I had obtained it, but I was afraid to tell them I was employed. At the same time I was becoming increasingly influenced by my aunt Violet's view of the world - titles, landed families and the British class structure. The *S.E.* despite its conservative slant reflected also the rebellious side of the Canadian Lord Beaverbrook who was well known for liking to set a cat among the pigeons. Thus the *Express* newspapers waged a bitchy campaign against the old landed upper-class families, and I under the influence of Aunt V's snobbery was appalled. When the assistant managing editor suggested that we should suspend my Saturday employment, I was not sorry. What would Aunt Violet and her upper-class friends say if they thought of me as a squalid hack on Fleet Street? I would be excluded from the world of old families, and no deb, who had been presented at court, would ever marry me.

While I was trying to get a permanent job on the *Express*, I had also been in contact with the London bureau of *Newsweek* magazine. They had sent me out on a few assignments such as attending an international whaling conference in Oxford and covering the opening night of *Othello* at Stratford starring Paul Robeson. His reputation very recently restored after being smeared as a Communist, he perspired a lot in his dressing room after the performance. My main value to *Newsweek* was to play cricket on an American amateurs cricket team, organized by their chief European correspondent, Eldon Griffiths, who later went on to become Minister of Sports under Prime Minister Edward Heath. Eldon was a gangling red-head, and chose me because I had played the game until I left England at the age of 10 and three-quarters. Eldon did not however offer me a job on *Newsweek*. None of the other Americans had ever played it at all, but Eldon was Welsh, and passed himself off with everyone's agreement as an "American."

Our first match was against the Lords Taverners, a prestigious cricket club, and we played for an urn of Boston tea leaves. The industrious Eldon had found the original tea company that had sent out the consignment of tea to Boston, Mass., which the Americans had tossed into the harbor, starting the Revolutionary war, and a little man ran out onto the field with the package. I was quickly bowled out by Alf Gover, a famous retired bowler I had never heard of.

One of our next matches was in Ruislip, a suburb west of London. By this time Eldon's team had become a status symbol for some American executives in London, who vied for a spot on it. Despite my insignificance Eldon allowed me to stay on the squad, and I found myself standing in a line of my fellow American players facing another line of our British opponents. Appropriately I was at the end of the line, and opposite me was the English umpire, a wizened 90-year-old man, and next to him a British children's TV star, Mr. Pastry. "When she comes in front of me," said Mr. Pastry. "I'm going to faint." He was referring to Jayne Mansfield, who was going to throw out the first ball. She undulated between us, coming down the opposing parallel lines, smiling prettily, showing her delicious cleavage, wearing a tight red and gold dress, shaking hands with each of us. After me she turned to the umpire, and said in a soft breathless voice, "What a doll." In true British fashion he batted not an eyelid, and showed not the slightest emotion as this Hollywood bombshell stood a few inches from him. Then she stopped before Mr. Pastry, who collapsed on the ground.

Newsweek sent me to an auction at Sotheby's conducted by Peter Wilson, the chairman. Susie's friend, who was his secretary, went to his flat one morning to deliver some papers. Entering her boss's bedroom she found him in bed with his butler. By the standards of those days the paintings by van Gogh, Monet, Picasso etc. fetched very large sums, but I incorrectly reported that there appeared to be a decline in their prices. After the auction I went to the rostrum to interview the tall elegant charming Wilson. Beside us were the paintings. I was nervous. Wilson said, "Please be careful. You've just kicked a van Gogh."

Mrs. Welch had given me an introduction to P.L. Travers, the author of the Mary Poppins stories. She nicely gave me tea in her Chelsea house probably financed by the enormous royalties from the children's books and the movie profits, and I guessed she was a follower of Gurdjieff. When I left she introduced me to her big son who was about 20 years old, as he came up the dark staircase. "Is he going to become a writer?" I said, trying to flatter her. "Oh no," she replied. "Nothing as stupid as that. I'm very glad he's going to be a banker."

My fixation that writers were mostly silent led to Shaun and Anthony behind my back seeking to oust me from the flat. I had only myself to blame, as at meals I would sit silently watching them. John Ward told me later, "I opposed their plan, and urged that you be given another chance." I was grateful to him for years afterwards for such loyalty. However, I took the hint and started to participate more in the joint conversations.

Then Joe Bottomley, my erstwhile Princeton roommate, visited our flat. Already he had some kind of corporate job for an American firm in Europe. I felt very inferior. "Peter," he said, looking around our flat. "You live like a Bohemian." His remark amazed me. By English standards my roommates and I lived a respectable middle-class existence.

My family on my father's side penetrated my consciousness slightly. My father's brother, Uncle Dick, had bitterly resented in 1933 the main bloc of the estates being left to his older brother, my father, even though primogeniture was still the custom in those days. He would storm into our Priory Hill mansion, holding the bible, protesting that all he got was a small trust. My father's defense, or so my mother told me, for bagging almost all of the riches was that Uncle Dick was regarded as financially irresponsible by our grandfather. He had allegedly been profligate with money as a young man, and his private life was even more disordered than my father's, though both were skirt-chasers. Uncle Dick had committed the further sin in my grandfather's eyes of converting to Roman Catholicism.

Nevertheless, he and his third wife, Aunt Sylvia, who was considerably younger than him, invited me frequently as a weekend guest at their farm house in Alconbury Weston, which was about 10 miles north of the main Rowley estate. I enjoyed this hospitality, even though it included taking a bath in a hip bath, which was a quaint half-tub where one sat on a ledge with one's legs and hips in lukewarm water. In the somewhat unheated bathroom one's flesh above the water level froze, while the rest of one stayed warm.

In their living room during the day or in the evening my aunt might take a nearby shotgun out of its case on the wall and wielding it like a club, hold the barrel and strike the stock against the parrot cage, if the bird whose cage was often covered with a black cloth made too much noise for her taste. "Shut up," she'd shout. "Shut up." Like many hunting people she was a forceful personality, and shared with her husband a love for the sport and a tendency to blunt behavior with humans as well as animals. However, sex between them was another matter. Their private parts might be intimate with the back of a horse, but my uncle told me, "We live as brother and sister." This was because Dick believed he was still married in the eyes of God and the Roman Catholic church to Violet, his first wife, who had left him during the First World War to become the Second Duchess of Westminster (there were four in all by the same Duke).

At night after dinner before watching TV my uncle said, "The Rowley family have fallen a long way." I could hardly disagree. Then he remarked to his wife that he had been campaigning for the election of so and so to the parish or district council. For some years Dick had been an elected member of the Huntingdonshire District Council. "I told the villagers he was a gentleman." Aunt Sylvia snapped, "I've told you not to say that." But Uncle Dick with his white hair around his balding handsome head was so obviously a gentleman of the old school that I doubted if even the most left-wing voters were offended.

During the day he would lend me his shot-gun, give me a handful of cartridges, and I would go out onto the farm and try to slaughter innocent pheasants, rabbits and pigeons, who were usually smart enough to run or fly away before I came within range. As I had never been taught how to fire a shotgun at game, I was singularly inept, and even I was disgusted when I murdered a pheasant hiding five feet from me in fear inside a hedge, feathers, bones and blood scattered throughout the branches and twigs. The remains of the carcass were inedible. By late afternoon my uncle observed, "You used up a lot of cartridges and got almost no birds, Peter."

Even wearing my U.S. Army flak jacket was of no help. Why did I think this made me more manly and therefore a better shot? Aunt Sylvia and I drove in her car up to Rutland to observe Dick pursue foxes with the Cottesmore Hunt. He was about 70 then, and still boxed regularly in a local gym for fun. From the roadside gazing over a hedge I watched him go over a five-foot high fence on his horse. Sylvia and I stopped by the gates of Morcott Hall School, where I had lived for the first year of my life. "I'd like to see it," I said. Sylvia said, "I'll park the car by the entrance. Walk up the drive, and say you're John Rowley's brother." Morcott Hall was the very house which Dick and Sylvia felt should have been left to him by our grandfather. It was rented out to a girl's school by my oldest half-brother's Receiver and his trustees, Coutts bank, while John lived in his sanatorium. I had on my Army jacket with the name "Rowley" sewn onto the front pocket above "U.S. Army."

What Sylvia did not tell me was that only about a week earlier an American Air Force sergeant at a nearby base had been convicted of raping an English girl. My boots scrunching on the gravel, I approached the large, impressive Georgian facade. It was a Saturday afternoon, and girls stared out of windows at me. Ringing the bell, I said in my American accent to the middle-aged woman who opened the door. "My name's Peter Rowley, and I'm John Rowley's half-brother." She took one look at my name tag, and slammed the door in my face. I trudged disconsolately back to my aunt's car.

Late one Friday evening as dusk was settling over the flat Huntingdonshire landscape Uncle Dick and I went to Priory Hill to see if we could find George. Dick wanted to talk to George about some jewellery, which was in my uncle's possession. The diamonds and emeralds had been worn during her life by grandmother Rowley and had been buried by her in 1940 to prevent an invading German army from seizing them. In 1945 after the war George, knowing she was not far from death, persuaded her to go out into the kitchen garden. She pointed out the spot, and he dug them up. Although some of the jewellery was owned by her, several valuable items including an emerald brooch and necklace belonged to the small trust of my father's and were therefore the property of John, George and me. In typical male fashion it was custom in those days not to allow the wife ownership of too much, and thus, although Alice Nina Corbett Rowley had the use of them during her life, they legally reverted to the trust on her death. After she died, Uncle Dick took from the St. Neots mansion not only her personal jewellery, which he inherited from her, but also the trust items. There were hints by my uncle that he wanted to discuss this subject with George. Uncle Dick and Aunt Sylvia did not like George. "He's very odd," they would remark. I could hardly disagree. George hated Uncle Dick. "He runs a sheep into a barn and screws it."

We went to the decaying main house, but there was no sign in the deepening gloom of George, and so we decided to walk across the little railroad bridge, where I as a child had watched steam engines pass underneath on the main line from London to Scotland, and see if he was on the farm land. We passed a thatched cottage. About 800 yards to the right we could see a copse in the near darkness and two figures - one very fat and the other a normal shape. We approached them. Because of his girth George was struggling to trudge across the thick furrows, aided by a walking stick. Uncle Dick and George exchanged a few cold words while the farm manager and I stood by.

Dick and I drove back to Alconbury Weston, and George, who could not drive because of his bad eyesight or inability to pass a driving test, either returned to the mansion to lock himself in behind barbed wire or be driven by the employee to The Sun, a pub in St. Neots, where he would fill himself up with beer before returning to his brother's lonely stately home, where the plaster was peeling. Burglars had already broken in on several occasions, stealing shot guns and old gold watches.

Around that time I was out on a date in London with a girl friend, Susie Buchan, daughter of the Lord and Lady Howard de Walden who had decided a few years earlier I was eligible to attend deb dances.

"Let's see your fingernails," she said. I held them out to her. She had been trying to stop my habit of biting them, even though thanks to Calista they were at least clean now.

"That's better," Susie said with a friendly laugh.

Suddenly she said, "Why don't you visit John?"

I was flabbergasted.

"He's your brother," she said. "You should go visit him." I probably knew at that time that John had been transferred a few years before from his previous mental hospital Ticehurst, in East Sussex, to The Priory in Roehampton, a suburb west of London.

The idea of my going to the hospital was so unthinkable, and I had been so trained to regard John as an unspeakable subject that I could not think how to answer her question, which even to me sounded reasonable. But I knew I was right.

"It would be impossible for me to see him," I said. "It would not be a good idea." Deep within me, seeing my insane half-brother, being in his presence, was a prospect that terrified me.

Susie, sensing she was up against a blank wall of my psyche, did not press the subject..

Then my aunt and uncle's only child, Rosabelle, married. She and her fiance had met when they both fell off their horses at the same time at the same fence on the same fox hunt. Slightly plump and happy in her white wedding gown at the reception on the grass in the summer beside the tent, she came up to me, saying, "When are you going to get married, Peter?" This question infuriated me.

The spirit of John hung in the air that night when I had dinner at Lady Myra Fox's mansion, Croxton Park, whose 3,000 acres adjoined John's 2,000. Myra had been a good friend of my mother's in the days when she and I lived at Priory Park. Staying with Myra was Lord Dundonald, who was the nephew of John's mother, Lady Marjorie Cochrane Rowley, my father's first wife. The man was in his early thirties with dark black hair smoothly pasted across his head. He was of slightly above average height, wore a tailor made dark suit and possessed regular features. He looked and acted the role of a peer. As we stood for cocktails in Myra's splendid drawing room, it was clear that he was a superior being to me, and with him was his fiance, a pretty young redhead. I was jealous. I was made to realize that I was very lucky to meet Ian. Not a word was mentioned during drinks or dinner of our joint crazy relation, although our hostess, who was a more distant relation of the Cochranes, the family name of the Dundonald peerage, had certainly known John and George before the Second World War. Myra did say of George, "He's so eccentric. I couldn't possibly ask him here." So George resided on the weekends in John's crumbling big house a few miles away ignored by her and everyone else who had known the two brothers before the Second World War.

At least Uncle Dick, Aunt Sylvia, Rosabelle and her new husband Richard Picton-Warlow lived a relatively normal life. Although they received only a small part of the Rowley fortune and were still bitter over the apportionment years earlier, they were better off than John, George and me. John, the heir, was locked in his sanatorium, sleeping in a ward with the other nut cases. His life was totally controlled by The Court of Protection since he was legally certified. He was not given any money. The trustees, Coutts Bank, who also acted as Receiver, collected their fees, and the family lawyers Bird & Bird received their fees. The estate agent profited from their fees.

No effort had been made to raise the farm rents as the years went by, and thus the tenants were paying far less than the market value. The Bank rented the home farm and Priory Hill house to George, but with his disabilities George made no money as a farmer, and the Bank neglected the maintenance of the mansion. George hoped that raising pigs would be the answer to his money shortage.

Left alone George was able to cut the old stamps from the letters in the estate boxes and sell them to dealers in London. Secretly he sold paintings of Fydells - a branch of the family - which belonged to his older brother. He guessed that since Fydell was a different name from Rowley, the family lawyers and the bank employees would be very unlikely to notice their disappearance from the house or even their listing in an auctioneer's sale catalogue. He needed the money to pay for his prostitutes, cigarettes and alcohol and support his London flat. It was very unfair that John should inherit everything. John got no benefit from the fortune, George very little, and I as the younger brother lived off my two small separate trusts, which were sufficient to allow me half a bedroom in a London flat.

The Alconbury Weston Rowleys were in real terms far better off than we three brothers, and so I gave as a wedding present to Rosabelle an inexpensive framed print of an impressionist famous painter, but I sensed my aunt and uncle felt my gift should have been more generous, and the invitation on weekends ceased, though they used as an excuse that now they had to invite their newly married daughter and her husband.

About once a month George phoned me in my London flat.

"Can we meet?" he said in his part-cockney accent.

We met usually in a middle-class hotel just off Sloane Square in the evening. He would arrive by taxi, and I could see him dismounting with difficulty from the vehicle through the saloon bar window. He was dressed in a brown three-piece tweed suit, a dirty green mac covering his massive bulk. If it was raining, he wore a squashed down black fedora. Otherwise I noticed his black hair pasted across his brow and white skin. When he entered, all the eyes in the lounge focused on him. I was acutely embarrassed.

"Hello, George," I said in a strained voice, shaking his soft hand. I was afraid of him, even if he was my half-brother.

"'lo, Peter," he mumbled.

Settling his near 300 pounds into an arm chair, he ordered a large lager. He lit a Player cigarette. I smoked too.

Knowing the answer even before I asked the question, I said, "There's nothing that can be done for John?"

"No," he replied, gazing at his unpolished shoes. "He's been seen by the best neuro surgeons. If they operate to remove the bullet from his head, they might kill him."

"Is the .22 bullet the reason he is the way he is?"

"Maybe," he said morosely.

"He's blind in one eye."

"He nearly killed a nurse at Ticehurst. He's very violent."

"I'm the heir."

There was silence between us.

I said, "Is there any way of transferring some of John's money to us?"

"No."

After dinner I helped him into a taxi. After the door closed, he slid the window down and said, "When you're my age you'll have a lot less sex drive, Peter."

One night he asked me to come to his flat. He lived at 20 Hyde Park Place on the north side of Hyde Park in a service flat. The management was supposed to clean his apartment, and supply meals when he wanted them. His rooms were on the fifth floor, reached by an elevator. I sat on a stained blue couch. The phone rang. George picked it up. He said sharply, "I can't talk to you now," and hung up. I was puzzled as to why he was so rude to the person on the other end of the line. For the first time in my relationship with him it dawned on me that the caller was a prostitute.

I was always hoping that George would ask me to meet his mother, Lady Marjorie, who I knew he occasionally saw. She lived alone in a bed-sit off St. George's Square. But this was a forbidden subject - a black hole of anger, a feud stretching back decades between her and our late father. I was in the wrong camp. Some years earlier I had actually met one of Marjorie's sisters, Lady Grizzell. It might have been when I visited London the summer I was thrown out of Princeton. Her Pekinese dogs sat on cushions, and she politely gave me tea. She was courteous and curious about me. Then much later during the period when I was living in London as an adult George rang me and asked me to dinner at her flat, but unfortunately I already had another engagement. I hoped that the invitation would be repeated.

I read that Sir Winston Churchill, who had resigned as Prime Minister in 1955, was going to speak in a town east of London as part of the general election of 1959. While courting during the Second World War my mother and step-father had frequent arguments about Churchill, my English mother less than enthusiastic, my American step-father an admirer, while my mother liked Roosevelt and Jack - like his mother - loathed him. As a 14-year-old on a private tour of the House of Commons I had been allowed to sit for a second on the very cushion of the front bench where "the great man" sat during parliamentary debates. Then in 1958 *Newsweek* had sent me down to Chartwell, his country estate, for the day to learn about his daily activities - a fruitless trip, as the local shop-keepers knew little, and, if they were aware of more gossip, weren't talking if they hoped to keep the Churchill family's business. Everyone knew the wartime leader was in poor health. I said to a girl friend, "Let's go listen to him. It may be the last time ever we'll be able to see him."

The political meeting was in a large cavernous hall, and Jill and I sat in the balcony. There on the stage was Churchill sitting in a chair along with a few local party officials.. The speaker was the local M.P., and Churchill was only there to lend his support and prestige for his politician neighbor's election. For an hour and a half he said not a word, a plump figure dressed in black while the other politicians orated. Near the end of the meeting somebody made a joke about reading glasses, and the famous man twirled his spectacles, mumbling a witticism we could not hear. Those in the crowd closest to him laughed.

I thought Eldon had promised me a job as a foreign correspondent for *Newsweek's* London bureau. After the *Sunday Express* adventure I went to the newsmagazine's office in the Haymarket, but Eldon was not there. I waited for four hours in the reception area, brushing off suggestions I return another day. When Eldon finally returned, he said, "I can't offer you a position here, but, as I have just been made foreign editor in New York, come back with me, and I'll guarantee you a position as a writer." My dream of becoming a novelist in Europe outweighed the glamor of being a journalist in New York. So I declined, but then a friend in the London bureau recommended I apply for a mysterious job as "Near Eastern Correspondent" for an unnamed news organization. I wrote to the box number of the advertisement. "You'll have to do espionage for the CIA and M15 if they hire you," my friend said. But I never heard from whoever placed the ad.

So during the day I studied how to write novels, reading three times all nine novels in the Galsworthy trilogy, starting with *The Forsyte Saga.* Occasionally there were assignments from *Newsweek*, but to maintain my self-esteem as a writer it was necessary to see something published. So I started to write articles with photo illustrations by me for American Catholic magazines. They were not *The New Yorker*, but my name was in print. I devoted months trying to write an article for *The Reader's Digest*, interviewing sick and disabled persons. One middle-aged man lay in a hospital bed and painted with a toothbrush held in his teeth, unable to move hands or feet. His predicament left me speechless with embarrassment and fear. The hero of the proposed article was Leonard Cheshire who founded homes for unfortunates such as the paraplegic. Cheshire, who had won the VC, had flown an extraordinary number of missions as a British bomber pilot during the Second World War. Then he had found God. He was now a quiet gentle man. The *R.D.* might have paid a lot of money for my story about him, *if* they had bought it, but I had to settle for *The Catholic Digest.*

An article I wrote for the American Knights of Columbus magazine described a Benedictine abbey in Gloucestershire, whose abbot planned to build a cathedral on a hill of their grounds which would be second in size only to St. Peter's in Rome. Every year the cleric visited the U.S. to raise money for this project. When I visited the site there were a couple of young monks working on an excavation plus a few feet of brick wall. They were quite happy with their lot in life. The abbot rarely raised more money than would cover the expenses of his trip around the U.S. Behind his back within the community he was known as "The Abbot of Tours," though of course I did not write this in my piece which assured the readers it would be built even if it took "a lifetime."

I overcame my lack of belief in Roman Catholicism, whose tenets over sex were more than I could bear, a state of mind that had developed from the time I entered Princeton. At lunch I went to a pub, and ordered the cheapest lunch possible, annoying the hard-working middle-aged man who made the lunch and served us at the counter by leaving the smallest tip I could possibly get away with. This left a little bit more money so that I could afford to take girls out on dates.

And there was my mother's English family - seemingly more normal than my father's. My mother's mother lived with her sister in a large flat opposite Westminster Cathedral, a Roman Catholic church. Grandmother Eyre, her spinster sister Dorothy Norris and their Catholic paid companion Miss Kelly had chosen the location in order to be close to God and his priests. Great Aunt Dorothy had been kept at home by her mother for decades in order to care for that old lady. Her marriage prospects ruined, she devoted her life to religion, even saving string and boxes for the poor, knowing every cleric from the cardinal on down she could ever hope to meet, serving on lay committees for charities.

A thin lady dressed in variations of black and grey with rather beautiful, delicate features, she talked rapidly in a whisper one could hear easily, and was kind. She seemed to sense that religion had been the only answer to her mother's determination to keep her home until death claimed the older woman. The two old sisters frequently asked me to tea, sitting at opposite ends of the dining room table, in between less wealthy old creatures of both sexes. Miss Kelly, who was more agile but only a few years younger than her employers, bustled around, trying to be important and useful, helping with tea and scones.

With nothing else to do on a Sunday afternoon I would attend, attempting to make boring conversation, the only young man present. After about an hour or two I would need to urinate. "Can I please use your bathroom, grandmother?" "Yes," she replied in her aging slightly shrill voice. "It's that door there." I knew where it was, but I was always hoping she'd send me to a bathroom far away from the dining room. Her preferred one for me was a small toilet directly off one side of the dining room, and once inside I knew that the sound of my water hitting the bowl could be heard by the guests. So I was forced to kneel.

Conversation with my grandmother was invariably superficial except for the one time when she said to me, "Is your mother a good cook?" "No," I said. She laughed in a horrified way. "I'm sure she's a good cook," she insisted. "I'm sure you don't mean that." "No, she's not." However, her sister despite her lack of husband and children was able to speak intelligently particularly if the subject was the Roman Catholic church and its members. Great Aunt Dorothy had been an ally of grandmother Eyre in all the years that the latter had had to endure her husband's tyranny and infidelity until he died in 1953. She had lived with them whether it was Ireland, Bath, London or their country house in Hertfordshire. At the latter residence the two women had spent hours walking up and down the drive every day saying the rosary.

When necessary Great Aunt Dorothy Norris included family members among her charities. The nefarious Lieutenant Colonel Francis Norris, the presumed helpmate of Hitler, was her brother, and she always hinted there was not much hope for him while he contemptuously regarded her as a nuisance.

There was a relatively distant relation who was an epileptic - a man in his mid-forties, slightly stooped and quiet, who had a smallish trust fund and a fat wife, whose job was to care for this distant cousin. "Peter, dear," said my great aunt, "please go to their house in (a northern suburb of London the name of which I have forgotten), and accompany them to Badminton. You'll enjoy it. And you'll be doing a good deed." I took the underground out there. I had never met the couple before, and they lived in a brick bungalow. Then the three of us took a train.

I found myself going to the west of England. Conversation was strained, and on arrival at the Badminton station I encountered a retired major general and his wife who was an uncle of Lady Fox. I was enough of a snob to be humiliated by my companions. Badminton was the center of horse trials on a large estate, tents and thousands of upper and middle-class horsey types milling around in the mud. It had been raining. The epileptic's wife got stuck in the thick slime, and, even though I was there supposedly to help her and her sick husband, I was afraid if I walked the 30 feet to where she was floundering I too would be trapped. Bewildered, I looked around the crowd, hoping for help. Fortunately a fox hunt employee, who wore thick waders, sloshed out and dragged the plump Norris woman to firmer ground.

A girl friend was Daisy de Lettre, who lived in Paris. She was only 16 with angelic child-like features. Her father was a well-known French radio announcer, and her parents owned a chateau far from Paris, but her mother preferred the French capital while the father liked the mansion. I had met Daisy through my aunt Violet, as her daughter and Daisy had stayed at each other's respective English and French homes, ostensibly to learn English or French The English always alleged the French insisted on talking English with their young visitors. Daisy was very sultry and kissable, and I even crawled after her through the heather of the Yorkshire moors, but our lips never met. She was seductive, flirtatious and not particularly nice.

But she asked me to stay at her grandmother's house in Nice. I liked Daisy's mother, Nicole, more than Daisy though I had no sexual designs on her. Daisy's grandmother had lived in the chateau with her grandfather until one night she climbed down a ladder placed there by her lover, a colonel in the French army, and fled. She married the officer, and eventually settled - as a widow - in Nice. The grandmother had flaming red hair and lived in a cottage which literally occupied most of a Nice pavement but was not big enough to be on a lot of its own. At dinner whenever the mood struck her she sang bars from French songs. Her knowledge of English consisted solely of "Yes… no… beautiful…sexy." After she had delivered these words she was very pleased with herself. Nicole and Daisy tolerated her. One night they offered me at dinner more food than I could eat. "Je suis plein," I replied in my beginner's French. Bursts of laughter. I had just said I was pregnant. "Peetterr," said Nicole kindly, "vous dites, 'Je n'ai plus faim.'" During the day on the rocky beach a mile away I tried to get close to the cold Daisy, but her mother quickly gave me a stern warning shake of her head.

I attended the ballet frequently in London - practically always at Covent Garden - and loved the grace and beauty of the Royal Ballet in those days under the direction of Ninette de Valois. This was around the time of the last performances of Margot Fonteyn, who I saw once and found somewhat slow and unexciting, and I think I saw her once with Nureyev, who was at the peak of his powers. But the ballerinas who really caught my heart were the younger ones such as the English star Antoinette Sibley and Svetlana Beriosova. I developed a crush on Sibley, and dreamed of meeting her at the stage door or at a party. She was a delicate slim blonde with an utterly entrancing flirtatious smile plus a strength and precision which I was sure would be ideal for me. I knew I would never meet and marry her.

The ballet was where I usually went when I wished to impress a girl friend. I tried to get seats in the middle of the orchestra about 12 rows from the stage, where I could be surrounded by the music and become happily transfixed by the flowing female bodies. There was a lightness and peace to the performances which soothed my troubled disposition and gave me hope for the future.

Changes occurred at 26 Buckingham Palace Mansions. Shortly after my reprieve won for me by John Ward a new roommate appeared. The more roommates meant each of us had to pay less rent. He was Nicholas Carr-Saunders, the son of a very well-known British economist. He had waves of very black hair which fell over one of his eyebrows. He was tall and amused by life. He was only about 19, and was supposed to be attending university in London, but emulating his father's successful career did not seem to be his ambition. Beside his bed in the dark room he placed a tape recorder, and devised a system whereby it played automatically a song of Eartha Kitt early in the morning in order to wake him up. I think the song was "C'est si bon."

John Ward himself was fond of music, and possessed a moderately good tenor, which he occasionally sang in the chorus of an amateur choir. Although I always slept in the same bed against a wall on the opposite side of a room looking onto the mews, several of my roommates changed around their sleeping locations. One night I returned rather late to the flat, and opened the door of a bedroom to find John sound asleep singing "I'm so pretty" from *West Side Story*.

As the numbers in the three-bedroom flat grew, available space lessened, and one day one of us invited to stay for a few nights a young man whose last name was Murray. Like the others he was a public school boy. He was a tallish, solidly built fellow. As a 10-year-old he had been playing with another child inside a cave. The earth collapsed, and Murray was able to escape, but the other boy was trapped and died.

After two weeks Murray was asked to leave by my flatmates. It was over a weekend, and, when we returned on the Sunday night we found that he had installed an electric light with bare bulb in a closet above the kitchen cupboard. This had been used to store suitcases, which he had removed. Then he obtained a portable ladder, put some sheets and blankets in the suitcase cupboard and slept there some seven feet above the kitchen. Nobody had the heart to forcibly evict him. Soon he was spending the odd night with whatever girl friend he could find, and then at breakfast time the young woman would climb down the ladder, which was held from above by Murray, her legs and skirt visible to us sitting at the table. Murray would follow. In the embarrassed silence nobody said anything until finally someone - it may have been Murray - said, as if nothing at all unusual had happened, "Good morning."

There were parties. "Bring your own bottle" was the rule. Blankets were hung in front of the windows in order to deaden the noise. There had been complaints from the other occupants of the flats above us. There was even an allegation from people in apartments higher up the inner courtyard made of dirty white bricks that they had seen objectionable sights in the bedroom that faced on it. At the parties one of us guarded the front door, allowing in only those we wished to attend, and once only pretty girls were permitted to enter.

During the day I wrote a few chapters of my first novel which was about Calista. In Stanley Kubrick's *The Shining* the writer types over and over the same sentence endlessly, leading his wife to infer that he is mad. I crossed out almost every word, wrote above it, crossed that out, and then wrote above that, rubbing out with a black pencil *that* version, and then writing on top.

One night I was picked up by a pretty whore in her Jaguar on Stafford St. The next day I saw Dr. Moynihan, convinced I had contracted a venereal disease. He sat behind a desk, and above him on the wall were a collection of enamel bleeding bowls. He persuaded me I was still healthy.

Another night I necked until dawn with a very fast girl. I was exhausted from the late-night partying and the endless re-writing. I began to feel guilty about the Catholic magazine articles, as I did not believe in the religion I was proselityzing for. Around noon one day I went to the Jesuit church at Farm Street, and found myself in a confessional box, confessing my sins, and to my amazement and anguish sobbing and pulling my hair. The Jesuit behind the screen gave me absolution, and told me to see a doctor.

Dr. Moynihan prescribed some pills. I felt as if I was in a state of electric shock, though the sensation was at the same time pleasant. Every nerve in my body was alive. At the same time I was rigid.

In this new state of religious fervor I was invited by Daisy and her mother to Le Bal de Grand Siecle in Paris. I decided I should marry a Catholic girl. Madame de Lettre said, "You will have to be approved by the ladies of the ball committee, Peetteerr." Two small groups of middle-aged French women eyed me carefully in separate apartments, as I sat before them. Then Nicole said, "Ahh, Peetteerr, it would be so nice if you had a title. Couldn't you be Lord Rowley?" "Oui," I said weakly.

The dance was held in the Orangerie at Versailles - a very long room. Daisy wore a white dress. We stood in a line in order to be announced by the major d'omo at the top of carpeted steps to the crowd of dancers in the hall below. I said to the uniformed butler, "Lord Peter Rowley." He cried, "Monsieur Maude Peter Rowley."

For most of the night Daisy and I sat in uncomfortable silence at a table beside the dance. I proposed to her. "Merci," she said coldly. "I will think about it."

Of course, soon after a letter reached me in London from Daisy, turning me down.

I flew to America to stay six weeks with my mother and step-father in Princeton. According to Roman Catholic theology, I had decided Jack's marriage to Katherine was valid, and that therefore his relationship with my mother was sinful. When they would take me to the New York airport so I could return to England, I intended to tell them as my parting words, "You should live together as brother and sister." However, a few days before my departure, my mother showed me an airmail letter from her sister, the reverend mother: "You should put Peter in a mental hospital." "Why?" I said to my mother. "I wrote my sister Violet that I was concerned about your obsession about being on time. Violet contacted Dorothy, and said she could not be responsible for you with your breakdown. What should I do?" "Nothing," I said. I realized my proposed advice to my parents to be celibate would cause an explosion.

On returning to London I went to mass every day. I read books of theology. Every week I went to confession. I left 26 Buckingham Palace Mansions and moved into 49 Lupus street solely because the other flatmates were Roman Catholics. Their system for the apartment telephone was to have a pay phone. One could only use it by putting in coins, although there was a key to the coin box. One could put in a pound note to replace change one needed.

I felt guilty that I had avoided successfully training in the United States Army Reserves. If I had been in America, I would have had to go to an army training hall one night a week and in the summer spend two weeks on a base. But there were no Reserve training units for low-ranked persons such as myself in Europe! I took a trip to Orleans just to get a new private's uniform, as the regulation uniform had changed. While waiting three days for it, I sat by a French river and prayed and daydreamed.

At the U.S. Army base at Orleans I spent two weeks in an office. Every afternoon we were ordered to stand outside in the semi-circular drive to welcome the arrival of a general, as the base was the rear command for NATO. My fellow American G.I.s were so wealthy compared to the local French that they hired peasants to do k.p. for them. My fellow soldiers referred to the statue in the square of Joan of Arc astride a horse as "Joanie on a pony."

On the French train back to England as I stood in the corridor I was convinced that the sudden swaying movement of light back and forth from the sun through the carriage windows correlated with whether I was having holy thoughts or not. Then I went up to Newcastle to stay for three nights in a hotel near my Reverend Mother Aunt Dorothy's convent and college, where she commanded 1,500 students. As we walked one afternoon she said, "I apologize for trying to lock you up in an asylum." Gradually I was unwinding from the breakdown.

Shortly after that my great aunt Dorothy arranged an interview for me with the Roman Catholic cardinal. It was her idea. For 20 minutes I was alone with his eminence. He said, "Have you thought of the influence of the Romans on the British character?" I had not, but the cardinal wanted to talk about nothing else. I had forgotten that at the very time I was seeing the great cleric, my reverend mother aunt, who looked like her own mother, was standing on a street corner waiting for me to pick up her in my car and deliver her somewhere. I arrived 45 minutes late. "I forgot," I said to her. "I was with the Cardinal."

Over the phone George told me, "A prostitute tells me that you are hiring two prostitutes at once for kinky sex. She and her friend, another whore, say you are part of a ring that has orgies with that homosexual Lord (I don't remember his name, but this particular peer was notorious at the time)." I was so upset I went to Father Walkerley, the Jesuit I confessed to weekly. "Go see a lawyer about it," he said. I had to tell the young solicitor that I had had normal sex with only two prostitutes in my life on two separate occasions. "Tell your brother," the lawyer said, "You'll bring a slander suit against the girl who said that to him." I relayed this information to George over the phone. He grunted.

George meanwhile was being constantly approached by the farm tenants. "The barn is falling down. The estate doesn't do any repairs on my house." They knew he craved attention alone in the big house on weekends with the occasional call-girl as a companion. George persuaded the Court of Protection to fire Carter Jonas, the estate agents since before the Second World War. He persuaded the Court to remove an executive of Coutts Bank as the Receiver, although the Bank and the family lawyers Bird & Bird remained largely in power, collecting their fees, as Coutts could not be dismissed legally as the trustee for John's money and estates. The Court appointed a tall massive tough accountant from Bradford in the north of England as Receiver by the name of Kenneth Marmaduke Moss. To support his girl friends, London flat, alcohol, cigarettes the renting of his mad brother's St. Neots mansion and the tenancy of the Home farm George was running out of money

One of my new self-imposed rules for strict adherence to Roman Catholicism was to force myself to take out Roman Catholic girls at least half the time. One of them was Elly Mazur - a gentle, dark-haired creature. She was also quite pretty with a pure white creamy complexion covered with a very slight down. She had been in the same convent school as Daphne, the redoubtable Aunt Violet's eldest daughter, and was a friend of hers. In my snobbish way I felt Elly because of her foreign parents and lack of money and a title was not quite good enough for me. But she was so nice I usually forgot this when I was with her, and one day she and I drove to the downs overlooking the British Channel, and she took a photograph of me sitting on the grass looking handsome and pensive, gazing out to sea. Only a year or two after that she was killed in an auto accident.

By the spring of 1961 I realized I was about to lose my American citizenship. The U.S. law in those days was that if you resided in your native country for more than three years and were a naturalized citizen as I was and were not employed by an American corporation, as I certainly was not, the United States government fired you, on the theory, I guess, that you didn't deserve to be an American. I would then be a citizen of no country, as I had renounced the Queen. In a panic I decided to return to the U.S.

I had nowhere else to go but New York City. I traveled by the cheapest fare on the S.S. United States. Accompanying me was a beautiful English girl, Rinalda Baird, another friend of Daphne's. She had a full, luscious figure and dark reddish brown hair and fulsome dark cherry-colored lips. She had persuaded my parents and me to sponsor her to America so she could get a job there. We had separate tiny cabins. She was engaged to an Englishman, who had serious doubts about her going with me. He need not have worried. Every day and evening, as the ship's powerful engines made a steady drumbeat through the walls of Rinalda's cabin, I read out loud to her Graham Greene's *The Power and Glory*, raising my voice above the background noise. She sat on her bed, knees and legs raised, a pillow behind her back, looking very tempting, while I sat on a chair, but I never touched her.

My mother was 21 years younger than my father.

*Even while at Eton my father suffered from asthma and bronchitis
and died of a heart attack at age 56.*

*Morcott Hall, Rutland, in the 1930's, where I spent the first year of my life.
The tree and the ivy are gone.*

My mother and me on a sundial on a lawn of our other manor house in St. Neots, Huntingdonshire.

Myopic, unhappy George Rowley at about age 12. He stands before front steps of Priory Hill mansion in St. Neots which was razed in 1965 by the St. Neots Urban District Council.

Sitting cross-legged is John Rowley at his Eton house in about 1933.

An Eton athletic photo. John is top left.
Later at Trinity College in Cambridge John (upper left) rowed in the Third boat.
After Dunkirk he lived for 40 years in mental hospitals.

*In all of the Eton photos John – unlike the other boys –
never looks at the camera.*

The war is on!

When I was 20, Calista was a sophomore at Wellesley College outside of Boston, Massachusetts – an early love.

In America in the 1950's crew-cuts were fashionable for young men.

A cigarette helped me lecture my friends on the status of the world.

Entering the U.S. Army with a crew-cut meant there was little more to be shaved off. On discharge I grew it out – to my mother's relief.

I am on a beach in California. Barry Goldwater was running against Lyndon Johnson for President of the United States.

Jane Wyatt was a star of "Lost Horizons" *and* "Father Knows Best." *The photo is at her house in Los Angeles. Jon Kubichan was a TV producer. His wife, Marion Thompson, an actor, was a friend when I lived alone in NY.*

Ronnie Plummer, a partner in the London law firm of Allen & Overy, led the legal battle to rescue the Rowley estates. Second lieutenant John Rowley inherited the manor house in Huntingdonshire and Rutland on his father's death. John's shell shock at Dunkirk led to a financial mess.

Terez's sister became a city councillor in Geneva, Switzerland. F.M. Esfandiary, the best man at my marriage to Terez, was a well-known Iranian writer and futurist who predicted that after the year 2030 we would live for ever.

Terez at my half-sister Dorothy's wedding in Princeton, New Jersey. Terez's mother fled with her as a baby from Hungary to Austria at Christmas, 1944, escaping from the Russian army. Then – to their subsequent regret – the family returned to Hungary in 1947.

Terez in a magazine advertisement. After her parents were in prison for three years she escaped from Hungary in 1956.

Chapter 4

New York

My mother's garden in Princeton was her evocation of the English life she had left. Before finding somewhere to live in New York I sat on her terrace typing the opening chapter of my first full-length novel, *Life at Lord*, destined to be an all-out attack on Princeton University. She had dug flower beds in the somewhat sandy New Jersey soil. Despite the hot American summers a variety of pretty specimens grew in them, and my step-father had constructed a stone patio behind the two-story house to please her. This was also useful for him so that he could drink several cocktails in the evening and smoke cigarettes. He was rarely able to cut his smoking down to less than two packs a day. The rear of the garden was what might be called untamed New Jersey jungle with trees and creepers, though through the foliage one could see a neighboring house.

My novel began with a red helicopter hovering over Carnegie Lake (given by Andrew Carnegie and vulgarly described by the students as the only rubber-bottomed lake in the world), and of course I had my anti-hero necking with a red-haired girl in the early summer heat in an Adirondack boat which tips over. The only nice person in the book would be a fictional representation of Neal Peirce. All the rest including my alter ego would be varying degrees of "shits." The faculty would be treated kindly, including a "communist" professor.

Before I finished the first chapter I went to New York. Where would I live? My enthusiasm for Catholicism led me to a party at *Jubilee* magazine, a liberal glossy monthly for Catholics, where I met John Reynolds, a nice young importer of Japanese umbrellas, and nearly signed a lease with him for a two bedroom apartment. But then Anne Fremantle said, "Go and have tea with Mrs. Wyatt. She's a friend of mine. She has rooms for rent. You'll like her." The house was 310 East

50th Street, an old brownstone near the corner of 2nd Avenue. Her full name was Euphemia Van Renssalaer Waddington Wyatt, and she was an elderly lady with white hair, very white skin and a pretty face. We sat in her library on the second floor. On the couch beside her was a white poodle. "This is Beaumont," she said in her upper-class American voice. The animal snapped off and ate a flower from the vase beside the tea tray. "He likes tulips, but he prefers orchids." We agreed I would rent a bedroom upstairs for $50 a week, including breakfast and dinner. There would be several other young paying guests. Her butler and cook did not live there.

Why did I give up the opportunity to share an apartment on the upper east side with a friendly respectable young man? John was outgoing, and a fellow Catholic. His features were regular, and he had a ready smile and laughed frequently enough to be pleasant. I suspected I would be lonely. He would be out a lot during the day. His family lived in the environs of the city. He had a number of friends. I knew very few people in New York. At Mrs. Wyatt's I would only have one modest-size room on the third floor with a bed, desk, closet and chest of drawers looking out on the red brick exterior of a modern apartment building across the street. I would not be allowed to invite girls up to my room. I had yet to meet any of Mrs. Wyatt's four other young persons, but I guessed at least one of them would be there in the evening. We would have breakfast and dinner together. Mrs. Wyatt would also be present during the day. She was a convert to Roman Catholicism. She had the elegance and good manners of old family New York. I would be safe.

I always addressed her as "Mrs. Wyatt," though her friends of the same age as her called her "Effie." When she talked with them on the phone, she would often say, "Poor dear." Thirty seconds later I would hear the "Poor dear" again. She was 77 years old and somewhat bent, but the stairs from the ground floor, where there was the kitchen and dining room, to the library and drawing room on the second floor and her bedroom on the third floor were no barrier to her. Nor did she hesitate to walk her poodle, who yelped frequently, from 310 almost the length of the block to 1st avenue and back. Beaumont defecated anywhere up and down the street. In the morning she opened the front door. The animal ran to the lamp post across the sidewalk from our steps and urinated against the metal base. There was invariably a row of parked cars there.

Paddy, the butler, was a very thin short man who had worked for her for about 25 years. His skin was shriveled and pale, and frequently he smoked a cigarette leaning out of an open window before resuming work. He spoke with an Irish accent and always obeyed her in his soft voice with a slightly resigned, "Yes, Mrs. Wyatt." He did the cleaning, cooked breakfast and waited on table at night. He was married to Bea, the cook. She was plump and friendly. She shopped. Otherwise she rarely left the kitchen which looked onto the rear garden. Along the paths there was ground ivy, and there were a number of trees. Additional shade was supplied by an awning over an outdoor stone table where we ate on warm summer evenings. Eating with silver cutlery most of the year we were in the dining room illuminated by candles, a small chandelier and sconces.

By 1961 there were probably no other boarding houses for young persons left in Manhattan, and Mrs. Wyatt's was certainly the last of the society ones. There were still a few wealthy parents who preferred to put their daughters in a respectable residence run by a widow whose name was in the *Social Register*. Most of the paying guests were young ladies, but there were always one or two men. Qualifications for a man were less rigorous provided he was of good character. I had one of the three regular size bedrooms, and there were two small ones, costing $35 each a week. We were allowed to use any part of the house and garden except Mrs. Wyatt's bedroom and drawing room. The latter was decorated in a white and gold motif, where hung an original portrait of George Washington by Gilbert Stuart. In the library was a primitive-style painting of Mrs. Wyatt's direct ancestor, the last of the Patroons. He lost his title when the British captured New York from the Dutch in the early part of the 18th century. The first one, a Dutch minister, had arrived in the 17th century with a boat load of settlers, and was given 50 miles of land one mile wide along the Hudson River by the Dutch royal family. There was also a photo of a very pretty girl in a white wedding gown. She was married to one of Mrs. Wyatt's grandsons.

As a teenager she had become a Catholic because her European nurse was one. As a young woman she had been married to a stock broker from another *S.R..* family. They had two chauffeurs, and an impressive house full of servants. He also had a mistress, causing her much distress. After the depression struck in the early 1930's, finding himself penniless, Mr.Wyatt jumped out of a Wall Street window or shot himself. She was left with three daughters and a son, the oldest less than 20. First of all the widow wrote a Broadway play, which folded in New Haven. Her second oldest daughter, Jane, left Barnard and became an actress. She converted her large house into a residence for the grown-up children of those families who had not lost their fortunes. The staff was retained. The male "guests" wore white tie for dinner, the young ladies evening attire, and Mrs. Wyatt presided. There were as many as 13 boarders.

By the middle of the century she was growing older, and sold the mansion, and bought two adjoining town houses on 50th street, renting out one, and using the other as a smaller version of her previous residence. The Ruppert brewery sold its premises on the East river to the UN, the rats fled from the demolition site, and one of them bit a baby in one of Mrs. Wyatt's rental apartments. A lawyer friend said, "Pay the parents anything they want." She did, and then sold that brownstone.

I met the other paying guests. Among the other young people was a pretty rich girl from Pennsylvania and a girl whose father was German and mother American. She had been raised in Chile. Mrs. Wyatt led the conversation at dinner. It was sometimes intellectual, usually lively and always fun. She tried to draw each of us into whatever was being discussed. She did not allow bad language or what she considered unseemly subjects. Once one of the girls, who was studying to be a nurse, started to describe with excitement the birth of a baby, but our hostess politely and firmly said, "That is not a suitable subject at dinner."

Sally, the wealthy ex-debutante, became involved with a Hispanic fortune-hunter, who regularly came to our residence to take her out. He was allowed inside the front door in order to pick her up, but, when he returned her sometimes as late as 2 a.m., he had to kiss her good night outside the entrance. The German American girl was soon a close friend of the heiress and advised her on her predicament, as her parents strongly opposed the suitor. The rest of us, including Mrs. Wyatt, observed the romance with interest.

At breakfast outdoors that summer Mrs. Wyatt read the *New York Herald-Tribune* (now defunct) and then gave it to me, while she looked at the *New York Times*. In the morning I wrote my novel, frequently staring out the window at the apartments opposite. At night I noticed a young couple who started to kiss, and then they lowered their Venetian blinds. I was tortured with jealousy. My view was looking north, but usually there was sunlight on the facade across the street.

Nearby I could hear the roar of the traffic on 2nd avenue. One of the commercial establishments on the west side of 2nd between 50th and 5lst streets was "DANNY'S DELICATESSEN: CELEBRITY RENDEZVOUS WHERE THE ELITE MEET TO EAT." Inside there was a garish red decor, formica tables, plastic chairs and a few customers who were clearly not famous.

At lunch I would escape, walking down the staircase past Mrs. Wyatt who might be at her desk typing a review of a Broadway play for a provincial Catholic weekly. She was able to go to the second night after every Broadway and off-Broadway opening. Or, while sitting on the couch, the dog beside her, she might be cutting with a pair of scissors every advertisement from the current issue of *The New Yorker*. If Beaumont tried to commit some minor crime such as eating a page, she would gently slap his nose, saying "No, Beaumont." She was a supporter of the anti-vivisectionist movement. She added, "I would be a vegetarian, but I don't want to be an inconvenience to my friends when they ask me to dinner parties. They would have to cook a separate dish for me."

I sat at the counter at a newspaper shop combined luncheonette at 1st avenue and 50th, ordering the cheapest sandwich or hot dog. I left the smallest tip I could get away with. However, the owners, the Leffs, a late middle-aged Jewish couple, tolerated me. They were proud that her sister was married to Allie Sherman, the coach of the *New York Giants* football team. At the counter I struck up a friendship with Albert, the local window cleaner, who was lanky and unshaven. Beside him was his pail, ropes and safety belt. Talking with his guttural Bronx accent he would say of Julie Harris, the famous actress, who had a house between 50th and Beekman Place, "I just done her windows." If I happened to pass by when he was hanging outside her residence 20 feet above the street, he would gesticulate with his finger to show she was inside her living room, mouthing the words "She's in there right now." I also went to the same snack shop for a tea or coffee in the morning or afternoon. This only cost about 20 cents, while my lunch bill for a sandwich and tea was about one dollar. I traveled by bus and subway, costing 15 cents.

Then at 5 p.m. I went for a walk. Initially I explored the area around Beekman and Sutton Places. I envied the rich in their apartments and town houses with their spouses and children, their country houses and cars, even their numerous friends. I sat on a bench along a walkway between the East river drive and the buildings, dreaming of a lovely nice girl who would be my wife. I looked at the tide going in or out.

The water had a calming effect on me. Occasionally a sailboat, tug boat or freighter passed by. But even I knew my reverie had to stop at some point, and I continued my exercise. My other incentive for traversing one street after another was to find an attractive restaurant where I could take a date. By saving every cent I had just enough to pay for a dinner once a week for two.

The Honourable Julia Stonor was a member of an old Roman Catholic family in England and was spending a year or two in New York, working wherever she could find a job. She was younger than me. I liked her, but had no wish to kiss her. She invited me to go to Newport, Rhode Island for the weekend. We visited her grandmother, Lady Camoys, who lived in one of the famous mansions. Her ladyship was American. As a young woman she had married Lord Camoys at a time when many American heiresses were offering themselves and their fortunes to European nobility. The rumor was that as a young man the peer had been told by his trustees that funds were low and that in order to save the estate he must wed a wealthy Yankee.

We walked into her dark patio. After Julia introduced me, the old woman declared, referring to the late President Franklin D. Roosevelt, "This country's gone to the dogs since 1932, don't you agree?" I did not think so, but I was afraid to disagree with her. What if she exploded with anger, or ordered me to leave her splendid villa, embarrassing Julia? We then had tea.

The next day we stopped at the Livingstone's house. Julia's cousin, a relation of the Camoys, was married to Mr. Livingstone, a member of a very prominent Washington D.C. family. Julia said, "They've had to cut back their servants from 12 to six." Following Betsy, her cousin, inside Julia said so only I could hear her, "She's often nasty to the staff. I've told her not to be rude."

We were invited to go sailing with the John Nicholas Browns. He was a scion of one of the state's oldest and wealthiest families. They lived in a copy of a French chateau. We came out of the other side of the big house into the sunshine. There was an immaculate green lawn which descended in a gentle slope down the hill side to the water's edge. There was a dock, and beside it was the Brown's yacht.

Mr. Brown was tall, well-proportioned, deeply tanned on his long wrinkled face, and had a reddish brown beard. Wearing a captain's hat, he was affable and sat in a chair, holding the wheel. His wife was plump and also friendly. We motored out into the harbor, and set sail. There were several other guests including the pouting Betsy, and her younger brother. I was nervous. I might say the wrong thing, and finding my balance on the sloping deck was a challenge.

Late in the afternoon Jackie Kennedy's mother, who was a pleasant pretty woman, gave Julia two tickets to a charity dinner. It was to take place in a very long big house copied from a famous English stately home. The owner was an elderly single woman. She employed 24 servants. The purpose was to raise money for the English Speaking Union. Julia said, "The man who runs it is James Beck. You can see him sitting there at the head table." She pointed to a solid-looking middle-aged figure. "He's probably already drunk. His wife, her sister and he live in a mansion, and his wife likes to keep white rats as pets. There are hundreds of them, and they live under the lawn and in the basement under the dining room. Every night the butler brings a silver platter of sliced meat. There is a hole in the dining room table, and they come up from below, and he feeds them. The other day some of the rats burrowed under the fence and got into the local high school. They bit some children. So the fire department had to be called to kill them."

Returning to New York, I resumed my life at Mrs. Wyatt's. Then I went to England for a short visit. George said, "Can you help me get our jewellery back from Uncle Dick? It's hard to prove it's ours, but in Priory Hill there are some oil paintings of our ancestors where the women are wearing diamonds and emeralds." I said, "Maybe they're the same ones Dick has. With my camera I could take pictures of them." I drove him to St.Neots in a small rented car. I was always uncomfortable in his company, but the fact that we were on a joint mission - our first such - reduced the tension somewhat.

Unlike the rest of the house where the paint was peeling and dust lay on the furniture, the dining room was in good condition. The dozen chairs with the Rowley family crest were repaired and polished, the curtains were clean and the pictures hanging on the walls restored. "The St. Neots Urban District Council has been trying to grab the house, but I've been advised to say it's being used. That's why I've fixed up the pictures and other stuff." There was a full-length portrait of our great grandmother Caroline Rowley as a young woman, wearing a necklace and brooch. There was another one of three young ladies, and one of the girls had a ring on each of her fingers. I photographed them.

George and I went out to the circular drive. He moved slowly across the gravel, leaning on his stick. It was a sunny day with some haze.

Stopping, we stood together, a tall young figure and a somewhat bent very fat middle-aged one. I was bareheaded, but he wore his squashed black "pork pie." There was mystery in the air. We looked at the oaks, chestnuts and elms rising above the rough grass. I walked to the railings. The park stretched down to the road at the bottom. In the branches there were two herons.

After I returned to Mrs. Wyatt's, I received an airmail letter from George. I knew it was from him because of the dark blue ink and the very small lettering. "There's a rumor John has had a heart attack. He's not expected to live." I felt a chill. A few days later another letter arrived. "It turns out it was not a heart attack." I was relieved.

I had developed what was diagnosed by Doctor Welch as an ulcer. I was in some pain. I then went to see Dr. Irving Ehrenfeld in Passaic, New Jersey, who my mother and step-father recommended. He said it was an acid condition of the intestinal tract and prescribed a tranquilizer and a strict diet of mild foods. Mrs. Wyatt told Bea to cook for me only certain kinds of food.

One day Jane Wyatt came to stay at her mother's house. An air of electricity filled the normally quiet atmosphere. Only a year or so earlier she had finished making the final episode of *Father Knows Best*, starring Jane and Robert Young - one of the most successful TV shows in history. She did not like Bea, and the feeling was mutual. Everyone knew who she was, and Jane would use the telephone on the landing just outside of my bedroom, talking in her confident excited way. Mrs. Wyatt was proud of her, and treated her as an equal. She usually said out of Jane's hearing, "Jane has done very well in Hollywood, but she should have stayed in New York on the Broadway stage where she could have become a great actress like Cornelia Otis Skinner. That's where her greatest talents were." After being lured from New York by the California movie industry, she had her first film success as the ingenue star in the classic *Lost Horizons*. I instantly liked Jane, and admired her energy, looks and spontaneous laugh.

Since my return to America I had been required to report for military training one night a week, and all day Saturday every month. My unit was the U.S. Army Reserves on West 42nd street, and my job was in personnel, bringing files up to date and filing them. Most of the time there was nothing to do but gossip. After a while I was awarded a stripe. I was rather disappointed because previously my brown uniform had none at all, and, if I took a girl into a restaurant or bar, the headwaiter had no idea what my rank was and sometimes - to be on the safe side - assumed I was an officer.

That summer of '62 I found myself on a crowded train with a lot of other reservists heading up to Camp Drum, which is in the western part of New York state. It is a remote area, very cold in the winter, with forest extending in all directions.The pain of my acid condition and the shock of the impending two weeks' military training led me to give up smoking, as I sat with my fellow sufferers on the overnight trip.

I spent virtually the whole time in an office, shuffling personnel files, and a fellow reservist, a Jewish friend, and I spoke loudly of what we would do when the two weeks were over and "we return to the real world." However, one day I had to do "kp", and I sat on a wooden step outdoors peeling potatoes by hand. My eye flicked over the headlines of the local paper. Step-Uncle George, having resigned voluntarily from Eisenhower's cabinet as Secretary of the Treasury a short while earlier, had been summoned before Senator Stuart Symington's committee and accused of profiteering during the Korean War. It was my step-father's brother versus Democratic senators. Backed up by an army of lawyers and accountants, George addressed them as "you boys." They retreated.

In 1962 the Cuban missile crisis began. My political views had moved gradually from being an anti-Senator Joseph McCarthy moderate Republican to the far left. I opposed President Kennedy's blockade of Cuba, feeling that since the U.S. had stationed nuclear missiles in Turkey I did not see why Russia could not put theirs in Cuba. My unit might be ordered to go on active duty. We would go as a back-up force to Florida. I stood in formation, very afraid we might receive such a command. I planned to refuse the order. I would be jailed. Whether I would survive prison and whether this would be another humiliation in the eyes of friends and family were painful thoughts. Some reservists were called up, our division was not.

Barry and Ellen Block, who were now married, told me that Calista and Philip were divorced, and she was living in New York. Feeling cautious as a result of having been badly burned, I phoned her. "Will you have lunch with me?" I said. I did not want to take the risk of asking her out for a date at night. "Yes," she replied. "I'd be delighted." I was curious as to what she would be like, and my hopes rose a little.

There was a restaurant almost directly opposite 310 East 50th street, where the food and decor were good and not too expensive. When she arrived, she looked the same, not surprisingly a few years older, and there was a look on her face that I can only describe as both slightly harder and wiser. She did not tell me why her marriage had failed, and I, though friendly, was careful not to show a lot of enthusiasm for her. She had a job. I was not a success in the world, but she did not seem to hold my relatively humble way of life against me. I found her attractive, and her laughter, jokes and remarks about life were appealing. We enjoyed ourselves. We agreed to meet for another lunch.

In the same restaurant the following week I mentioned my political views. They were not hers, but she was polite. Calista said, "I'm an admirer of the Black Muslims. I read their newspaper every week. Do you like them?" I had to confess that I knew very little about them, but I said I was not one of their supporters. Our meeting was pleasant, but there was a slight atmosphere of mutual disapproval. Nevertheless I decided a few nights later to phone her and ask her out on a date. "This is Peter," I said in an even friendly voice. Sounding frantic, she snapped, "I've just been fired. I'm very upset. I can't talk to you now." She hung up. Her abrupt manner reminded me of how I had suffered. I swore to myself I would never call her again.

At dinner one night Mrs. Wyatt in her clear patrician voice said, "In the 1930's I remember going to a wedding up the Hudson. President and Mrs. Roosevelt were guests. When they left in their open car, driving away along the drive, nobody in the crowd cheered for them, except for me. They hated him. But he was our President. I thought it was terrible."

Around this time the Governor of New York state Nelson Rockefeller announced that he was leaving his first wife and would marry a Mrs. Murphy, whose husband was a scientist working in a Rockefeller research institute. There were four Murphy children, and her nickname was "Happy." Mrs. Wyatt said angrily, "I am a Republican but that man will never set foot in my house." A year later the governor lost the battle for the nomination as the G.O.P. candidate in the 1964 election to Barry Goldwater.

Daisy wrote me from Paris to ask if she could stay a few nights at 310. Mrs. Wyatt generously agreed to have her as a guest. One evening I took Daisy out for dinner. She wore very little makeup and a nice, ordinary dress. The following night a man came to the door as her escort. I noticed she had on lots of lipstick and rouge. Her hair was beautifully done, and she wore a pretty dress. I was hurt.

My Princeton novel was finished. It had taken two years, and I had rewritten the manuscript twice. I had high hopes for it, and I took it to Mavis McIntosh of the literary agency Otis, McKee and McIntosh. Mavis was a friend of Louise Welch. Elizabeth McKee helped by Mavis had been John Steinbeck's agent. About three weeks later Mavis asked me to come to her office. She said, "If you are writing to make money, you'd do better to go to the racetrack. However, I like *Life at Lord* (that was my title), but I think you have been rewriting it over and over. Am I right?" "Yes," I said. "If you will restore it to the first draft, I will try it out on a few publishers." A month later I gave her my original version. "There's an editor at Scribner's named Hutson who went to Princeton. I have an idea he might like it." To be taken on as a client by such a prestigious agent made me happy and hopeful.

My state of nervous optimism was short-lived. Mavis said, "He turned it down. He wrote me that Princeton was both better and worse than your novel. I'll try it out on a few more publishers." Their responses were also negative.

During this period while still doing the occasional article for American Catholic magazines I wrote a few pieces for the *New Statesman, The Spectator, The Nation* and *The New Republic.* The disappointment of my failure as a fiction writer was softened somewhat by the very modest prestige associated with these distinguished periodicals.

On another short visit to England I saw Bernard Williamson, a partner at Bird & Bird, the family lawyers, referred to as "Birds" by George. I had first heard of Williamson immediately after the Second World War when my mother regarded him as the bright young hope to enliven the older partner, G.F. Higginson, who in turn I remembered being looked on as the bright young hope of the firm in 1941 when my father died. Williamson had been an officer on active duty in the British Army for the six years of the war. Of average height and physique with a round face and dark hair, his eyes twinkled and he liked to roll the words in his mouth in a sort of soothing drawl while explaining the intricacies of the law, which he supported on balance. At the same time he maintained a slight air of cynicism towards the legal world. A few years later he was to cause me quite a lot of trouble. One of his pleasures in life, which he had ample opportunity to indulge in, was to observe the antics of the Rowley family. He said, "Your uncle Dick walked in here one day, and said, 'I feel guilty. My conscience bothers me. I'm giving you these jewels which were my mother's for life.' They belong to John, George and Peter." Smiling, he handed me a package. I looked at the contents. There was an emerald necklace and bracelet, and a diamond necklace and brooch. They were beautiful in their old settings.

Returning to New York, I met the editor of *The Nation*, Carey McWilliams, a delightful plump man of about 70, his wife Iris Dornfeld, the novelist, and their son, Jerry, a tall, very thin person with a boyish manner and a black cowlick. Younger than me, he was an aspiring writer. He was given a $500 advance by a publisher to complete a novel he was writing. I was consumed with jealousy. Mrs. Wyatt spent four hours one evening reassuring me of my talent.

Renting a Chevrolet Impala with Tom Carson and an Irish girl I had met at Mrs. Wyatt's, Bridget "Can-Can" McCann, we drove across America on a holiday, Tom and I splitting the driving. It was the summer of 1964, and as we entered the western states, we said with a laugh, "This is God's country - Goldwater country, where the men are men and the women are women." In Los Angeles we separated, and I was invited to stay at Jane and Eddie Ward's house. Jane Wyatt had married Edgar Ward, and they had two grown-up sons. Eddie Ward was a very pleasant man whose manner said, "I married the movie star."

Sometime earlier Mrs. Wyatt had told me, "Jane thinks you're the best-looking man she's ever seen." I was excited at the prospect of staying in her house. The Wards lived in a lovely part-Spanish, part-English style house in Bel-Air with a view towards downtown LA and the Pacific. It was above the haze of smog. On two sides were lovely lawns and beds of flowers with English and native California varieties.

The Wards took me to a party given by a well-known producer called Martin Manulis. Inside the house were original impressionist paintings by such artists as Renoir, Monet and Picasso. There were a number of beautiful women, some of them blondes. Several of them had their legs in white plaster casts as a result of skiing accidents.

The lunch was on the terrace, and we were told where to sit, and I found myself at a table for four. The other three were Hollywood writers, and one of them had written the script for *Lilies of the Field*. A year earlier Sidney Poitier had won the Oscar for best actor, and the film the award for best picture. Even though I knew that Hollywood writers were supposed to have sold out for money, I still felt overwhelmed during lunch by my middle-aged companions. They were confident, well-dressed and well-fed. The conversation during most of the lunch among the other three men was about Dirk Bogarde, the

British film star. The LA writers gave a variety of reasons as to why Bogarde was not an international star. They agreed that he probably never would be. After lunch I tried to talk to the Manulis' pretty daughter, but she was not in the least interested in me.

In the late afternoon Jane said, "Would you like to go for a swim? We don't have a pool, but Cary Grant lets me use his." She drove me to his house, which was also in Bel-Air. Grant was not there. We both swam and chatted, lying by the pool side in the sunshine. Jane had a good figure. Her vivacity was as delightful as ever.

After dinner with Eddie and Jane at their house I was alone with the star. "I'm going to bed," she said. "I will too," I replied. I climbed a few steps up the staircase. I stopped and said, "Good night, Jane." I looked down at her. Her face and lips were only about one foot from mine, as she smiled up at me while talking and laughing. Resisting an urge to kiss her, I went upstairs.

I was 30. My trustees in London handed over the capital from my two small trusts to me. Since 1941 they had lost most of the money due to a combination of inflation and investment in bonds rather than stocks, not to mention the steep decline in the value of the pound versus the dollar. The trustees of one fund were Coutts & Co., and the trustees of the other one were Captain Linton who had died of drink, Joss Wickham who had died of a heart attack, Uncle Dick and for only a few years Mr. Turton. George said, "Don't give the money to your step-father. I wouldn't trust him." On a trip to England earlier in the year my mother and step-father saw George, and without being asked to give his opinion Jack said, "George, you need medical help with your eating, smoking, and diabetes. And your weight problem. You should go the Mayo clinic in Minnesota. They have a terrific reputation. They would help you." He pressed this argument repeatedly during the evening. Although he did not show his feelings, George was enraged. Persuading me to take my $35,000 account away from my step-father and not transfer the English capital to him, as I had always said I would, was George's revenge.

Around the same time George was told by the owner of 20 Hyde Park Place in Paddington that he would have to leave. The block of flats would cease to be service flats, i.e. delivering meals to the apartments. By then George had already sold one of John's paintings, the portrait of our great grandmother, to the landlord, Sir Charles Rowley, a distant relation. He did not tell the Court of Protection and the Receiver, but kept the money for himself. On his last night George ordered seven desserts, ate none of them and plunged a half-smoked cigarette into the top of each. He then moved to Artillery Mansions in the Westminster area of London. This enormous block of flats, which catered to M.P.s, offered daily maid service but there were no meals.

Every day at lunch time he took a taxi across the park to the pub he had always frequented in Paddington. Every Friday night he visited his favorite call-girl, though I did not know this at the time, and wrote her from five to nine checks, alternating between Coutts and Barclays banks. These sums ranged between 100 and 200 pounds in total. In today's money these figures would be multiplied by a factor of 10. She said she needed the money to support her parents, sisters and a brother who was a drug addict. Sometimes he wrote her letters, saying, "You only get me drunk. I won't give you any more money." Every now and then he wrote a will leaving everything he had to the lady in question. I knew none of this.

I transferred all my modest assets to an investment counselor in New York. Despite my explanation to my step-father that the minimum account the new advisor required necessitated transferring even the small sum under Jack's supervision, Jack said, "You are welcome to come and stay here on weekends, but you can no longer bring girls."

Moss persuaded or forced George to give up being tenant of the Priory Hill house. He sold it and the park to the town. Moss' motive was to reduce his work as administrator, although he said John needed the money. The local politicians said they were going to convert it into a residence for unwed mothers. Then they changed their minds. Some of the park land and the mansion were sold to developers for middle-class housing. There was land nearby, also owned by John, which could have been used for housing, but the most powerful town councillor, whose own home bordered on these fields, did not want his view spoiled.

The house was razed, but before the demolition crews arrived, an auction was held. "Birds" sent me the sale brochure, suggesting I might like to buy a set of antique plates which had the Rowley name on the back of them, but I was still convinced I was going to be a great novelist and such family matters were irrelevant. The farm tenants bought some items for their own smaller houses. George wandered through the rooms among the crowds, looking for the last time at the furniture, paintings, walls and windows which had been part of his life for so long. Some of the county families attended the auction. Lady Fox, for example, saw

George but did not say "hello." The lawyers, Moss and the Court decided not to sell the family portraits and a small amount of the furniture. These were placed in a local warehouse, called Brittain's.

Great aunt Dorothy died. I was in New York. The news came as a surprise and a slight shock. She had always appeared to be healthy, constantly bustling around on goodwill missions. She was about 70. None of my English family ever told me what she died of. With their policy of secrecy they were not likely to tell me even if it had been an overdose of heroin or in a shoot-out with the police.

On one of my now infrequent visits to Princeton on a weekend I saw on television that the Viet Cong had killed six American soldiers in Vietnam. I sensed that President Johnson would use this tragic event as grounds for sending large numbers of American troops to Vietnam. Jack, who happened to be watching the news at the same time as me, was obviously happy to greatly increase our presence in Vietnam.

That summer of '65 a group of friends and I rented for two weeks a Greek caique, advertised as a yacht but in fact a fishing boat, but before arriving in Athens I spent a week in London staying with my friends Susie and David Buchan. The Conservative Prime Minister was Alec Douglas-Home, formerly a lord, and I said to my hosts, "He's not too bright. He has to use match sticks to figure out economics." David, a very tall, hearty squire from Aberdeenshire, became quite annoyed at me. We then watched four beetles crossing the TV screen. It was the start of the weekly show starring the Beatles, who were just achieving fame.

On one of those days George telephoned me. To my surprise he said, "Will you come with me to my solicitor's office?" It was in the City of London, the financial district, but the offices were a bit like a rabbit warren. The firm was called Yarde and Loader. I had never heard of them. Mr. Loader was the stocky senior partner, and his articled clerk, a Mr. West, a taller, solidly built character, obviously wielded some power. Though dressed in modern clothes both middle-aged lawyers could have stepped out of Dickens' novel about the law, *Bleak House*. How my brother had found such a seedy, raffish pair to represent him I had no idea. Led by Mr. Loader, they explained carefully that George wanted me to cooperate in a legal attempt to break John's trust and transfer some of our mad brother's riches to us. Loader said, "Most of any money we obtain will go to George, but you will get some." Sitting in an arm-chair my half-brother first nodded silent approval. Then he grunted. Then I went to Greece.

I came back to New York and Mrs. Wyatt's from my very cheap "yachting" holiday. The eight of us who had shared the cost of the fishing boat had had to sleep on narrow boards covered with thin blue foam rubber mattresses.

I became friends with Annette Weld. A Roman Catholic and a painter, she was a tall English blonde about five years old than me. She was a daughter of a retired Major General in the Indian army, who was British. She had a clear cheerful voice with an upper-class accent, though not affected. Though she had very little money, she was always fashionably dressed and pretty, and she had an innocent quality. She was usually fun and optimistic. Try as she might, she was not a good painter, which was almost her only source of income, and even her portraits were of marginal quality, though occasionally she caught one of her subjects correctly.

She invited me to East Hampton to stay one night with an English girl friend of hers who was a secretary/personal assistant to the movie star Dina Merrill. Her boss was away and the friend welcomed us into the ultra-modern luxurious house with its sunken living room just behind the sand dunes and the ocean. In the background the crashing of the waves made a rhythmic drum beat. Dina and her husband Stanley Rumbough alternated visits there on weekends with their respective partners. The film star was in love with another movie star, Cliff Robertson, while Stanley, according to Dina's "Girl Friday", had a different girl every other weekend - a redhead, blonde etc. The next day Dina returned to her home at about noon, and before her arrival our friend quickly hustled Annette and me out to the beach under the hot sun, climbing over the dunes to bring us sandwiches and cokes whenever she had the opportunity.

The glamorous setting and the liaisons inflamed my imagination, and I started to write a new novel, *Camel Through the Needle's Eye*. The plot was about a very rich young man, son of a Dina Merrill-type character, who gives up his fortune and becomes active in anti-Vietnam war protests. He is drafted into the Army, nearly dies from meningitis, goes AWOL, joins left-wing protest movements and is finally murdered by the police and right-wing thugs. While sitting on the beach, reading the manuscript I congratulated myself on my "masterpiece".

I also read some correspondence from England about Yarde & Loader's attempt to break my grandfather's trust. They had sought an opinion from a prominent young barrister, a Mr. Browne-Wilkinson. He

said that breaking the trust was impossible - problems of unborn
children, distant relations, difficulty of determining life spans etc. I was
very depressed. I was by now aware that my future career as a great
novelist was far from certain, and I needed the money if I was ever
going to marry and have children. Mr. Turton had kindly agreed to
represent me in my collaboration with George, and now he offered to
go to another barrister for a second opinion.

In the afternoons I volunteered to campaign for a Mr. Schwartz, who
was one of the Democratic candidates in a primary for a political office
like state senator or U.S. Congressman. Schwartz was the only one of
the candidates to oppose the increasing number of American troops in
Vietnam. He was a hopeless candidate, but from a shabby downtown
office for six weeks I telephoned registered Democratic voters to ask
them to vote for him. Usually the person who answered was polite,
though sometimes they hung up. I was aware that I was tilting at
windmills, but at least I was doing something to oppose President
Johnson, and I felt better. (I had by the way voted for LBJ in '64.) I
even wrote a few press releases for my man. Of course, he lost.

A new "guest" arrived at Mrs. Wyatt's. Jackie DeVoe had dark curly
hair, a creamy complexion and drank heavily. She was above average
height and overweight. She was about 26 and a daughter of a family
who had owned the DeVoe Paint Corporation. She had a sweet nature
and was shy and gentle. She was similar to Tennessee Williams' heroine
in *The Glass Menagerie.* She had been married for three weeks when
she was 18 and slim. "Once I was very pretty," she said sadly. "Even
Ernest Hemingway asked me for a date." There were several framed
photos in her bedroom confirming her self-description.

After dinner every evening Jackie would go out and buy a six-pack
of beer, carry it surreptitiously in a brown paper bag and then walk up
to her bedroom, hoping Mrs. Wyatt wouldn't see her. She and I lived on
the top floor. Later in the evening she went out again. By eleven at night
she could barely stand up, and her speech became slurred. Mrs. Wyatt
was aware of her weakness, and was very kind to her. She would call
up the stairs to her, "Are you all right, Jackie?" Jackie would reply,
summoning every effort to sound sober, remaining as sweet and polite
as ever, "Yes, thank you, Mrs. Wyatt. I'm fine." Occasionally during
the night Jackie lost control of her bowels, and the walls and floor of
the bathroom she shared with me were smeared with excrement. Mrs.
Wyatt insisted on cleaning it up herself, and apologized to me. I assured

her I was not angry. Jackie had a sister, Madeleine Talley, who was married with children. Beginning a career as a financial manager she became very well-known and highly respected.

My fascination with the Hamptons, the long beautiful beaches, the social life, the exclusive WASP clubs like the Maidstone and the Meadow club, the dreamy F. Scott Fitzgerald mansions, the glamorous women in their Pucci-Gucci prints and shoes and their high-powered boyfriends led me to rent a tiny cottage literally on the wrong side of the railroad tracks in East Hampton. It cost very little. It was through Jackie DeVoe's family I heard of it, and it was so bad that once I put up for one night a fashionable male guest of theirs, a German art dealer, who could barely hold his nose down he disapproved so strongly of where his hosts had put him. There was a tiny living room and bedroom with chintz curtains, and it was shaped like one eighth of a railroad car.

I was dating occasionally an English girl who worked for a realtor who specialized in expensive holiday homes. She was worldly-wise, divorced, attractive with wide full lips, sultry brunette hair, a tan, and a good figure, and in her New York apartment we would argue about birth control and abortion. We kissed. But I was careful, so I thought, not to be passionate. I asked her to come for the weekend to my little cottage. I gave her a pullout bed in the living room. I got into my double bed in the bedroom. After we had said good night, to my astonishment I felt my sheets and coverlet turn partly aside and she started to climb in. "Let's make love," she said. "I'll do everything." Her hand reached for the opening in my pajama trousers. I felt a flash of desire. Then I refused, and she became very angry. "How can you ask a girl here for the weekend and not make love?! It's <u>understood</u>. Why else do you ask her? <u>You can't do this!</u>" I could see her point, but my religion was everything to me.

After I had arrived in New York, through an introduction from Farm Street I had gone to a new spiritual advisor, who was a stocky, genial Jesuit at the Church of St. Ignatius Loyola on Park Avenue. He was late middle-aged. Once a month he would hear my confession. We would have a friendly conversation, he would give me advice and I would give him a little money. I had begun to read about the brothers Daniel and Philip Berrigan in *The Commonweal*, a Catholic intellectual magazine. Dan was a poet and also a Jesuit. They were starting to be active in the anti-war movement. On a visit to O'Prey I said, "Ten percent of all the apartments and town houses on the upper east side should be taken over by the blacks from Harlem. They are 10% of the population." O'Prey's face darkened. He condemned my idea angrily.

I telephoned Dan and went to see him for the first time. He greeted me with a gentle smile and handshake. At his request I called him Dan, rather than Father. Dressed as a priest in a black top and trousers, he was about 45 years old with small sharp features. He was diminutive with dark short hair combed slightly over his brow. He had a kind, non-assertive way about him, but spoke with quiet conviction, leavened with flashes of humor. On occasion he was slightly amused and cynical. Besides being erudite and charming he was a rebel. There was an impish quality, something of the leprechaun about him. He heard my confession but said such a rite was no longer necessary in the present day. We agreed on politics and the Church. I decided to visit him regularly and support him.

Mary Yost became my literary agent. She was the wife of a psychiatrist, and one of her clients had written a well-reviewed book of short stories. An editor at Viking, Cork Smith, a tall, reserved, nice WASP, showed an interest in *CTNE*. I met him and took him to lunch a couple of times. He said he needed the support of his fellow editors. He assured me that it was very likely my novel would be accepted. My hopes rose, and once again I began to dream of literary fame. The months dragged on. Cork reassured me and Mary. Then Cork and I met for lunch again, me paying the bill. He carried with him a box. I guessed my manuscript was inside. "We just can't publish it," he said. I was so upset that I wrote a letter to the president of Viking, Tom Guinzburg, complaining of the long, misleading (as I saw it) delay. I said it was discourteous to Mary and me. He replied that he was sorry, but these things would happen again.

While in Princeton for the weekend I went to a party and met an ebullient blonde girl with a curvy figure. Her name was Donna Jenkins, and very soon she said, "I am a Vanderbilt. My mother is a granddaughter of the Commodore." I was slightly impressed. She had a strong talkative personality but appeared to be confused. I said to an English cousin who happened to be staying and also met her, "I like Donna. She's trouble. I'm not going to get involved with her." I then took Donna out on a date.

Soon she asked me to accompany her on a trip to north central Pennsylvania as guest of her mother, Barbara Jenkins, in a rented private plane. Donna and her mother were patients of an English psychoanalyst, Dave Brown. His practice was in Tioga near the

Lackawanna river. The two-engine propeller plane flew us west from Teterboro Airport over the suburbs of New Jersey and southern New York state, across the Delaware River, and the hundreds of miles of green forest and deep into Pennsylvania, eventually landing on a grass field. During the flight Mrs. Jenkins, sitting in the front passenger seat, said, "Communism is a terrible danger. *Life* magazine is Communist. I belong to the John Birch Society."

Mrs. Jenkins had discovered Doctor Brown through a book in which he was described as "Doctor X". She had learned the real identity of this wondrous psychoananlyst. The analyst had cured previously hopeless patients through the administration of a drug.

His car parked nearby, Dave was waiting by the field. About 45 years old, slightly stooped, he looked like the devil. He had very dark hair, dark horn rim glasses, tanned wrinkled skin and a charming smile which curled down at the edges. He was also tall, and wore a black suit with bow tie. He spoke in a cockney accent but with a certain sing-song quality and it was immediately obvious that he was highly educated and intelligent. He was very sure of himself, and greeted the two women, warmly hugging them.

As part of their therapy he injected LSD into his patients. Provided there was a prescription the drug was legal in those days, and Dave's partner was a local osteopath, who wrote out the prescription. Dave made the hallucinogenic himself. He then went off with Mrs. Jenkins for what would be a nine-hour session in his office in the osteopath's building in the town. His fee was $50 an hour, which in today's money would be about $250. After the treatment Barbara Jenkins went to sleep. The next day she returned by plane to Teterboro, and then her chauffeur drove her to her estate in Far Hills, New Jersey.

Donna and I stayed on for a few days. Donna was also Dave's patient, and she then had her nine-hour session. One of Donna's brothers was also a patient. There was one other regular patient, a middle-aged lawyer. I stayed at the Browns' house which was about two miles up a stream. One had to travel along dirt roads. Their home was called Rivendell after the one in the Tolkien books. Dave, his English wife Sofia and their friends had chosen Tioga "because the air here is clearer than anywhere else in America. We can tell because the lichen on the rocks is so pure." About two years earlier the Browns had built the large two story house right on the edge of the creek. There were no immediate neighbors. The water ran past, rippling over the rocks, forming tiny bubbles. The forest surrounded us. The only sounds were the wind in the branches, the birds and the stream. Occasionally a branch fell into the water, or a fish jumped. I was entranced by their world, and grateful to Mrs. Jenkins for giving me a free ride and particularly to Donna for introducing me to her friends.

There was a party at Rivendell, and I met the science fiction writer Theodore Sturgeon. Donna told me she had sex with him. She was my girl friend, and it was obviously just a passing incident, as she was not close to Sturgeon, and they were little more than acquaintances. She had just wandered down a hall and into his bedroom. In the free and easy atmosphere I became so drunk that I had sexual intercourse with Donna. However, the next day I assured myself it was not a mortal sin as I had been too inebriated to have done so with full awareness of my will.

Around this time Donna and I went swimming in a pool in the stream, and she swept her hair to the side. On one side she was bald. She explained, "I just lost it. My father gave me $25,000, which I gave to a young movie producer, who promised to make me a star, but he ran off with the money." At Rivendell I was determined not to smoke marijuana or take LSD. I was deeply afraid of their effect on me.

Returning to Mrs. Wyatt's, I received a letter from Mr. Turton who said that the barrister he had approached thought it was possible to break my grandfather's trust. I was very thankful to him, and greatly relieved by this news. Instantly I knew that if the case remained in the control of Y&L George and I would never succeed. Mr. Turton lived in Yorkshire, and I felt he was too far from London to continue as my solicitor. I felt guilty, but I sent Mr. Turton a check as thanks for all his help over the years, but said I would have to find a new lawyer in London. My aunt Violet said, "You should never have done that." Mr.Turton was disappointed but accepted my check and seemed to understand my viewpoint.

On the New York City buses was an advertisement offering a sort of "computer data dater." There were slips one could tear off with an address and telephone number. I assured myself I was only doing this as a joke. I then received a form with many detailed questions about my tastes in clothes, food, movies, the kind of girls I liked etc. I sent it in, expecting to be told to contact girls with similar interests to mine. Naturally I expected them to be middle class and living in Manhattan, hopefully on the upper east side. However, the computer sent me a letter telling me to contact five young women, and they lived in

Queens, Brooklyn or the Bronx. I finally took one of them to a matinee of an anti-Vietnam war play in the Village, but we had little in common. I then told a friend of my mother about who the computer thought was suitable for me. She replied, "I'm not in the least surprised the machine calculated you were lower class Queens."

Among the girls living at Mrs. Wyatt's was Marion Thompson from California. Dark-haired and energetic, she was a tall beautiful actress with a fresh-faced regular look which was not in style at that time. She and I discussed how one day we would be famous. There would be two plaques in front of 310 saying that we had lived there. Marion went every day as a student to the Stella Adler Acting Studio. An important figure in the theatrical world, Ms. Adler was also reputed to be cruel to her students, particularly the female ones. About once a week Marion would return to our house in tears.

One day the lamp post opposite our front door keeled over, crushing the roofs of three parked cars in a row. No one was inside them. Beaumont's daily urine had gradually over the years eroded the metal base. When I suggested to Mrs. Wyatt that Beaumont was responsible for this atrocity, she replied sharply, "Beaumont had nothing to do with it." Life continued as usual for the dog. Once a week Bea gave him a bath, and the animal was covered with white soap suds. He was then rinsed and dried, emerging as the fluffy white poodle he was.

Brice Clagett was by now a partner in a Washington, D.C. law firm. He asked another partner for introductions for me with two New York law firms who might be able to help me with John's English trust. I went to see a gentleman at Sullivan & Cromwell, one of the most distinguished firms in the city. He was a senior partner and sat behind a large desk and spoke in measured powerful tones, considering every word. Late middle-aged, he wore a waistcoat and watch chain. A tall substantial figure, he was willing to help. But he was a little too pompous for my taste, and I wondered how interested he really would be.

Then I went to another very well-known firm, Cravath, Swaine & Moore. The partner, George Gillespie, was about 35, slimmer than the S&C partner, and alert. He said, "In the U.S. we cannot take money away from the incurably insane, but maybe the British system is better." He approached one of his colleagues, another partner, who was the son of the famous Judge Medina of the Hiss case. Medina recommended Ronnie Plummer, a partner at a London law firm called Allen & Overy. He had done business with Mr. Plummer.

Ronnie had a large well-furnished office which he was at ease in. Below average in height he was about 45 years old with dark hair and a round strong ruddy face above a stocky body. He was very energetic with an aggressive manner which was pleasing. Other than a few pleasantries at the start he was strictly business. Then he asked his assistant to come in. Ernest Jowett was a very tall man in his early thirties who was thin. The two men could not have looked more different. Ernest was eager, quick and always ready to make often brilliant suggestions, not that Ronnie was not equally intelligent.

To my surprise Ronnie said, "I am willing to take this case on one condition. I want you to all agree to accept one third each if we win. This is a test, and in the actual negotiations percentages may change. But now you must agree to accept one third each." I, who had expected to receive much less than George, consented. I expected George to be unhappy. The third party was our uncle Dick, who intended to give his share to his daughter Rosabelle. He had only just been informed of the matter, and had previously never expected to receive anything.

In order to divide the diamond and emerald jewelry between the three brothers, "Birds" sold it with George's and my approval. Mr. Moss, representing John, agreed. I could have kept my share as one piece of jewelry, but I said to friends, "I have no wife to give it to." The auction raised 2,400 dollars for each of us. Since then the value of emeralds has skyrocketed. This was enough for me to take a trip to South Africa. I was nervous about going there alone, but I felt I had to find out if I could survive without my parents, the Welchs or Mrs. Wyatt. In the meantime Ronnie would learn whether Uncle Dick and George were willing to compromise.

Carey McWilliams gave me an introduction to Ruth First, who was a white South African exile living in London. She had been imprisoned for 101 days in solitary confinement by the apartheid government and had written a book about her experience. A pretty dark-haired woman of middle years, she gave me the names of five friends in South Africa. From other friends I received about 60 introductions.

On BOAC, now named British Airways, I flew to Nairobi, Kenya, where the plane refueled. I then flew non-stop to Johannesburg, seeing the sun rise over the horizon and illuminate the light brown landscape of Africa. Before landing the stewardess gave me a form. There was a question, "Are you carrying any explosives?"

My middle-class hotel was in downtown Johannesburg. From my

14th floor window I looked down on the railroad station. At the morning rush hour there was the white entrance where a few whites came out. An enormous stream of Afro-Americans poured out of the black entrance. Like the Afrikaans I felt a shiver of fear to be so outnumbered, but at the same time and more strongly I could see how unfair the situation was. Before destroying the paper on which I had written Ruth's contacts, I memorized them.

I went to a dinner party in a wealthy suburb of South Africa. The hostess was a glamorous American young woman Mary McFadden married to a young executive, and there were a number of older guests. While the African maids served dinner, they said, laughing, "Our servants are very stupid. They are like animals They don't even know how to use knives and forks. They cook their meals over an open fire, and eat with their fingers." I seethed with anger, but did not dare object.

The next day I phoned a white South African lawyer. I had two separate introductions to him, and one was from Ruth. However, I used the other in order to see him. Inside his office I said, "Ruth First also asked me to look you up." His face turned white. Then he decided to trust me, and we talked about the political situation.

Everywhere I went, the Afrikaans accent was sing-song and yet lyrical with a very slight cutting sharpness to it but delightful unlike any other accent of an ex-English colony I had ever heard. It was like listening to a song.

I was given an introduction to a couple who lived in the Transvaal. I had only met their son briefly at a cocktail party in New York. They invited me to stay. "Would you like us to take you to Kruger National Park?" For the next five days I was their guest. We stayed in comfortable rondavels, round huts, and I was given one. The food was good, and I saw a lot of game, including a few lions, though the high grass obscured the view. At dinner the couple said, "The niggers are just like children. They are incapable of governing themselves. Our kaffir cook prepares our meals in our house, but then goes outside and cooks over an open fire for herself and her family." They pressed their argument every night at dinner, and I am ashamed to say I nodded agreement occasionally when I had to.

I took the famous "Blue" train from Johannesburg to Capetown, which was a comfortable overnight one with sleeping accommodations, stopping briefly at the Kimberley diamond mine where there was an enormous hole in the ground.

In Capetown the atmosphere was relaxed, there were many charming villas on the slopes above the beach below Table Mountain, and the ocean was beautiful. Because the prices in South Africa were so low compared to those in England and America, I was able to rent for two nights a hotel suite by the sea. One of my introductions was to a pretty sharp-faced South African girl, and on the couch we kissed a lot, listening to the waves outside. A long way to the right on the horizon was Robyn Island, where Nelson Mandela was incarcerated. During our necking she told me that her boyfriend was an informer for the white South African police.

I met a group of young American members of the "Peace Corps" who were on holiday. We agreed to share the cost of renting a car, and drive north up the Indian ocean towards Port Elizabeth. They were convinced I was with the CIA. I suppose my secretive, reserved manner, suit and tie led to this misconception, but, try as I might, I could not persuade them I was not a CIA agent. Finally I gave up and came to rather enjoy my new role. They were very nice guys. The beaches were lovely, unoccupied, and the waves so perfect that they were chosen as the best in the world in the classic surfing movie *The Endless Summer*. One of the reasons the beaches were empty was because blacks were not allowed to use them.

The American consul in Port Elizabeth was the son of a friend of my mother in Princeton. He and his wife invited me to lunch. During the meal Horace Burn, a six foot four, sincere, likable man, said, "Would you like to come with me on my visit to the Transkei? I do this for the State Department regularly." The Transkei was technically an independent nation within South Africa, home of the Xhosa, a tribe who spoke with a clicking sound. One of them was Miriam Makeeba, the singer.

Horace regarded the tribe as split into the good guys and the bad ones. The head of the good guys was Knowledge Guzana, a charming, well-mannered lawyer, who was for democracy, and the leader of the bad guys was Paramount Chief Kaiser Matanzima, a very tall black, who was the Prime Minister. He was polite but suspicious of Horace. There was a Parliament, and 12 white South African civil servants sat on a raised dais beside the benches for the M.P.s and made sure the blacks didn't do anything to upset the white apartheid government in Pretoria. The debates were in English, Afrikaans and Xhosa. Progress was slow because each interpreter addressed the whole body.

I drove alone to Durban farther north on the Indian ocean. It has a tropical climate, and even though it was the winter it was still humid and warm during the day. I went to see a white South African editor of a newspaper, who was outspoken in his opposition to apartheid. Not too long after that he went into exile. He arranged for me to visit Alan Paton, South Africa's most famous writer and the author of *Cry the Beloved Country*. I had tea with Paton and his wife in their house in a suburb. White-haired, brimming with indignation at his country's racist policies, he was very worried because his wife was obviously extremely ill. Night fell. From his home I drove back to Durban. Looking in my rear view mirror I could see a car follow me most of the way.

By then I had developed a theory that a revolution would occur in a few years. Guerrillas, I thought, would come down from the north along the eastern and western sides of the country. I thought I would drive north towards the Mozambique border following the coast. I had to stop about 50 miles from Mozambique as the roads became increasingly sandy, and I became afraid my small rented car would be stuck. This took about four days. I knew no one, and I grew so lonely that I thought I would go mad. With great relief I flew from Durban to Johannesburg and was able to phone a few friends.

Then I flew west to South West Africa, known today as Namibia. My plan was the same. Drive north towards the Angolan border. On arrival in Windhoek, a small airport in this very wild under-populated country, I rented a car, but the agency people said, "You'll never survive on your own. There are no petrol stations. There is no food and there are no hotels. There are wild animals. It's very dangerous."

For $300 a week I was given a jeep, food and a German safari driver, Wernher, who was about 35 years old with dark hair, a solid physique and a friendly manner. He packed provisions and extra gasoline, including a tent and sleeping bags. We drove hundreds of miles over sandy roads, our dust billowing a quarter mile behind us. There were some mountain ranges, but it was mostly scrub brush as far as the eye could see. Very occasionally we would see a black and a village. It was the way the world must have looked a million years ago. At night we slept under the stars and gazed up at the Southern Cross.

We stayed one night with Zacky Eloff, his wife and family. He was a painter and game warden in the Etosha Pan, a vast game reserve. The Pan itself is a salt lake second only in size to the one in Utah. Zacky described how a leopard had broken into his compound surrounded by a high wire fence. He shot it before it killed his two small children, his wife and himself. Communication was by radio, and their nearest neighbor was 50 miles away. During the day we drove through the reserve. The bushes were only two or three feet high, and it was easy to see elephants, giraffe, lions, zebra and all kinds of antelope-type creatures like springbok and wildebeest. In the evening we waited by a water hole and watched the animals drinking. They were watchful for lions.

There were stories of Bushmen living in the semi-desert. A party of African thieves had tried to escape across the Pan, but their foot prints gave them away. Zacky, Wernher and I drove out onto the dry lake. The vehicle sank about three inches into it, but could move slowly. The sun cast long shadows from Zacky and Wernher wearing their Stetson hats, Zacky's four wheel pickup and me across the salt surface. As the sun slowly went down, there was an exceptionally beautiful sunset. Then darkness fell, and Wernher and I retreated to Zacky's compound. Lying in my sleeping bag, I listened to the occasional roar of a lion and the soft rustle of the wind through the grass.

In his spare time Zacky painted skillful impressionist oils of the animals and made numerous drawings of them. From him I bought four drawings and an oil of at least 13 elephants grazing on the veld, that he had painted from the top of a kopje, a small hill.

On the way back we stopped in a tiny town surrounded by wind and the semi-desert that looked as though time had stopped in the 1920's. We ate in a kind of curious bar restaurant outside, and there was a wild middle-aged woman who made a pass at me and insisted on dancing, which I reluctantly did. I resisted her charms, but I knew I was in the middle of nowhere and would never be there again.

After an unproductive three nights in Lusaka, the capitol of Zambia, where along with constant references to Kenneth Kaunda the nation's president the evening TV news was devoted to the latest activities of elephants and omitted world news, I went to Dar-es-Salaam, the capitol of Tanzania, like Zambia a free African country. There was dancing outside in all of the nightclubs under the stars. On the floor were spies from America, Russia, China, Eastern Europe, England, South Africa and free Africa.

In neighboring Mozambique there was a guerrilla war against Portuguese rule, and two of the northernmost provinces were now in rebel hands. After visiting the headquarters of Frelimo, I was driven to a guerrilla training camp 50 miles north of the city. There was sand, some huts and some men standing around. Ruth and one of her friends had given me an introduction to the head of Frelimo, Dr. Eduardo Mondlane in Dar. He was a Mozambique black who held a Ph.D. from the University of Syracuse, where he had been teaching. His wife was a white American, and they had three children. I phoned for an appointment. When I arrived at his villa, the guard was a bent old black man who moved with difficulty. Dr. Mondlane was charming. He said, "The enemy will be crushed as easily as Mad Mike Hoare." He was a British major and mercenary who had been captured in another African nation.

I flew to Algiers where I met an African in exile from South Africa. He said, handing me a blue airmail letter, "Can you please post this for me from London? It's to my family in South Africa. If I send it from here, the South African police will read it and not send it on." Algeria had recently won its freedom from the French. I went to the casino, but did not gamble. The gambling rooms were drab. I found the atmosphere depressing. In the streets the only people who looked well-dressed and well-fed were the blue uniformed police.

In London I told Ruth about her friends I had seen, and posted the airmail letter.

About two years later Dr. Mondlane opened a parcel. When it exploded he died. A few years after that Ruth and her husband Joe Slovo left England and moved to a free African nation. A few years later she received a parcel, which killed her. Many years later after the South African blacks took over the government from the white apartheid regime, Joe Slovo became one of the first Cabinet ministers.

While I was in England and Africa, Paddy had died of cancer. Mrs. Wyatt hired a big, very nice Haitian woman to cook breakfast and make the beds. She was competent and friendly.

I went to Tioga for a weekend. Donna told me she was sleeping with Dave. Sofia had her own lovers. Dave also slept with his secretary, Sally, who bore him a baby. Sofia cared for her and Dave's small son and daughter, Christopher and Naomi, in the Rivendell house while Sally lived in the Tioga office building with her baby. I learned that Dave had never attended any university, had no medical qualifications, and that the Oxford Institute of Psychoanalysis which he had founded was entirely his invention. Donna said happily that she and her mother during the LSD therapy were able to remember their births and even time in the womb.

In England George and uncle Dick had agreed to accept the hypothetical one third. Ronnie and Ernest started the trust-busting case. George had felt for years how deeply unfair it had been for his older brother to receive almost everything, and he very little. To add to the wound was the fact that John had ignored his wealth by living in a mental hospital. So no one benefited. George had been unable to marry and have children and lead a normal life, George thought. If the trust could be broken and some of it taken away from John, then George insisted to himself that most of what was recovered should go to him. He told his "girl friend" and her sisters this.

Uncle Dick's anger at the Rowley state of affairs was of even longer duration. My grandfather had given him a pittance in relation to his older brother, my father. And then Owsley had died, and Dick still did not benefit. "Birds" did not want any change in the status quo, which might reduce their annual fee. Coutts Bank, the trustees, who were also the Queen's bank, had the same viewpoint. For that reason the Receiver, Mr. Moss, was also opposed to any alteration. In addition "Birds", Coutts and Moss did not want their power and any prestige attached to running the Rowley estates to be lessened. The Court of Protection took a neutral position. Ronnie, Ernest and I hoped to persuade everyone to cooperate.

My lawyers asked me to move to London for five months to help them. In 1957 Aunt Violet had introduced me to an old (in both senses of the word) friend of hers, Evelyn Ramsden. She lived in a small penthouse at 105 Onslow Square only a quarter mile from the Wickhams. Barely five feet tall, she was born with a club foot, and moved with the aid of a stick with difficulty. She had gray hair, a round wrinkled face and a wide mouth. When she smiled - along with her kind eyes - the effect on me was soothing and delightful. We quickly became friends, closer than her and Aunt Violet, about whom we sometimes talked and joked. Evelyn's father had been a British diplomat in Scandinavia.

Although she had a small private income, her occupation was translating Scandinavian books, particularly novels, into English. She gave me one, *You Are Mine*, about a Norwegian girl who is forced by her parents to give her baby for adoption and then years later tries to find him. She was badly paid for her work by publishers. First she would do a literal translation. Then she would rewrite the text into an artistic, readable prose. Then she would give it to a friend who had usually been a native of Sweden, Norway or Denmark to search for errors and clumsy phrasing. At the end of this the publisher would pay her the equivalent of a starvation wage. Evelyn also had at least one other translator competing for the same business. Occasionally she went to the British channel and stayed in a hotel for a rest, and she gave me her flat in March, 1967, for a month.

My solicitors asked actuaries to calculate the likelihood of each Rowley inheriting if nothing were done. They replied that Uncle Dick's chances were about 10%, George's about 32% and mine about 58%. The reason I appeared to have the largest share was that I had been born after our grandfather's death in 1933, whereas my two half brothers were born while he was alive. After the Second World War Parliament had passed a law to prevent persons in their wills from affecting the lives of those who did not even exist yet. Previously a will's "entail" could insist the money go to the eldest son of the eldest son for ever, for example. I was thus theoretically able "to bar the entail," i.e. dissolve it, and freely receive the capital. Even if there had to be a trust for him, George was absolutely certain that John his insane older brother would be the first to die and that he, George, would inherit everything. He had waited all his life for this, and it was only the very slightest angle of the path of a .22 rifle bullet that had cheated him so far. Rushing to Y&L, George was furious and vowed to fight.

The month was up, and I had to find somewhere else to live temporarily. In *The Times* I saw a classified ad for a basement flat in The Little Boltons, a fashionable area in west London.

Almost daily I phoned Ronnie and Ernest - with ideas. What a nuisance I must have been!

Ronnie said patiently, "Yes, Peter?"

Trying to be a serious mature man with a razor-sharp mind, I said, "What about increasing my percentage? We know George is in bad health. His chances are not good."

"We'll have to see," Ronnie replied. "I'm sorry. But I have to take another call. I'll pass you over to Ernest."

Ernest said, "We're looking into every possibility, I assure you, Peter."

George rang me.

"I'm the heir," he said angrily. "I'm a solicitor…" He launched into a long legal explanation of how wrong my claim was.

"Yes, George."

I said this a number of times.

Finally he hung up.

Then I rang Ronnie and Ernest.

The Honourable Lady Fox invited me for lunch and to spend Saturday night. I first remembered hearing about her as a child when my young mother complained that the young Myra had demanded that her maid be allowed to stay at Priory Park for a shooting weekend. She only lived three miles away. "There wasn't room in the servant's quarters, and Myra was livid when I said her maid would have to come over daily to dress her." Myra's father had been Minister of Agriculture under a Conservative goverment, was made a lord, and thus when Myra married Sir Gifford Fox she was able to add "The Hon" to the "Lady." They had one daughter, Jeanna, age six, who may have rescued me, age four, from drowning in Myra and Gifford's small pool by extending a pole with net for collecting leaves to me as I floundered. Sir Gifford during the Second World War was "debagged" by his fellow officers. This was a custom in the mess among some of the British upper class whereby an unpopular man had his trousers forcibly removed.

Myra had arrived for lunch in the early 'fifties wearing a wide-brimmed Ascot hat and accompanied by a pansified man at my parent's Princeton house, seeking comfort from her divorce. She kept Croxton Park and the 3,000 acres, which she had inherited. She became the first land owner to farm her land herself using a foreman and laborers which was economically far wiser than having tenants under Socialist governments who kept empowering them.

By 1967 her hair was yellow, her mouth wide with slightly turned down corners, but she still managed to look quite pretty, using lots of rouge and white powder, wearing couturier clothes. She smoked a lot and drank whiskey to relieve the loneliness. If there was a large party for lunch, though there were only a few the day I was there, she would come onto the lawn, saying "Lunchie…lunchie." When Myra toured her estate, showing it to guests, she opened a barn door with her gold key. That day the butler was young, handsome and black-haired with a long sharp jaw, and he passed the strawberry bowl to her ladyship, who said, "I've told you to pass it on the other side."

"You weren't talking to me that way last night, milady."

I watched her face. She registered the remark for less than a second in a placid way.

Then she ignored it.

At dinner after the fish she said with a smile, "I'm feeling chilly. I'm going upstairs for a moment to put on some more pearls."

During coffee in her drawing room where the antique tables were covered with hundreds of tiny ornaments she said, "Peter, darling." She addressed everyone except for the servants as "Darling." "Let's go to a dance. My chauffeur will take us. It's in Norfolk."

I knew that relatively recently she had ordered an earlier chauffeur to drive her to London for a party. Reaching London, she decided the party would be a bore, and told him to drive the hour and a half back to Cambridgeshire. When they were within a mile of Croxton Park a little before midnight, she suddenly decided to go to the party after all. The chauffeur stopped the Bentley by the side of the road, got out and walked away. She did not know how to drive, but she somehow managed to get the car and herself back to her mansion.

When we arrived at the large country house and entered the hallway, the hostess was climbing the stairs. She looked down at us.

"The toilet on the floor above is overflowing," she said to Myra and me.

She gazed penetratingly at us. I felt highly embarrassed because I was sure she thought I was Myra's paid lover.

Myra and I danced, but I was careful not to get too close to her, and she for her part kept her distance, smiling graciously and widely.

"What a lovely dance," she said. She said this several times. "So many friends here." I had only noticed one or two come up to her.

In the Bentley on the way back, as we sat side by side in the rear seat, she said, "Peter, you should be a diplomat."

A few weeks later my mother arrived in England to visit my grandmother, who had broken her hip while gazing up at a new holy frescoe on the ceiling of a side altar in London's R.C. Westminster Cathedral. She had neglected to notice a small step behind her.

Myra invited my mother and me to lunch at Croxton. Before we arrived we drove past Priory Park. There were now dozens of houses near the newly named "Rowley Road" but the manor house was gone.

"To think of the money we spent putting electricity into that house," was my mother's only remark. Until his death my paternal grandfather had refused to have electric lights and modern plumbing.

There was a different butler - older called Palmer. Myra said brightly, "I think he's hung his hat here." At lunch the two women eyed each other, although my mother usually looked straight ahead rather than directly at her ex-friend. Myra lived in splendor. My mother lived a middle-class existence with Jack in New Jersey. Feeling inferior, my mother was pleasant to Myra. Myra was delightfully patronizing to her.

On returning to London, Ronnie said to me during one of my phone calls, "George is capable of fathering children."

"How do you know?"

"Yarde and Loader told me."

I was worried because if George produced a son, he would inherit everything.

In my next phone conversation with Ronnie he said, "Uncle Dick's lawyer came to see me…"

"Are they going to cooperate?"

Ronnie chuckled.

"Yes. All he wanted to talk about was how pretty Rosabelle was."

"I'm not getting anywhere with this case, though…"

I felt a chill.

"Mr. Williamson at Bird and Bird won't answer my letters."

A few days later Ernest said, "Ronnie sent copies of his ten letters to Mr. Williamson to Mr. Woods, the managing partner."

A few days later Ronnie said, "Because of George's bad health we think he should get less than 32%."

George produced a medical report. "George's heart is as good as a jet fighter pilot's," the doctor wrote.

"We'll demand a reputable physician examine him," Ronnie said.

I visited Father Walkerley, S.J., the priest who had heard my confession when I burst into tears. I told him about George.

Walkerley advised, "Why don't you show some mercy."

The flat I had rented was owned by David and Fleur Gibbs who occupied the town house above it along with their children and nanny. If I stood on tip-toe I could just see the level of grass on their lawn behind the residence from one of my two bedroom windows. After a while the Gibbs and I became friendly, even though I was their tenant with a separate entrance below them. One of Fleur's best friends, who was staying above me as their guest, was Liza Hill, a sensual Australian girl of about 25. She was attractive and just-divorced. Fleur was Australian too. Liza's divorce had been unpleasant, and Liza's brother had told her, "You've been avoiding sex. What you need is to make love to a man. That'll shake you out of your divorce blues." Her ex-husband was said to have treated her badly. Liza had started dating. One afternoon I met over tea on the lawn one of her new admirers. He was a very respectable, well-meaning stockbroker type who tended to waffle his words in a sort of constrained upper-class accent. "He's flabby and boring," she said to me after he had left. "Why don't you come downstairs and have a drink with me this evening?" I said. "I can't. Gerald (that was the stockbroker's name) is taking me out for dinner tonight. But I'll insist I'm home by eleven. And then I'll come down to you." I went to bed about nine, but I couldn't sleep, and listened to the wind and her eventual hoped-for appearance. Suddenly she appeared at the door of my bedroom in her nightgown, slipped between the sheets and blankets, and we made love three times in two hours.

However, Liza was a divorcee, and even though under the influence of Berrigan and another modernist priest I had just started to relax my prohibition against sexual intercourse I could never marry her.

While my affair with Liza and the battle over the case were going on, I started to take out to dinner a tall pretty girl with dark hair, who was an heir to the Reed paper fortune. I was convinced I was in love with her. I wanted to marry her. I gave her a copy of Henry Miller's *Tropic of Cancer*. The next time I saw her she said, "I read some pages. They're <u>revolting</u>." I could tell from the way she looked at me that she had decided I was too weird to be a future husband.

Then came a girl whose build was slighter than Ms. Reed. I fell in love with her. She was a very attractive blonde. I planned to propose. She worked for Amnesty International. I may have even kissed her a few times. "I love to get clothes from…" She mentioned a store on Beauchamp Place. I gave her a light brownish pink dress in her size from there. She accepted it, but I could tell she had decided not to see me any more. I had invaded her space.

I then proposed marriage to Allegra Kent-Taylor. I had known her slightly for several years. She was a tall lovely girl with blonde hair. Fleur Gibbs had said of her, "She's a classic English beauty." I had not even dared to kiss her, even though I was in love with her. Allegra said in her lightest, most charming way as if she wanted to fly away. "I'm so complimented. I couldn't possibly."

Before I left England, I resumed smoking.

Returning to New York, I remembered that three strikes and you were out. At Mrs. Wyatt's I learned that Beaumont had died of natural causes. He was buried in the back garden. Except for Mrs. Wyatt no one missed him. There were two girls living there, Erin, who I liked, and a friend of hers, who I also liked but whose name I can't remember, and the three of us went on a non-amorous weekend to Orient Point on the north branch of Long Island.

"Do you think I need a psychiatrist?" I said to them innocently.

To my surprise they both said, "Yes."

At about the same time as this disturbing advice I was realizing that it would be much more difficult to find a wife while living in a single room at Mrs. Wyatt's. I had to have an apartment of my own and live alone, where I could take girls, bed them and marry one of them.

I said to Mrs. Wyatt, "I'm sorry, but I'm going to have to move out into my own apartment."

"Yes, my dear. I quite understand."

I then learned through the grapevine that my decision was an important factor in her selling 310 and moving to California to live with Jane. She gave me some of the furniture from my room.

I found an apartment with a bedroom, living room and terrace looking towards the East river, the UN and the Chrysler building a block away. I was determined to be within two blocks - north, south, east or west - of Mrs. Wyatt's old house. I also took with me her Haitian maid for two half days a week. Immediately I was lonely.

I went to see Mrs. Welch with the idea of resuming my old treatments. But after one pleasant session I had my doubts that she was the one to help me find the love of my life. I knew she was important in the Gurdjieff movement, but now with my Catholicism I was suspicious.

Berrigan said, "There's a shrink I like. He's a friend - Mark Stern."

That summer Tom Carson, taking a quarter share, and I rented a new cottage in Bridgehampton. It had four bedrooms, an open kitchen, counter and living room with fireplace and an almost unobstructed view across the grass, sand and dunes a quarter mile away of the ocean. Only one small house obstructed the vista. There were also blonde-colored dune rushes between me and the beach. One could not hear the sound of the waves, but one could see a few white caps.

Out of gratitude for introducing me to Allen & Overy I welcomed as weekend guests Brice and his wife, who was an elected official of a Maryland county. She was a pretty woman shorter than him, and he was a supporter of the American troops in Vietnam. The war was in full flower - if that is the word. Relations between Brice and his wife and me were already slightly strained that night because of the conflict when I took them to a nearby party. Brice was a very skilled lawyer, and I was afraid of his verbal mastery.

Among the other guests was Fereidoun Esfandiary. At 18 he had been on the Iranian Olympic fencing team. He had muscles, a magnificent chest and a strong-jawed face with black hair and eyebrows. He was the author of two novels. The first, *Day of Sacrifice*, had been chosen by the *NY Herald-Tribune* as one of the 10 best first novels of the year. His second, *The Beggar*, described a man minus limbs in country like Iran. A third was on the way. An argument about Vietnam broke out between Brice and Fereidoun. I thought Esfandiary talked circles around Brice. I was delighted. By Sunday the writer was a new friend, and relations between Brice and me were not what they had been.

Another guest on a subsequent weekend was Sofia. Dave was due to arrive with her, but then opted to come the next day. She had short darkish red hair and might be described by the French as "jolie laide." She had a pert mouth with rather sensual smallish lips in the shape of a bow or the opening to a tunnel. She was only about five foot four inches tall with hips that were wider than her breasts which appeared to be small. She had an energetic way of moving her head up and down rather like a bird. She of course spoke with an English accent - educated - with an excited trill quality.

"What a pity Dave had to postpone his flight," I lied.

The sun was setting to the west.

"Yes, isn't it?" she said with a naughty smile. "He'll be flying in Barbara's plane to Teterboro airport, and then he'll come by limousine for the drive here. We'll miss him dreadfully."

Then we kissed several times and went indoors to make love.

I felt a certain rage but I couldn't have said whether it was towards her, Jim or myself.

Dave arrived the next day, and I pretended nothing had happened. Sofia did likewise, and Dave went along with the game.

Returning to New York to my empty apartment, I welcomed as a guest a friend of the Browns - an English mathematician in his mid-thirties with two black front teeth - Chris. He gave me a plastic pouch.

"It's the best marijuana - Acapulco Gold."

I had heard that marijuana was best smoked while having sex. There was a wealthy Jewish girl, Mimi Matsner, I had been dating. In her apartment, which was only a few blocks from mine, very late in the evening we smoked one cigarette together, and kissed frequently, but my hopes for intercourse were ended when she insisted I go home, even though we had by then finished a second weed. I got into my leased car. After I had gone a few feet, the street seemed to stretch away endlessly while the sides of the buildings expanded to left and right. Frightened,

I managed to park it by the curb and walked home to my penthouse and fell asleep.

The fact that I was living alone and starting an adulterous relationship must have been in the back of my mind when I went for my first appointment with Dr. E. Mark Stern. His office was on the second floor of a somewhat murky building on University Place in Greenwich Village. The room was darkish. He stared at me steadily in a very penetrating way. He had black hair and appeared to be in his late thirties with a medium build. I interpreted the gaze as a deep concentration about my welfare. Referring to the three English girls who had turned down my proposals of marriage - said or unsaid - he commented, "Don't they have names?"

I then drove the seven hours to Tioga. I felt the existence of Mark, as he asked me to call him (by the way the price was right), was a counterbalance to my involvement with the Browns. After purchasing about $70 worth of food stuffs in a Tioga supermarket as my gift to the Browns, I arrived to begin a life style whereby Sofia made love to Richard Englesteen at about 11 p.m. and then had sex with me in my second floor bedroom (Richard was in a first floor bedroom along the same hallway where Donna had her liaison with Ted). Because I was the latest in her romances each night, I felt I had an edge on Richard, and she said, "I just make love to him so that he can go to sleep." During the day I sometimes tidied up as much of the Brown's house as I could. During daylight hours Richard taught me how to throw a spiral pass with a football. I had known since my days at Asheville that my manhood was lacking because I could only throw a wobbly one. Dave frequently came to dinner at night, although he spent his nights with Sally in his office, sitting at the head of one end of the table, though I sat at the other end. Dave said, "Norman Mailer's novel, *An American Dream*, is so appalling..." Another evening Dave, Richard and I composed a letter during dinner with Sofia's enthusiastic approval attacking Ivan Gold, Sofia's New York City lover, for covering his bed with plastic before making love to her when she had her period. Ivan was Mary Yost's star client, and the short story about the girl who had made love so often to a gang of young men and then been shipped to a rest home had been titled "A Change of Air." So we titled our letter, "A Change of Story." It was because Sofia had previously assured Ivan she had no other lovers, including Dave.

I returned to New York and related the above activities to Dr. Stern. He listened silently.

"Why don't you laugh?" I said.

"I didn't want to upset you."

Then I returned to Towanda for what I expected would be another four day visit before returning to my cold NY apartment and Mark. It was the beginning of the hunting season in Pennsylvania, and the rural roads looked as if the guerrillas were forming for a major assault on civilization. However, they were only the local deer-hunters, though doubtless some of the heavily-armed men in their baseball caps and wind breakers came from farther afield. Dave said, "Stay out of the woods. It's very dangerous. A year ago near here a nephew shot his uncle across an open field at a range of 200 yards, inheriting the family farm, mistaking him for a deer. The judge said, 'These hunting accidents are regrettable. I suspend the defendant's hunting license for a year.'"

After about two months of relating to Mark my life story once a week, I said, "I notice you treat me less seriously when I don't have a tie on."

"That is so superficial. Among your problems are ..." He then proceeded to dissect my character in an unfavorable way.

"I am like a surgeon," he said.

I was furious.

Finally he concluded by saying, "I worry a little that you have come to me as you seem to get involved with psychoanalytic quacks like Dave. As for Mrs. Welch..." He then made some less than complimentary reference to her. I was too afraid of him to point out that even though Mrs. Welch only had a masters in psychology, whereas he, Mark, had a Ph.D, Mrs. Welch's husband was a doctor.

I returned to Towanda and related my current experience with Mark to Sofia and Dave, who were sympathetic to me.

That fall to my amazement my mother asked if she could come and stay for three nights in my Long Island cottage. I couldn't understand why, but the visit was uneventful until the end when she suddenly said, "When are you going to make something of yourself?"

I was surprised to read in *The New York Times* of the engagement of Mark. The story was nearly half a column. There were a number of impressive details about him and his fiance, Virginia, and their families. I was instantly jealous.

I went to England. Ronnie and Ernest asked me to fly up to Bradford, Yorkshire, to see the Receiver, Kenneth Marmaduke Moss. "He's refusing to supply me with any figures about John's income and assets," said Ronnie. Moss was a big man, at least six foot three inches tall, with a powerful beak nose, and a bachelor. By American standards the office building in the center of Bradford and Moss's office would have been classified as quaint, if not an outright throwback to the 19th century. The exterior of the building had dirty white tiles, and the accountant's office with its old furniture and clutter of files was on the fifth floor with a view of the square. "You should give me a thousand pounds for so successfully selling Priory Park and the mansion," said Moss. "Okay," I said, "But can you speak to Ronnie and Ernest on the phone?" I made the phone call, and the Receiver dictated some figures to them. When I returned to London, I said to Ronnie, "I'd better send him a cheque." "Certainly not," said Ronnie. "You're under no obligation. It's coercion." Whether Moss received kickbacks from the tenants we were never able to prove, but what were facts were that he received free shooting and they asked of him the minimum amount of work.

I refused to go to Princeton for Christmas but instead spent it in Towanda, although I did send some gifts to my mother, Jack and Dorothy.

Not too long afterwards I spent the weekend with my erstwhile family in Princeton, regarding the Browns by then as more of a real "family". Somehow I found myself on the living room couch, talking to my mother, my head in her lap, looking up at her face. She referred to my "wicked psychiatrist," meaning Dr. Stern. I did not agree with her, but I was unable to reply as I felt that she had cast a spell over me.

By January, 1968, Donna Jenkins had told her mother that she was having an affair with Dave. Mrs. Jenkins was not pleased. She always paid for her and Donna's "psychoanalytic" sessions with Dave. Her son, who had also been Dave's patient, had married the Browns' baby-sitter, a 17-year-old Tioga girl with a clean complexion, creamy breasts, a sweet nature, and a lower class background. He had ceased to be a patient. The middle-aged lawyer had terminated his therapy with Dave. At the same time Berrigan asked me to a sort of group therapy conference at Cornell in Ithaca, N.Y. The person running it would be Stern, though Berrigan acted as a kind of consultant to the affair.

Dave needed patients, and asked if he, Sofia, and Richard could attend the gatherings. Stern supervised a couple of hundred participants including Dave, Sofia and me. "Can you please form into a semi-circle around me depending on how close you want to be to the center. This is a game," he said. "Those on the outer fringe are in hell." Sofia was on the rim. "Me!?" she exclaimed with a bitter laugh. Fortunately I was closer to Mark in the crowd, and Dave frequently engaged him in learned discourses which I did not understand.

Ithaca was freezing, the temperature below zero fahrenheit. Berrigan invited me to his university suite of rooms for a drink, where Stern was also present. I was embarrassed by his presence and noticed he seemed to talk naturally and at much greater length with Dan than he did when he and I were alone in our therapy. Sofia refused to spend the night in my motel room.

The next day Berrigan and I drove to Tioga, and he spent the night at Rivendell. I admired his open-mindedness. I then paid for a small private plane to take him to the New York area.

My sister phoned me. "Can I borrow your Long Island cottage with my boy friend for the weekend?" I said, "Yes." A few days later she phoned me again, "My father is threatening to stop paying my bills at Bryn Mawr. He says he'll tell the Bryn Mawr authorities so I'll be expelled. He says if Uncle George heard of my behavior, he would stop giving $3,000 every year to my parents." I said impulsively, "I'll pay for your tuition." Stern said, "Do you really want to pay her college fees??" However, Dorothy cancelled the weekend.

Frequently I had fantasies of being in a fist-fight with Jack, but he always won.

My aunt Violet arrived in Princeton as a guest for a week or two to aid my mother and step-father as Jack was ill. He had for several years been having polyps removed from his internal organs. To combat these symptoms he had been receiving injections of something like monkey glands. He could not afford to go to Switzerland where there was an even more advanced treatment using other living-organism infusions. He had cancer. My mother said on the phone, "Won't you at least come down and see your Aunt Violet?" "Alright," I said reluctantly.

My step-father was clearly a very ill man, though he could walk. "I hear you've joined the Knickerbocker club in New York," he said. "That's for snobs." Then he showed me a photo of Dorothy with a young man at a dance. I knew he was not the same one she had planned to spend the weekend with in Bridgehampton.

My aunt Violet greeted me as usual, and then it was time for me to take the train back to New York. My mother drove Jack and me to a barbershop in town. He got out, and moved slowly across the street to the establishment. I noticed the fringes of his hair on his monk-like bald head, and wondered how much longer they would need cutting.

I said to Sofia on the phone, "Why don't you come and visit me in New York instead of me going to Towanda?"

She said, "I'll fly to Teterboro airport."

Then she phoned me shortly before her flight.

"I can't come."

I knew the affair was over.

Fortunately Annette was staying for a few days in my apartment. I began to suffer stomach pains. I took a small dose of librium, which I had stopped taking three years before when my acid condition had improved. I had been convinced the librium was affecting my eyes. I limited myself to numerous Gelusils every day. But the hurt from Sofia's decision was so intense that I took a larger dose of the tranquillizer. Finally I collapsed on my bed, and Annette held my hand, but the pain grew worse. I took a third dose. I was now up to about "60 ccs." Finally I fell asleep.

Annette returned to Guatemala, where she was now living and painting.

That April Martin Luther King was murdered. The night of the assassination I saw on the street corner of 51st and 2nd avenue a small group of blacks playing loudly from a music recorder to anyone who would listen King's famous "I have a dream" speech. Something about their bravery in proclaiming his message in what was "enemy" territory, the upper east side, moved me. I had to admit that I knew not a single black socially or in the very limited business and artistic circles that I frequented. Berrigan by then had - accompanied by his brother and seven white followers of theirs - burned the draft files of a board in Catonsville, Maryland. He was now under indictment for a felony.

One week I took out six different girls on successive nights. Often I went to the same restaurant. The biggest pleasure of each of those evenings was watching the expression of the headwaiter, as I arrived with a new one. I related to my dates my experiences in Towanda. None of the girls seemed interested in me.

Chapter 5

UN

"A man as handsome as you should be able to get a date," said Dr. Stern.

Around the time of this remark I heard that Great Uncle Francis had died. Well into his seventies, he had fallen over a banister on a second floor landing of a hotel in Folkestone. Frances had been there. To the relief of my English family there was virtually no publicity except in the local paper, noting a "Lieutenant Colonel Francis Norris…" etc. They had missed mentioning his career in the 'thirties, whereas, if he had fallen in London, some astute Fleet Street reporter might have sent to the morgue for the clippings. I was a little disappointed that such notoriety had not been given a last flash of light on the world's stage. I can't say I grieved, as the journalist in me had still not forgiven him for not telling me about the mysterious bonds. The former "Colonel Lawrence of High Finance" had left what was left of his money in trust to Frances and then after her death to the Wickham family.

One of the six girls I had taken out some weeks earlier was Emoke Kiss. She was a very handsome Hungarian, almost the same age as me, and, although I may have been a pain to the girls of the world in terms of the marriage market, Emoke was somewhat guarded as to her deepest thoughts and feelings. I had not been able to penetrate her reserve. She was very popular, and many of the young men I knew had gone out with her. She was vivacious, beautiful, and intelligent with dark hair sometimes piled high on her head accompanied by a fall. Nevertheless, we remained friends.

In order to meet girls I decided to give a party. I phoned Emoke.

"Can you come to my party?"

"I can't," she said firmly in her delightful Magyar accent in a tone which implied that I was no longer dating material. Her voice had a throaty, powerful timbre to it. "I'm giving one myself that night."

"I hope you're planning to ask me," I said. Normally I would not have been so aggressive, but I was desperate and lonely. I don't think she had had any intention of inviting me.

"Yes, of course." She gave me the details.

I had always planned that <u>my</u> party be a sort of after-dinner one, while Emoke's was an earlier cocktail gathering. She did not seem interested in attending mine.

Emoke lived in an apartment on East 36th street between Park and Lex on an upper floor of a town house. An old elevator with iron gates took one to it. The furnishings were "antiquey", sort of smart but far from luxurious. I had kissed her there once briefly. The living room was crowded with people in their twenties and thirties, and I was immediately nervous. But rare was the party I went to that I was not jittery about. However, Emoke's friends were highly respectable, socially desirable, and this added to my unease. They were mainly WASP Americans. How would I ever match up - particularly when they started to talk to me and I had to say something to them? An additional problem was wending one's way among the living bodies just to get a drink or find someone, preferably of the opposite sex, to converse with. At least, after I had secured a scotch and soda, I could light up a Marlboro. The noise was of a high level.

I recognized a few faces, most of whom were connected in one way or another with the Knickerbocker club. The "Knick" did not admit ladies as members, but girls associated with its men carried a certain cachet. A more terrifying group it would be hard to imagine - for me. There wasn't anyone there I could call a friend, except possibly Emoke.

Emoke introduced me to her roommate, Barbara, and then quickly moved away to talk with more eligible, personable guests than me.

Barbara was about five foot nine inches tall, well-dressed and Hungarian. She was thin and attractive, but I did not find her sexually exciting. But thank God she was willing to chat with me. In fact the conversation continued for some while.

Suddenly a beautiful girl approached us, wending her way through the crowd, her hips undulating out of necessity, her blonde hair glinting in the half light. I was immediately struck by her luscious red lips. She also had rich greeny-brown eyes, balanced cheekbones and a tanned lustrous skin on her perfectly rounded face. Her nose was impeccable, not haughty, but strong and straight. Her beauty alarmed me.

Barbara said, "This is my sister, Terez."

I gathered she was younger than Barbara, and she was very slightly shorter than the older girl.

Finally Terez drifted away from the conversation. Had she been bored? Had she found me unattractive? She had appeared to like me.

I said to Barbara, "I'm giving a party later this evening. Can you come?"

"I'd be delighted. Sure." She smiled. I had not dared to ask the sister.

When Barbara entered my living room after my party had started, she was accompanied by four of her friends, including Terez. I took heart. I couldn't be that bad if Terez was willing to join others at a party of mine. When she left an hour or so later, accompanied by Barbara and one or two others, I said to her in front of the group just in front of the door, "Will you have dinner with me?"

"Yes," she said smiling.

Even I was astonished at my effrontery in seeking a date from her while ignoring her sister and braving the stares of the others in the departing group.

"Next Tuesday at 8 p.m.? Where do you live?"

"85 East End Avenue. The apartment's under the name of Ann Loud."

On the Friday I played tennis with Sheila Graham's daughter, Wendy Westbrook, who I had dated once or twice. Though not as famous as Hedda Hopper or Louella Parsons, her mother, an ex-chorus girl from London, had been F. Scott Fitzgerald's mistress and a Hollywood gossip columnist of some power. Her daughter also proved to be a better tennis player than me, and, after I was defeated in the morning on a red clay court on the west side by the Hudson river, I suffered a back spasm, barely succeeded in driving to the east side, and taking the elevator to my apartment. Once inside I collapsed on the floor, and could only just reach with one arm the telephone. A Dr. Arnold ordered an ambulance for me. I must have been able to unlock my front door, and before the eyes of my nice homosexual neighbor, the well-known Broadway actor Ben Govern, I was transported to the physician's office. He taped me up. I then returned on a stretcher to my empty apartment. Ben said, "Can I buy some groceries for you?"

"No, thank you," I said.

I retired to bed to spend the next three days and nights alone watching the funeral on TV of Bobby Kennedy.

By Tuesday night I was well enough to be able to go to 85 East End Avenue.

Her name was Terez de Tuboly. I said to her, as I looked around the well-furnished apartment, "How can you afford such an a residence on a UN salary?" I knew she was a guide there, speaking French and Hungarian. Despite my rude question the evening was a success.

A few dates later I gave another party, and sitting on my couch was a beak-nosed girl wearing a white dress with black polka dots, and next to her looking adorable was Terez, and the sensation came over me, as my eyes glanced over the two of them, that Terez was "It.", the girl I would marry. This flash or brainstorm was like a happy expansion of some very pleasant beige-colored cloud in my consciousness.

After the party we made love on my golden beige-colored couch. I think she was reluctant to start an affair with me, but she enjoyed our intimacy

When we drove out to my Bridgehampton cottage, I said to her, "Can I call you 'TT'?"

"Why?" she said in her strongly Hungarian-accented English, holding my right arm, as I drove.

"It's short for Terez de Tuboly."

"Yes."

"My name is spelt T-E-R-E-Z, not Theresa. When we arrived at McGuire Air Force base in New Jersey after the '56 Revolution, the immigration officials changed the spelling."

"To me you will be Terez," I said, emphasizing the "z."

Although she said nothing, I sensed she liked the restoration.

She told me she had done only one semester of a community college near Poughkeepsie, New York, where Terez and her family had settled in 1957. She had also taken some courses for a year at the Sorbonne in Paris. "I've been accepted in the General Studies program of Columbia University this fall."

I decided to educate her informally, passing on my extensive knowledge, such as it was, to her of politics, history and literature. Most of the time, she listened happily, but one evening - perhaps I was tired or suffering from a hangover - I said, "You bore me."

She was very hurt, and with great difficulty I eventually persuaded her I did not really mean it. A few days later she gave a birthday party for me in the cottage replete with lavish gifts. I was in love with her.

One night in late August Terez and I went to a Hungarian restaurant on the east side, which had chequered red and white table cloths.

"Can we get married?" she said.

I stalled.

We continued the conversation as we walked to my car. She burst into tears. I felt anyone who could cry over me was worth seriously considering as a marriage partner. Impulsively I said, "Yes."

We returned to the cafe.

"Can Berrigan marry us?"

"Yes."

It was less than three months since we had met.

"September 10th."

"September 10th."

I only learned later that one of her best friends from the UN, Lynn Esmay, having met me, said to Terez, who was wondering whether she was wise to marry me, "Terez, you're lucky. Peter's kind." Returning from holiday, Dr. Stern said, "Did you marry her?"

I invited him to the wedding, but I was sure he wouldn't come, and he politely said, "No."

Barbara told Terez who told me, "'When I told Emoke, she sat down on her bed in shock.'" I heard that a friend, Ashton Hawkins, remarked, "They're a very odd couple. They couldn't be more different."

One night a week or so before the wedding, Terez lying beside me, I woke from a dream at 2 a.m. At about eight in the morning my stepbrother Bill rang from Princeton: "Jack died at two this morning."

"The hated step-father dies, the hero marries the beautiful girl, his first novel is published," said Terez.

"Two out three is true," I replied.

I did not go to the funeral, though the notice in the *The New York Times* listed four sons and a daughter of the deceased. Three days before the wedding I phoned my mother, "I'm sorry about Jack."

I do not remember what she replied, but her voice sounded constrained.

"Can you come to my wedding tomorrow?"

She said she'd be there.

I had difficulty finding a Catholic church which would allow Berrigan to officiate. Eventually the pastor of the Church of St. John the Apostle, a small edifice on East 72nd street between 2nd and 3rd avenues, agreed to allow the indicted Jesuit to appear on his altar. He demurred, however, when I asked that a Beatles song be played.

The night before I sponsored a fund-raising dinner party in my apartment for Berrrigan, at which he spoke. Terez was there and a group of our friends, including Barbara, and their brother Louis, a very tall young man who was still in college.

By then I had met Terez's father, who insisted I learn the Hungarian word, "Egeszsegere," said as a toast meaning, "Good health." He was quite a tall man, gray-haired, about 60 years old, a programmer for IBM with a wide smile and a seemingly friendly manner. He was talkative in his heavily accented English, which was understandable. Terez's oldest sister, Maria, who had married in June, had gone away on a vacation with her new Swedish husband, though they lived in Upper Saddle River, N.J.

I had invited Albert, the window cleaner, as a guest to the ceremony and reception, and the morning of our wedding I woke in a daze, and remained in this state until four in the afternoon. What was happening to me, I wondered? I wore a dark business suit with yellow tie, my favorite color. My best man was to be Fereidoun, also known as "F.M." to his friends, including his close companion, Flora Schnall, the lawyer, who took him to the side of the brown stone church outside and persuaded him to wear a tie. He had not worn one for years. He looked strikingly good-looking and Iranian. I said to my old Asheville classmate, Bob Luchars, "Can you and Louis be the head ushers?" I had had to partially concede this honorary position under pressure from Terez to Louis, and of course Barbara was a bridesmaid.

Bob said angrily, "Why am I not your best man?"

I mumbled some diplomatic reply.

As I walked up the aisle to the altar, I saw Anne Fremantle, sitting in a middle pew with her son, Adam. I had not asked them, but as it was a church open to the public, I could hardly ask them to go.

Terez walked up the aisle on the arm of Louis senior, wearing a white dress to the knees decorated with filigree gold lace. Her blonde hair was supplemented by a golden fall, and her immaculate makeup was done by Elizabeth Arden. Berrigan married us.

We walked down the aisle, arm in arm, and it was then that I saw my mother. It was also the first time she had seen the front of Terez. My mother looked strained, hard and determined to do her best.

Outside, before climbing into the limousine, even though we had been limited to 45 persons, Terez invited several of her UN girl friends to the reception.

Our friends, John and Gabriella Isaacs, gave the reception in their penthouse apartment at 710 Park Avenue. Albert was not there, but Emoke came. Gabriella was an old friend of my new wife - physically a sensationally exciting girl. Mingling on the terrace were my sister Dorothy and step-brother Bill. Louise and Bill Welch were there, giving me as a wedding present Blake's *Songs of Innocence and Experience*. I knew that if it had not been for them 13 years earlier, I would not have been there. I saw Berrigan out of the corner of my eye. Terez and I then went alone to La Caravelle for dinner - again a gift from the Isaacs.

Our honeymoon began with the first night in a seedy hotel in Merida on the coast of the Yucatan. A bottle of champagne only made our feelings about the bedroom even more sour and angry. We then went to a hotel on the Isla de Mujeres, where the waves crashing against the rocks below our window made a thunderous, sinister drumbeat. We moved to a bedroom on the other side of the hotel, looking west, where the sound was less thunderous. One day we rented a rowboat with an outboard motor and a young guide who made no effort to conceal one of his balls protruding from his blue cutoff jeans, as he held the rudder. He grinned lasciviously. We went a few miles west to the uninhabited island of Cancun.

Cancun was a deserted crescent of perfect beach - white sand, a line of trees and behind them forest. We met a Danish wife, relaxing with her two small children under a palm frond leanto. We became friendly, and she shared her shade. She said, "My marriage is in trouble." She added, "My husband is the regional director of tourism here, trying to promote Cancun as a resort." A few hours later, as we chugged along an inlet, a middle-aged stocky Mexican, looking macho with his black mustache, accompanied by associates, passed by in a speedboat. "Eee's her husband," said our virile boy-man. The estranged husband glared at us.

On returning to the hotel Terez and I had a drink on the terrace, and sitting a few feet from us, opposite Terez, was a pudgy Mexican fellow guest who puckered his lips like a pig for my wife's benefit. I was smart enough not to hit him.

At Chichen-Itza Terez fell ill with a stomach disorder, and the doctor was summoned. While she was recovering, in the dark lobby I met the hotel owner wearing a white hat, who looked like a white man who had murdered someone in the civilized world. Alone I climbed the pyramid. At the top I encountered a boy of about 12 swinging a rope with a thick knot at the end. As far as the eye could see was the flat green jungle. Back in our hotel room Terez screamed when a cockroach-type creature scampered across the black parquet floor. "It's just nature," I said. She screamed again. As Terez got better, she said from her pillows, "You should change investment counselors." I bridled at this interference in our financial affairs.

Our honeymoon was to end in Mexico City. We had been given an introduction to a Mexican painter and his middle-aged blonde Polish wife. The artist only painted or sculpted feet, ankles and calves of legs. She was an attractive woman with a personality larger than life, and I became temporarily enamored with her. On the dance floor I kissed her briefly on the lips. Terez and her husband saw this. On our return to the table I could see that my bride was <u>very angry</u>. Shrugging his shoulders, the painter said to me, "This goes on all the time."

The Polish wife said, "You're not much of a husband."

On Terez's and my return to our hotel room she barely spoke to me. My pleadings that I didn't really mean it were to no avail, and at the airport the next day the icy atmosphere between us continued. We returned to New York.

Dr. Stern said, "<u>How could you!?</u>" He then said, "This is the trouble with getting married in such a short time after you first meet." I bitterly resented that *his* engagement had been longer.

A few days later Terez and I went to dinner at La Cote Basque, and she dug the nails of the fingers of one of her pretty hands into the palm of my right hand so hard that I thought our marriage was over. I thought, 'Well, at least I can say I was married for three weeks.'

Despite continual rages and arguments we soldiered on. Occasionally plastic cups and saucers flew, and every now and then a tennis shoe. I was usually the target, but sometimes I threw them back. Once she beat the ceiling of our apartment with the end of a broom stick, leaving a small dent. At a cocktail party we both attended I stood out of choice only with the male guests. For me this was very unusual.

Then we went to Princeton for the weekend, and my mother invited some of her friends and a few of mine to meet Terez. One of them was Bill Boyd Jr., the son of a newspaper chain through his mother's second husband in California and heir through his father to *The New Brunswick Daily Home News*. Bill was a handsome, dark-haired man about the same age as me. He said angrily, "How could a girl as beautiful as her marry <u>you</u>!?" I felt shocked and hurt, and that was the end of that friendship.

We flew to London, and aunt Violet, who suffered from migraines, met Terez, and when Terez was not in her living room she made it clear to me that she was disappointed in my choice of such a glamorous wife, but somehow I rather enjoyed this insult.

Soon there was a trial in camera in the Chancery court to decide if George, Rosabelle and I would be allowed to break away one half of John's estate, and Mr. Browne-Wilkinson, now a QC, the very same one who three years earlier had said we could never succeed, spoke eloquently for us. Moss had promised he was coming down from Yorkshire and would oppose the sane members of the family. "Birds" had told him he was forbidden to speak in open court, but he had planned to ignore this edict. However, on the day of the trial, driving down from Bradford, he stopped momentarily in St. Neots and severely sprained his ankle. The spectacle of the enormous Receiver elbowing aside Mr. Williamson and Mr. Woods from "Birds," his own solicitors, not to mention the portly barrister who <u>was</u> permitted to act for him, rushing into the pit of the court room and declaring loudly to his bewigged lordship that John was too poor to give money away to his rapacious relations never took place. Moss was charging the tenants rents at one third of the current market rate. However, a technicality prevented Mr. Justice Cross from ruling in favor of us, and the trial was postponed for a few months until some more documents could be obtained. The barristers collected their papers, and we went our separate ways.

Meanwhile, I introduced Terez at lunch at the Stafford Hotel to my guest Christopher Hollis, the Conservative ex-M.P. for Winchester, co-sponsor of the Parliamentary Bill in 1955 abolishing capital punishment, godfather to one of Evelyn Waugh's children, a well-known Roman Catholic writer, who I had known for several years. Once he had stayed at my parent's house in Princeton, and early one morning I came down stairs to see the gruff *literateur* holding a blue airmail letter. "My daughter's reproduced herself," he growled. He had told me I would be condemned for having such a rich hero for *The Camel Through the Needle's Eye.* I had money. "I only have one seventieth of what Sander gave away," I replied. I had arranged several lectures for Hollis in America, including one at the Catholic center for Princeton University, and the priest, a Father Murray when I mentioned Hollis's friendship with Waugh had replied, "Who's she?" I had another connection to Waugh. One of his daughters married John D'Arms from Princeton, N.J., who was one of my five classmates who tricked me into the fist fight 14 years earlier. As for Terez at lunch whenever she wasn't looking, Hollis leered at me. Our friendship wasn't ended, but it was weakened.

At a friend's flat I gave a small party so that the majority of friends and relations could meet Terez. Among them was my cousin David and his wife Gaye. About 12 years earlier he had married her over his parent's opposition. She was the daughter of a pub owner, of lower middle class background, and both Uncle Reggie and Aunt Jane had warned David, "She does not belong to our class. She'll never be accepted in the county. It would be a big mistake." While they were dating, they had asked to stay a few nights on separate occasions at 26 Buckingham Palace Mansions, which I had arranged. When I was alone with one couple or the other they bitterly attacked each other. I was neutral. At the wedding Aunt Jane, who earlier had said, "One thing I could never forgive David for is if he married a Jew," wept piteously throughout the service, and Uncle Reggie gave a speech at the reception which could only be described as unenthusiastic.

David held a series of jobs such as door-to-door salesman of hearing aids and employee of an outdoor gardening service. Gaye bore him three children. Then Uncle Reggie died, and under the terms of the entailed trust Aunt Jane was evicted from her attractive house in the Shropshire village to be replaced by her daughter-in-law with whom she was barely on speaking terms. She was forced to move to a one bedroom flat in London. But David, who was always thin, and Gaye came to my little party for Terez. I had put on about 15 pounds on my previously slim figure during my courting, marriage and the few months since then. Gaye had a very substantial figure. David and his wife got into the elevator to leave, and as the doors closed, grinning, he yelled to me, "Fatso."

The time had come for Terez to meet George. I invited him to the Stafford for lunch. From the moment George slowly approached the table the atmosphere between the three of us was infused with electricity. He sat down heavily, never looking at either of us. For once I ignored the stares of the other people in the restaurant. Terez began to laugh hysterically, but she was very careful that George not see her, and I was grateful and relieved by her tact. Despite his extreme shyness I sensed that George rather liked Terez.

Chapter 6

The Brothers Rowley

The U.S. Government tried Dan and Philip Berrigan in a Baltimore court house. Out of loyalty Terez and I flew to the city, renting a bedroom in a hotel nearby. I had never met Philip, and now I saw him sitting with Dan in a row with the other defendants while we observed from a bench for the spectators. With his crew cut and clean-cut manly features, his body bigger and stronger than his brother Philip, who was also a priest, reminded me of an F.B.I. agent, methodically working with honor for the bureau. At lunch time we went outside and joined a demonstration in front of the federal building. This made me nervous, but I guessed there would not be any violence, as we walked in an oval, holding placards - a futile gesture. There were about 50 of us.

Inside everybody connected with the trial played their parts as if by rote. The jury, a collection of ordinary-looking citizens, were highly unlikely to be swayed by William Kunstler, the defense attorney's, appeals to a higher conscience than the law. The prosecutors were suitably serious in warning how the system would collapse if people were allowed to take the law into their own hands and burn the files of draft boards. In his cross examination the prosecutor asked Dan how he felt about sending other young men to Vietnam because the ones whose files had been destroyed would have their future destinies delayed. Berrigan replied in effect that one had to use unusual methods to combat an illegal war. Kunstler, whose indignation seemed to be influenced as much by the publicity as the righteousness of his clients' case, orated impressively to the jurors, who voted to a man or a woman to convict. By that time Dan and Phil had been on the cover of *Time*. The whole affair depressed me slightly, even though we had dinner during it with Dan and some of his disciples. They were a rather sad-looking group of individuals who appeared to be ex-nuns and exbrothers. They seemed to be both lost and yet united in their admiration for their god-like leaders. Of course they were released on bail pending their appeal. Terez said, "What happens to Dan and Phil's followers when they go to jail too? They have no fame to protect them."

At the courts of justice in the Strand Rowley v. Rowley and Coutts & Co. reconvened - as usual in secret. The press would be denied the whole sordid story of John's attempted suicide and lifetime incarceration. The distant rumble of Dunkirk would stay within the panelled chambers. To no one's surprise John gave half his estates to George, Rosabelle and me, but he was not aware of his generosity as he paced the corridors of his sanatorium a few miles away. Coutts managed to keep their sticky fingers in the pie by remaining as trustee of most of the share handed over to us. The reason was that John might impregnate a woman, who would bear him a son, and then he would emerge from The Priory, decertify himself from the clutches of The Court of Protection, and marry her. These steps did not necessarily have to be in that order. He might marry her first.

As we walked down the stone steps from the Courts, Terez said to me, "We must go and see John."

Fear sped through me, but having just "stolen" half my half-brother's property from him I could see the justice in her proposal. Reluctantly I agreed, and we took a taxi to Roehampton. Fortunately the ride took about 20 minutes, postponing temporarily the meeting.

Roehampton was the suburb to the west of London where my mother and her sisters had attended a convent school of the Sacred Heart many years earlier. Among her classmates was Vivien Leigh, who my mother never mentioned. However, a friend of my aunt Violet's who lived in London once invited me to tea and said, "Vivien's parents sent her from India when she was seven, and she did not see them again until she was 17. She was always the star of the school plays." Aunt Dorothy, the nun, taught Vivien as a student but probably because of the star's subsequent marriages refused to say anything about her pupil, though it must be said in defense of the religious that by that time (when I mentioned the subject) she was suffering from the aftereffects of a massive heart attack which had left her partly paralysed. Aunt D, the nun, had been forbidden by her father to enter the order. In order to escape from his tyranny the moment she was 21 she enrolled as a novice, rising rapidly in the ranks.

"The last time I saw John was 28 years ago," I said, as the taxi approached the sanatorium.

"I know," said Terez.

Ivy covered the entrance of The Priory, a mansion that had probably once been a private house. There was a circular drive. An atmosphere of seedy wealth surrounded us. The institution was privately owned by a group of doctors and catered to alcoholics, drug addicts and the crazy, providing they or their loved ones had the money to pay the bills. We said to the receptionist that we had come to see John Rowley. We did not have an appointment. I was his half-brother, and she was my wife. The response of the receptionist was neutral tinged with boredom. We waited. Then a male nurse opened a locked door. Stretching ahead of us was a greenish-tinged corridor, and the nurse, whose face was disfigured with flaky skin, led us after a few steps into a small sitting room. There was John, sitting in an arm chair, wearing a brown three piece suit. I was in an even more formal dark suit. Behind him were French doors leading to a garden enclosed by a high wall covered with creepers.

Terez and I sat down on chairs, and the nurse leaned against a wall.

I said, "I'm your brother, Peter, and this is my wife, Terez."

Terez said warmly, "Hello, John."

John's mouth began to twitch. He put his fingers of both hands together in front of him rather as a professor might when listening to two of his students.

I said, "Are you happy here, John?"

John was silent, but the twitching of his mouth increased in frequency.

Terez said, "We're so glad to see you, John. If there is anything we can do to help?"

There was about five seconds of silence.

The nurse said, "John never speaks."

I leaned forward earnestly.

"John, are you happy here?"

John's mouth opened and closed rapidly, though the brown stumps of his teeth were rarely seen. He did not answer. In desperation Terez and I turned to the nurse, and from then on our conversation ignored John.

Terez said, "Does he ever have visitors?"

The nurse said, "Practically never. His mother and a friend of hers were here five years ago."

I said, "George stopped visiting a few years ago."

John unzipped his trousers while his facial twitchings continued. I was alarmed and glanced out of the corner of my eye at Terez.

Terez and I stood up.

Terez said, "What does he do all day?"

The nurse replied, "He eats, sleeps, walks. Occasionally he watches television. He turns over the pages of a book, but I don't know if he reads?"

I said, "Have you known him for a long time?"

The man said, "Oh, yes. Ever since he came here."

Terez said, "When was that?"

The attendant said, "About 15 years ago. I'm very fond of him."

I said, "He never talks?"

The nurse said, "Never. But he understands. I tell him to do something, and he usually does it. The other day he tried to run away from me when I was taking him for a walk in Richmond Park, but I caught him. He's a good runner, is John."

"I notice he has some sores on his leg."

"Yes, he scratches them."

Terez said tentatively, "And his teeth?"

The nurse replied, "We can't take him to a dentist. And when a dentist comes here, he won't open his mouth."

"Good-bye, John," said Terez kindly.

I said sincerely, "Good-bye, John."

We moved out of the door of the waiting room. At that instant with a grin John let out an animalistic and powerful roar, comparable to that of a gorilla. The nurse took us through the locked door while the roars continued, growing louder. He then returned to the ward.

Despite the wild sounds, which reverberated through the solid wooden door, Terez and I stopped.

I said, "I have an uncanny sense that he knows just what he's doing. I think he can be helped."

"You do?"

I said, "I know of a Doctor Bierer here in London. He's said to be fantastic with silent schizophrenics. They say he's a very warm man - loving - who just walks in on a patient and starts talking. Sometimes he talks for three hours - non-stop. And gradually the sick person starts to respond - over weeks and weeks of this direct confrontation with him. I'm going to try to arrange with The Court of Protection for Bierer to see John."

I had heard of Bierer from Stern. His name had come up during my therapeutic sessions in New York. Bierer, according to Mark, was such a forceful personality that once at a psychiatric convention he had rushed to the podium and hurled a book at a colleague. We had also talked about R.D. Laing, the then-famous psychiatrist who to the anger of many of his colleagues had advanced the argument that insanity was a sane response to an insane world.

After telephoning him, using Dr. Stern's name, I found Bierer in his office cum house in Hampstead. He was a stocky tanned man with a beard of advanced years.

"Let's go to a pub," he said.

There over lagers I described my brother. Bierer lived up to his reputation of being voluble and warm. If anyone could bring John back into reality, it was this amicable figure chatting in a friendly way. There was hope. Bierer was interested.

I made the usual phone calls to The Court of Protection, and they agreed to instruct Bierer to make a consultation visit to The Priory. I did not tell George.

We returned to New York. With his warmth and the informal atmosphere of the bar I was a little surprised that he had submitted a modest bill to me for our chat in the pub about John. Had he added on for the price of the lager which I had probably paid for but no matter? We came back to London again. Terez and I went to The Priory to see John, happily confident that there was new hope for my brother. In the front hall we were met by the portly physician in charge.

Angrily, his white face flushing red, he said, "Bierer had the nerve to come out here in a taxi. But your brother George as the closest relation had refused to give us permission for him to see John. I wouldn't let him in. Bierer's no miracle worker." I felt as if I had come up against a dead end.

We entered the dangerous ward. The attendant remarked, "There's a woman patient here who says John's her brother."

We passed a tall, late middle-aged man in the corridor, who said, "It's cold up here on the North Pole."

The nurse said, "He's a TV director. He says his producer is trying to eat his flesh."

We moved farther down the hall past the room where we had first seen John. This time we found John pacing in a large lounge area filled with brown armchairs and ordinary chairs. We greeted him, but he acted as if we were not there. There were about 40 feet between us. He was on the other side of the room. We watched for a minute or two and then left.

Epilogue

Calista died in a car accident in California. Mr. Fall fell down some stairs, and had to retire. George died in 1976 of alcohol, overeating, cigarettes and a heart attack. John died the day after Christmas, 1979, choking to death as the result of a side effect of an anti-schizophrenic drug. Eunice Roose Francis, whose existence had previously been unknown to me, gave an affidavit in 1981 to my lawyer, describing John's breakdown on the retreat to Dunkirk. Cousin David died in 1986 of alcohol and a heart attack. My mother died in Princeton, N.J., of pancreatic cancer in 1980. Terez, our daughter Caroline and I live in New York and Rutland, England.

INDEX